S0-ALB-427

FLEE THE CAPTOR

FLEE THE CAPTOR

By HERBERT FORD

Designed by
HOMER NORRIS
Updated Edition

REVIEW AND HERALD® PUBLISHING ASSOCIATION
HAGERSTOWN, MD 21740

Copyright © 1966 by
Southern Publishing Association
Additional material © 1994 by
Review and Herald® Publishing Association

Sixth printing

ISBN 0-8280-0882-5

dedication

To the men and women of Dutch-Paris, who, placing an ultimate value on human life, moved unarmed across occupied Europe during World War II to save hundreds of persons from death, this book is respectfully dedicated.

The Dimensions of This Story

A FOREWORD BY
DR. W. A. VISSER 'T HOOFT
General Secretary (1938-1966), World Council of Churches

I must confess that my first reaction on receiving this book was one of considerable skepticism. Would the author, living and writing in a world so utterly different from the Europe of the war years, be able to understand and describe the atmosphere of that period? Would he especially succeed in conveying to the reader of today an awareness of that unique experience of comradeship in total dedication to a deeply meaningful cause which characterized the Resistance movement and which made those years, in spite of all suffering, in spite of all failures, "the best years of our lives"? Would my friend Jean (for he became John only when he went to the U.S.A.) be portrayed as the unreal hero of a James Bond story or as the very human being he was and is?

But as I read on, my skepticism disappeared. I found that the story as told here brought that intensive experience of the war years right back. The author has of course used his privilege of writing a *histoire romancier;* that is, he reconstitutes events and conversations about which we have no detailed or verbatim records. But though I might here and there want to make a correction, I believe that the total picture he gives is basically truthful and reflects historical reality.

That is especially true of his characterization of John Weidner. He brings out that John was extraordinary in that he wanted to do a thing that ought to be very ordinary for any Christian, namely to help every man in need who crossed his path. It was this complete readiness to serve men without counting the cost which convinced me the very first time John came to me that this man deserved all the support I could possibly give him. I did not know at that time what remarkable results our collaboration would bring. When I had to organize the "Swiss Road," the organization to keep the free Dutch government in London in contact with the Resistance movement in the Netherlands, I needed a man of very great resourcefulness and courage to take charge of the courier service through the occupied territories.

John did not hesitate a moment to accept this very risky task. So he became one of the most indispensable links in our organization. The documents which he carried dealing with all aspects of life under German occupation in the Netherlands were a precious help to Queen Wilhelmina and her government in deciding what steps to take in order to encourage the Resistance and to prepare for the renaissance of the nation after the war.

The story has yet another dimension. Why was it that John accepted all these risks so readily? Why did he leave on these perilous journeys, each of which could easily have been the very last, as if he were going on a vacation trip? For those who have worked with him the answer is quite clear. He had that directness, that simplicity of faith, which made him realize that he was at all times in the hands of a loving God. He did not talk much about that. But he could show real astonishment when it was suggested to him that life in the Resistance movement was an uncertain affair. Uncertain? Not for one who read his Bible and knew about the divine care. And it was because of this dimension of John's life that he, a Seventh-day Adventist, and I, the Reformed pastor, regarded ourselves not only as comrades in a common human cause, but also as fellow citizens of the Eternal City.

Geneva
April, 1966

How the Story Was Uncovered

A FOREWORD BY

HASKELL LAZERE, *Director*

New York Metropolitan Council, American Jewish Congress

It is poetic that FLEE THE CAPTOR stemmed from an act of thanks. If it had not been written, the facts about the activities of a great humanitarian would have remained in the official archives of the Allied governments, rich research material for the historian, but hidden from the millions who should know about John Weidner. John does not parade his acts of heroism, his courage, or his decorations. It is a tribute to Herbert Ford that he was able to penetrate Mr. Weidner's modesty and capture so well in the printed word the wartime story of this amazing human being.

In 1963 while I was serving as the West Coast director of the American Jewish Congress, a Jewish civil rights organization founded by the late Dr. Stephen S. Wise, we conceived the idea of commemorating Dr. Wise's birth date with a program which would honor those individuals in the Los Angeles area who had rescued refugees from the Nazis during World War II. To find the rescuers, the American Jewish Congress publicized its search in as many newspapers as would carry the story.

Norman Rosen, a resident of Pasadena and a health food customer of John Weidner's, read about the search and wrote a long letter to the Congress detailing the exploits of John Weidner, whom Rosen alleged had saved 800 Jews, over 100 Allied airmen, and others during the Nazi occupation of France. In all, according to Rosen, Weidner had saved one thousand people. I recall thinking after I read the Rosen letter, "How could a man like this be in the Los Angeles area without anyone's knowing about him?" Members of our executive committee wondered the same thing. How could *one* man save so many and do so much under the eyes of the Nazis and their sympathizers? Why did he do it? Was he the virtual saint that Rosen described?

I arranged a meeting with John Weidner. He is ordinary in appearance, with thinning hair and of average build and height. His most distinguishing feature is his rather thick French accent when he speaks. He is friendly, charming, and animated, but quiet. One would never notice him on the street, and most of his customers not only would not suspect but probably would not believe that for a time he was one of the most wanted men in France because of his underground activities.

I wrote to people John Weidner said he had worked with or rescued, to obtain messages of congratulations for him on the night he was to be honored. (I confess that I wrote also to substantiate some of the stories he had rather reluctantly told me, because it was beyond my ken that a man who was so gentle could have been the fox who stole so many prizes from the Nazi grasp.)

When we announced that we had found John Weidner, newspapers all over the world carried the story and communications began to arrive from ambassadors, former colleagues of John in the underground, and from people he had rescued. One touching anecdote came from a woman whom he had taken with her family into Switzerland. She said that the night was very cold and she noticed that Weidner was not wearing socks. When she asked him about it, he evaded the question. It was not until she inquired about him from his co-workers in Switzerland that she found out he had none because he had given away all but the clothes on his back to the people he had saved.

I asked John Weidner why he had risked his life repeatedly to save so many. His answer was brief and to the point, "They were God's children; they were human beings."

In March, 1963, the American Jewish Congress tried in its humble way to say Thank you to John Weidner, with

Lee J. Cobb presenting him a plaque in the form of an open Bible and with a Biblical inscription. Before Mr. Cobb made the presentation, he said, "There is an old Hasidic legend that God has created in every generation thirty-six wise, pious, and just men, upon whom the world depends for its survival. They are called 'Lam-ed Vovniks.' Their identity is not to be known to any save God. Yet," continued Mr. Cobb, "I cannot help feeling that tonight we are in the presence of one of the thirty-six."

In a letter dated March 11, 1963, Helene M. Cornelisse, now of Houston, Texas, wrote the following about John Weidner: "There is a book to write about this man, . . . and the lesson I learned from him about 'serving,' which has become part of my own life, how little it may be compared to his example. He saved my parents life [sic]; he saved my life; he saved the lives of so many people, many of them Jews; but he did more: he gave us shelter and food, he gave us the courage we needed, and above all, he became the living symbol of a man devoted to his fellowman."

Herbert Ford has told John Weidner's story well, and in the telling he has shown vividly that one serves God best by serving his fellowman. FLEE THE CAPTOR is truly a great story of love and true adventure.

New York City
May, 1966

contents

introduction

OF THE MANY shocking examples of man's inhumanity toward his fellowman that came out of that great war which swept the world during the late 1930's and early 1940's, none surpasses in sheer horror the extermination by the Nazi war machine of some 6,000,000 of the 8,300,000 Jews living in Europe. In scope and methods employed, this massive lethal act has few parallels in history.

No one knew better that they were earmarked for death by the Nazis than did the Jews themselves. Many of these stricken people lived like animals in order to escape, at least temporarily, their deadly fate. Hundreds roamed the secret recesses of the countryside scavenging or stealing food and, when no food could be found, eating roots and bark and drinking the juice of grasses. Thousands lived completely immobilized through the day in cramped lofts or bunkers, venturing out to exercise their benumbed limbs only after the protective cloak of night had come. Yet, for all their fear, the Jews could do little to help themselves.

It is a credit to the name of humanity that out of the approximately 300,000,000 Europeans who lived under Nazi rule a brave group swallowed their fear and did something to help the Jews. For the most part these people made their first moves to give aid as individuals. They feared the consequences of what they did, but they feared even more facing the future as decent people if they did not help.

These people who helped were often blundering in their efforts. But their unpolished acts shine bright in the annals of man as his brother's keeper: the little widow passing her precious Aryan identification card to a Jewish mother, then marching off to the firing squad meant for the Jewess; the cattle dealer hanged in the public square for concealing thirty-five Jews; the watchman's wife who unsuspectingly whispered to her anti-Semitic brother that her husband was hiding Jews in the attic of a nearby office building.

Some 300,000 Jews lived in France in 1939. By 1940 between forty and fifty thousand Jewish refugees had also arrived in the country from Belgium and Holland. With the collapse of the French army in early June, 1940, the country was divided into two sections. The northern part was put under immediate German military occupation; the southern area took a supposedly independent status under Marshal Henri Philippe Pétain, whose headquarters were located in the town of Vichy.

The Jewish refugees fleeing from Belgium and Holland came by every mode of transportation into the southern section, or "Free Zone." Their countries were broken by the armored Nazi might, and their lives were stamped for extermination in the horror pogrom of death for all Jews. Most of the refugees were strangers to southern France. Few had friends in whom they could put their trust; fewer still had any type of shelter to which they could go. They were wandering exiles in a foreign land even as their Biblical ancestors had been. But no promised land awaited them; the best they could hope for was survival.

The incoming thousands were assigned to camps by the Pétain government. There they found a roof and a bed, little else. In one sense the camps were a blessing to the Jews. But in another sense, they became way stations on the road to Nazi death camps. The Pétain government, in its cooperative relationship with the Germans, committed itself to allowing the Gestapo to come into the camps and seize Jewish refugees for deportation whenever they desired. At first the pretense was made that only Jews with "political" backgrounds would be taken. This policy was then altered so that "foreign" Jews could also be taken. As the war progressed, however, all pretense ceased, and nonpolitical as well as political Jews were seized; the "foreign" Jews from Belgium, Holland, and other occupied countries were taken, along with French Jews.

It was at the ghastly beginning of this massive scene of fear and death that John Henry Weidner came into the picture in mid-1940. A burning young patriot who had already offered his services to the army of his native Holland on two occasions, Weidner knew better than most the price that must be paid for liberty. His offers to serve his country were rejected because he had been living in France for several years, and the Netherlands government could not take the chance that even a small number of its citizens who lived abroad might have sold out to the Nazis as spies for Germany.

Weidner, a devout Seventh-day Adventist, vividly remembered how his clergyman father had served a one-day term each week in Swiss prisons on several occasions over a period of years because his conscience told him young John should not be forced to attend state schools on Saturday, the day on which Seventh-day Adventists worship.*

John's heritage in liberty extended back to his grandfather, who had a distinguished career as a minister of the Dutch Reformed Church. His father frequently recounted to him the love of liberty that motivated his grandfather. For ten years the eldest Weidner had been chaplain of 's-Hertogenbosch Prison, the largest in Holland, where he fought for the protection and consideration he felt prisoners deserved. Later he became a minister of his church in Belgium; and everywhere he went, he preached love as the basis of all true religion and liberty as the unquestioned right of every man.

As he grew into young manhood, John's study of the history of Holland, with its distinguished role as a cradle of liberty, also had its impact on his life. Holland had been a land of fighters—fighters for great causes. For centuries the Dutch had fought the mighty North Sea to wrest their land from its encroaching tides. In the sixteenth century his country had fought against the Spanish Inquisition with its religiopolitical terrors which reached into every stratum of Dutch life. And it was to Holland, John learned, that the English Pilgrims first fled from England, seeking religious liberty. His country had always provided sanctuary for oppressed and persecuted people. His had been a land which vigorously upheld the freedoms given by God to mankind.

---

*Today full liberty of conscience is granted Seventh-day Adventists and all religions throughout Switzerland.

18

With this heritage of liberty and the deep spiritual belief that guided his daily life, John Weidner could not have sat by unmoved at the scene which was beginning to unfold in southern France in 1940. As he viewed the helpless Jewish refugees herded into the detention camps shortly after he arrived in Lyons to open his textile business, his entire background in life told him that he should give these people whatever help he could. That this help would soon be given at the risk of his own life made little difference to him. "You can't help only when it doesn't cause you to suffer," he reasoned. "When you want to help people in need, you can't be concerned if your hands get dirty, or if your life is in danger, for that matter. Helping those in need knows no bounds other than those of life itself."

The four-year nightmare that John Weidner lived from 1940 through 1944 to give help to the Jews, Allied airmen, and others in danger of death may seem to some a high price to pay. But to him the help he gave was a natural expression of the training he had received from his kindly father and beloved mother. Even when he was being beaten in Cruseilles or tortured in Lyons or was facing execution in Toulouse, John accepted these trials as part of the destiny he must follow in his desire to help those around him who faced death.

"The road of the benefactor is not always an easy one to travel," he says in explaining his deeds. "Very few of the people in this world who have done anything great for others have traveled a smooth road. Usually there are many trials if you want to do something that counts."

Through those tormented four years, most of which were spent in constantly trying to evade the sinister combination of collaborating French police forces and the Gestapo, while at the same time giving what help he could to others, John Weidner never lost his assurance that he was God's man doing what his heavenly Father would have him do. On numerous occasions, he recalls, "only the hand of God could have saved me from the things in which I was involved. I am completely satisfied in my own mind that God led me through those years of evasion, capture, torture, and fear."

Few will deny, when they learn John Weidner's story, that Providence was, indeed, by his side. There can be little doubt that the Father of the universe does give His special guidance and protection to those who, like John Weidner, demonstrate complete faith in His ways and works.

I

the mountain

A WEARINESS born of three days and nights of jam-packed train travel, and four hard days of plotting escape plans in Paris before that, slowed the feet of John Henry Weidner as he made his way along the rough path leading into the Saleve Mountain from the roadway between Annecy and St. Julien. Presently he left the trail and cut his way more steeply upward to the left. To the right ahead, he remembered, stood the control station on the road that ran across the top of the mountain, and he didn't want the gray-shirted guards at the control station to see him, not with the list of Jewish refugees he had in his pocket. It was imperative that the list be delivered safely to his friend at the Swiss immigration office in Geneva.

John paused to catch his breath and swung around to view the surrounding land that swept away in rolling verdant hills and valleys. Turning back toward the upthrust face of the Saleve, he felt a keen inner joy. This was "his" mountain —he knew its every secret; he had etched the features of its rugged bluffs and peaceful vales deep into his memory.

21

Pushing steadily upward, he soon worked his way behind a slope which concealed him from the control station on the mountain road. It was four miles from this point to La Croisette, the isolated little village atop the mountain where he would begin to look for the familiar route leading down toward the French-Swiss border. As he picked up his pace on the gradual slope, he topped the rising ground to his left and broke out onto the flat ridge he always followed toward the village. Here again he paused, this time to study the view on the other side of the mountain—the panorama that was Switzerland.

Spread out directly below him lay the green carpet of forest covering the border area. Farther away, set against a background of green like a diamond in velvet, lay the beautiful city of Geneva. Its spires and high-peaked buildings caught the afternoon sun. The dazzling League of Nations buildings stood out in the surrounding green like great blocks of white marble. To the right, angling away in deep blue splendor, was Lake Geneva. Behind the lake, rising toward the rugged Jura Mountains that framed the entire scene, was the Plain of Geneva. And far to the right the snowy head of Mont Blanc, Europe's highest peak, raised itself among the Alps.

The sound of his light mountain boots on the dirt was all that broke the silence of the afternoon as he turned once again toward La Croisette. He had little time at that moment for taking up his years-old love affair with the Saleve, however. There were other things that needed attention. The group of Jewish refugees waiting for him near the campus of the Adventist college at the foot of the mountain in Collonges was one. They had been there for several days already, and they had to be taken over the border that night, no matter how tired John felt. Both the Gestapo and the French police had stepped up their surveillance all along the border, and his friends were afraid the refugees might be discovered at the farmhouse where they were hiding. And the list in his pocket—that had to be in Geneva by tomorrow at the latest.

Jacques Rens was already on his way from Paris with another group of refugees, and if the names on Weidner's list were not entered in the registry at the Geneva immigration office before the group with Rens arrived, they would be turned back to France by the Swiss border guards. And back to France meant into the hands of the Gestapo!

Earlier that morning when he arrived by train in Annecy, he heard that reinforced control at every border checkpoint had been ordered. The Commandante General of the entire area was making an inspection, and special precautions were being taken all along the border. That is why he had decided to cross over the Saleve instead of taking the bus to Collonges via St. Julien, as he often did. There were control posts below Cruseilles and St. Julien, and another on the road from St. Julien to Collonges. If the searching of bus passengers at the control posts was being intensified, then John had no desire to go that way. The precious list of refugees, with its complete identification of each name, would make interesting reading for the Gestapo, and it would provide a ready-made trip to jail for Weidner. So he had gotten off the bus before it reached the checkpoint south of Cruseilles and struck off on foot toward the Saleve.

Now as he moved along the ridge of the mountain, he was startled by a voice challenging him from a nearby hill. He whirled around toward the sound. "Halt," yelled a black-coated Nazi SS officer through a megaphone. Behind the officer John could see the green German troop truck which had pulled to a stop on the road about a third of a mile away.

"Halt," came the distant command again. His attention now riveted on the truck, John could see SS troops pouring from it. As they leaped from the rear of the vehicle, he could see that they had dogs with them. Rifle barrels caught the lengthening afternoon sun as they swung toward him.

The situation telescoped through Weidner's mind. There were about fifteen Germans that he could see. The dogs began barking, and the first bullet slammed into a nearby tree.

"If I surrender, they can't do much to me," he calculated. "I have my papers in order. But what of the list, and the refugees waiting at Collonges? The SS won't release me today, that is certain. And I've got to go into Switzerland with the refugees tonight."

The Nazis were running toward him at top speed now, but they were holding onto the dogs' leashes instead of letting the animals run free.

He spun around and fled through the trees. "There may be more of them," John thought as he ran, "but I know the mountain better. If I can hold out long enough, I can go down the cliffs." Quickly he put more distance between himself and the onrushing Nazis. Bullets whined past as he hurdled fallen trees and rocks.

As he ran, he began to think of the course he would take. He decided to circle toward La Croisette, then cut around the village and try to go down the cliffs that drop behind the houses. It would be difficult for his pursuers to follow him there with the dogs.

La Croisette was still more than two miles away, and Weidner knew he would have to conserve what strength he had left. He began to count as he ran, trying to measure his running evenly to keep a constant distance away from the SS.

Then he saw the soldiers divide into three units. "They'll try to cut around me now," he thought. "I'll have to travel faster." Bullets sang their deadly song around him as he ran. He could hear the barking dogs, and from the sound he knew one of the groups was gaining on him. As exhaustion began to build up in his body, John started to calculate the distance to the houses of La Croisette: "Four hundred yards . . . three hundred . . . two hundred."

Suddenly he broke out of a small patch of trees, and ahead he could see the six or eight houses that made up the little French village. A hundred yards beyond the houses, chalky humps of limestone reared from the green undergrowth, marking the approach to the cliffs. One group of SS troopers was less than three hundred yards behind him now. He plunged past the houses and came upon the cliffs almost before he realized it. His time now would be measured in seconds. With the Nazis pounding out of the trees

25

behind, the old familiar crevasse in the face of limestone and granite had to be located immediately.

John stopped abruptly, glanced quickly across the face of rock, and spied his route down. It was a deep split in the rock face that, to the experienced climber, gave promise of hand and foot holds inside by which descent could be made.

Down into the split he crawled. Loose shale fell into his face when his hand slipped or groped for a firm rock. Far below, almost straight down, he could see the patch of green that was the peaceful campus of the college at Collonges, where he had spent so many happy days as a student. "Will there ever be peace again such as I had in those days?" he wondered as he clawed his way down the rock.

At last he reached his hiding place, a growth-covered outcropping more than one hundred feet down the almost vertical face. Below yawned nothingness for five hundred feet! "How I wish I had the proper tools for practicing *varappe* right now," thought the exhausted Weidner. "I can't hope to go back up, because the soldiers are sure to be waiting there, probably all night. I should have some real climbing shoes, pitons, and rope for going down. But I'll just have to chance it."

He knew he had to be as quiet as death itself. Any movement would let the Germans know he was still alive. He could hear the dogs snarling above. And the bullets seemed to increase as the SS men shouted in anger at the hidden man. But John was protected by the overhang above him so that the bullets struck harmlessly in the soft limestone or went whining off in ricochet when they hit a patch

26

of granite. He edged closer against the face of the cliff as he tried to stretch his exhausted body.

As he lay back in the small patch of bushes which made up his shelter, he noticed that the firing had diminished. Although the dogs still barked, they now sounded farther away, as though they were being taken to another area to look for the fugitive. Darkness was beginning to settle on the Saleve. Above, he could hear two soldiers talking. John, who understood German, heard one soldier tell his companion, "He has probably fallen down the cliff and is dead. The way he went over so quickly makes it all but certain. But our orders are to stay here until we're relieved."

Weidner turned his head downward from the little outcropping. The way looked dangerous, more dangerous than he liked to think about. As he studied the rocky escarpment for a route, his mind returned to other days on the Saleve when he had come to practice *varappe,* the mountain-climbing art of those who try for the highest peaks. Although the Saleve was far from the highest of mountains, its limestone-granite cliffs made it an excellent though dangerous practice area.

Before the war hundreds of climbers came from Geneva and the surrounding French countryside each week to practice on the Saleve for more difficult climbs. And each year a number who had not learned their lessons were carried lifeless from the bottom of the massive rocks.

As the welcome darkness continued to gather about him, thoughts of earlier days at Collonges flooded John's mind. One of the first discoveries he had made after his father had been appointed Greek and Latin teacher at the college was that the mountain held an exhaustless store of adventure. He was forbidden to climb the dangerous crags and outcroppings of the Saleve, but John was too much boy to follow the restrictions with any consistency. Many times he would slip away from the campus to try a new trail he had found or to scale a difficult face of rock with friends.

Once, when he was fifteen, he found himself at that dread moment of the mountaineer: he couldn't go farther up the rock wall he was scaling, and to go down meant certain death. The only answer was to jump to a jutting outthrust of rock on one side. If he missed the leap, he would fall to the rock-strewn valley hundreds of feet below. As was his custom at all times, whether in need or in thanksgiving, young Weidner closed his eyes and spoke to God. "My Father," he prayed, "my next moments are the most important of my life. I need Your help to guide my hands." With confidence born of the habit of prayer the youngster leaped for the rock and grasped its safety!

When John would return home after his early climbing experiences, clothes torn and boots scarred from the mountain's harshness, his father would ask the inevitable question, "Have you been on the Saleve again, son?" Schooled in honesty above all else, the boy would acknowledge that he had, indeed, been climbing. Then the thrashing would come. "I received more whippings than I can remember for climbing on the Saleve," he recalled years later. "My father had good reason to spank me; the mountain was very dangerous in places, and I was just a youngster, sometimes climbing alone. I can understand now that if I had been my father, I too would have been concerned."

The tense hours passed slowly, the silence being broken occasionally by German conversation above his place of refuge. "You stay here, and I'll take the dogs away," he heard one of the SS troopers say. "If that fellow is still alive down there, he will think we have gone when he no longer hears the dogs, and he will climb back up. When he does, you grab him."

Finally, with darkness fully come, John decided to go down the dangerous face of the mountain. By now only the night sounds—the birds, insects, and the wind playing through the trees higher up—could be heard on the Saleve. Cautiously he stretched out on the little shelf to flex his muscles. The movement sent shale and small rocks clattering down the face of the cliff. John froze, but when no reaction came from above, he cautiously shifted his body again.

As he moved, he looked out toward Geneva. The sparkle of thousands of bright lights startled him because they seemed so near. He saw a few small glows which marked the college campus, and the contrast between the almost blacked-out college and surrounding town with Geneva in the distance was striking. Geneva was purposely telling enemy air crews by its blaze of light that it was a neutral city, that there was peace in Switzerland; while the little French border city of Collonges tried to hide in the inky blackness of the night.

"Is it possible that so many people are suffering so much just a few miles from that city ablaze with lights?" John asked himself as he prepared to leave his tiny shelter. "There, just a couple of miles away, is Geneva. There is no Gestapo, no curfew, no death, no misery of evasion." As he slowly rose to his feet on the little outcropping, he whispered, "I'll be in Geneva soon. Wait for me, bright lights and peaceful streets; wait for me. I'll be there soon."

With torturing slowness he eased off the small ledge of rock back to the crevasse. That split in the rock, he realized, was his only route down, dangerous though it was. Fingers scraping raw on the rock, he began to inch downward. As he moved, he recalled a night some years before when he and a group of students had stood on the college campus watching the small light of a lantern in the hand of a climber moving slowly down the face of the Saleve. "He should stay on the mountain through the night," one of the students had ventured as the others watched in silence. "The only safe thing to do is to stay on the mountain through the night." Moments after the student's voice had trailed off in the quiet night air the little light had suddenly arched down, and with an awestricken gasp they knew the climber had lost his footing. The next morning they found him, skull crushed and fingers still clutching pieces of the loose lime-stone he had broken from the mountain's face.

Determined not to repeat such a performance, John now fought his way down with agonizing slowness. Below, he could see the lights, so close it seemed he could reach out and touch them. But that was another danger of the mountain he had learned. The bell-clear atmosphere surrounding the Saleve made lights which were quite distant look confusingly near. Exhaustion hovered close by him again; but each time it came, he would cling to the rocky face, not moving at all, and wait until the fatigue passed.

Finally, abruptly, John hit the bottom of the mountain. He crumpled in a heap when he realized where he was. He had been much nearer collapse than he realized before. Now, at least for the moment, he was safe. If he could keep going just a little longer, he could pick up the refugees and see them safely into Switzerland. The border would be no problem, not on such a black night as this one.

John's thoughts turned to the larger implications of his wartime involvements. His work, he decided as he rested at the base of the Saleve, had lately taken on real complications since he had organized his friends into groups to handle difficult assignments. It was so different now from the early days of the war when he was handling everything himself. Then he had been taking all the risks and had only himself to worry about. Now there were others: Jacquet in Lyons; Moen in Toulouse; Laatsman in Paris; and faithful, ever-helpful Marie-Louise Meunier in Annecy. He had to think of them and of how they could help rescue those whose death decree was written by the Nazis, and at the same time of how these friends could be protected from the Gestapo.

It was typical of John to think about others at a time when his own life was in great peril. Of rugged constitution, ruddy, dark-haired, and fast-reacting, he was in top condition at twenty-nine years of age as a result of his frequent mountain climbing, skiing, and hiking trips about the Swiss and French countryside and mountains. Now as he picked himself up at the base of the cliff and struck off toward the farmhouse where the refugees waited, he was thankful that he had lived healthfully and exercised vigorously. Mountain trips like this one were only for those in top physical condition.

As he came upon the farm road which led to where the refugees waited, John's weariness began to drop away again. It was nearing midnight, and the fresh night air seemed to give him renewed strength. Another ten minutes of walking steadily brought him to the little cluster of farm buildings and the house itself. He rapped out a prearranged signal at the door.

"You're late," said the small dark farmer who let Weidner in and then quickly dropped the blackout curtain behind him. "We were afraid you had been caught by the Gestapo. Everywhere they are tightening control of the area."

"I was almost caught on the Saleve, but I got away this time," John stated.

"Good, good!" the little farmer said.

The two men walked through the house and slipped quietly out of the back door to the barn, where the refugees were bedded in the hayloft. Anxious to reach Switzerland before dawn, they roused the sleepy people and led them into the chill of the spring night. They set off along a pathway which ran behind the barn, around the field and into the trees, bordering the St. Julien-Annemasse highway paralleling the border. Deep in the trees they paused to rest awhile.

THE MOUNTAIN

"I'll scout the road and see how the wires look," John said as he left the group. "Bring them onto the roadway, but stay well behind the trees until I give you the signal."

At the road John found no sign of either the French police or the Gestapo. The black night was at its protective best now; the other side of the road was barely visible. After his survey of the roadway, he ran across the strip of paving and down a little decline to the strands of heavily barbed wire separating France from Switzerland. "Lucky they haven't electrified this section yet," he muttered as he began to gingerly separate the lower strands. He crawled through, tearing the bottom of one trouser leg as the wires snapped back together.

Turning, he looked up the incline and back across the road, then both ways along the road to make sure it was still clear. When he saw no movement, he gave a low whistle, chopping the note off sharply at the end. One of the refugees ran out of the blackness of the trees, his body hunched low, his face a mask of fear. Behind him came an old woman, then a young girl, another girl, and an old man.

John put his foot against the lower strand of wire and pulled the others up. "Quickly, quickly; be very quick," he whispered at the formless figures pushing their way through the opening. "Keep going. I'll catch up with you. Don't stop. Hurry! Be quick! Keep moving!" Another old man, then a boy. "I'm last," the youth whispered softly as he slipped under the wires. The low whistle with its abrupt ending came from the other side of the road. The farmer was confirming that all the refugees had been sent across the road.

"Good-bye, good friend," John whispered toward the whistle, although he knew the farmer could not hear him. "I'm going to freedom now, to the precious freedom of Switzerland for a while. But I'll be back."

He turned from the eighteen ugly strands of double barbed wire and fled after the refugees. Racing through the broad, cleared no-man's-land used by the Swiss to expose border jumpers, John felt a sudden surge of joy well up inside. As he caught up with the refugee band, he pulled the leading member down beside him on the ground. The others fell exhausted.

"There is no need to hurry anymore," John told them. "We are inside Switzerland. It will be best to wait here until the Swiss border guards come and find us. If we are moving, they might shoot at us so that we will stop. There is no need to take a chance on their poor aim. Settle down and rest; we are in a free land."

The old woman slumped near the center of the group began to cry.

"That's all right," John thought silently. "Go ahead and have yourself a good cry, grandmother. Cry for whatever you will: for your freedom, or for your family still in France, or for your brother in the concentration camp, or whatever. Go ahead and cry; it will do you good, old one."

For two years he had been in the war, John reflected. Two years of brutality and sorrow—sorrow like that of the old woman weeping there on the hard ground of the Swiss border. Two years of flight by these poor people and thousands of others just like them. How he wished the senseless game of fleeing-from-death could be over! Why were men so brutal anyway? Didn't they know or care that the God of all creation was watching their black and evil deeds?

"How I wish it could have been different, these two years!" John mused. "I would like to go back to that sunswept afternoon in Paris in 1940 and have it all happen differently, beginning right there."

It was in Paris on a spring day that it all started; there in Boulevard de l'Hopital.

II

EXIT PARIS

THE SUNNY STREETS of Paris were teeming with people that June afternoon in 1940. They were in headlong flight to the south, traveling by any means they could find. Trains and buses were jammed; the price of cars was astronomical, and gas was close to impossible to buy.

In the street beside the Franco-Belgian Union Conference office of the Seventh-day Adventist Church at 130 Boulevard de l'Hopital, John Weidner stood by an eight-passenger black Renault, talking with a small knot of friends who were helping fill the auto with records from the church headquarters building. With the loading of the car almost completed, they paused to watch the hundreds of people riding and tramping past. Some families were using carts to carry their most valued possessions out of the city. Atop one cart, rigged with bicycle wheels, a child sat crying in the confusion and the heat of the late afternoon sun. Across the street a shopkeeper was putting up new signs advertising that the price of his merchandise had been reduced 50 percent. All across Paris the price of sugar, coffee, clothing—

anything not essential to flight—was being slashed almost hourly in an effort to sell out and get some cash before the Germans came into the city.

The flight southward from Paris was not exactly new on this June afternoon. For days refugees from Belgium had been streaming through the city with hair-raising tales of the armored German divisions that were sweeping through their country and into France. But the Parisians, remembering World War I, had been confident that the French army would stop the Germans well to the east of the city. It had been done before; why not again? So they had stayed in Paris and watched the pitiful Belgian refugees.

But now, with the Nazis not more than 150 miles from the city, the Parisians knew something had gone wrong. The Germans seemed to be coming with relentless drive; the French army showed signs of collapsing. They began to flee, a few at first, then by the thousands. "But the Nazis will be stopped below Paris," was the word being passed around as people packed their possessions. "We'll go into southern France for a few weeks; and when the French army starts driving the Germans back toward Belgium, we can return to Paris." That view motivated most of the little group that stood with John now, watching the hundreds move by in the street.

Pastor Oscar Meyer, president of the Franco-Belgian Union Conference of Seventh-day Adventists, one of those standing by the car, believed the Germans would surely be held at a line south of Paris. But most members of his church organization were leaving for southern France, so that was where the church headquarters should be, he reasoned.

Gabrielle Weidner, John's older sister, was Pastor Meyer's secretary, and she was needed wherever the church headquarters would be. Standing on the curb with Gabrielle were Elise Pache and Marthe Abgrall, both secretaries to officials of the church administrative headquarters. They were ready to move where their church needed them. Pastor Antoine Mathy, minister of a Seventh-day Adventist church in Paris, stood talking with the group. He would follow his congregation and minister to them as they began to locate in the southern part of the country. Also with the little cluster of people was Mrs. A. J. Girou, a church member who owned the automobile which was to be used for the trip. John, the only member of the group who held a current driver's license, was asked to drive.

John's feelings about the oncoming Nazis were based on more experience with the enemy than the others. All of the group were frightened at the prospect of living in a captive nation. But John could still remember with considerable clarity the World War I outrages of the Germans in Brussels, where he had lived as a child. He could recall how his father almost died because of starvation and the cruel treatment administered by the invaders. Had it not been for the miracle that God provided in the form of a young French army nurse who unexpectedly came to his father's home, the elder Weidner would have surely died, John believed.

"I want to get away from those mad people," he said to the group on the curb. "Here, alone in Paris, I can't do much to stop the terrible things they will do to France and Holland. But if I can get into southern France, perhaps I can do something there that will be helpful."

Since the others had heard so much about the German military might, they fell silent as John talked of his experiences with the invaders. All of them could feel, as they listened, that things might not go as they hoped, that the Germans might not be stopped beyond Paris.

Gathering by the car when Pastor Meyer had finally locked the building, the little group was led in prayer by the minister. In a simple petition he asked God's protection and care not only in their own journey but also for all those who were fleeing southward that day. When the prayer ended, the little company got settled for the trip. The sun was almost down as John nosed the big car out into the crowded street. It was Sunday, June 10, 1940.

John had been appointed "navigator" for the trip south as well as driver because he was familiar with a series of back roads which would take them in the direction they wanted to go more rapidly. Route Nationale No. 20 and other major exits from Paris were completely clogged. Carts, motorcycles, cars, and other types of transportation jammed the major routes. One was lucky to move even a mile or two an hour in the frantic confusion. John's back-road route lay on a series of interconnecting south, east, and west highways and farm roads. He moved the car slowly through the crowds toward the first of these byways. The oncoming night would also aid his plan, since during the day Germans were strafing some of the highways they needed for their advance. He didn't want to contend with a broad-daylight machine-gunning by the deadly Messerschmidts.

Pastor Meyer had decided that they should go first to the little town of Dammarie-les-Lys near the city of Melun, fifty kilometers south of Paris. There they would meet with officials of the French Seventh-day Adventist publishing house. Near midnight John maneuvered the car through the streets of the little town toward Les Signes des Temps publishing house. Rousing the officials in charge, Pastor Meyer went into immediate conference with them on the future moves should the Germans reach Dammarie-les-Lys.

The next day Weidner and his companions headed for Lamotte-Beuvron, about 150 kilometers away. At the small town of Briare they came to a formidable inspection area, where they were questioned, then sent on a detour which took them well around the little town. Scores of soldiers, military vehicles, and officials formed the checkpoint guarding Briare because a most important conference was being held in the town. Great Britain's Winston Churchill and Paul Reynaud, president of the French government, were engaged in one of the last war advisory meetings between the two countries before France fell. At this meeting the dreaded idea of a possible armistice came to some leaders of the French government for the first time.

When John and the group reached Lamotte-Beuvron, they went to the home of Mrs. Yvonne Dufau, a close friend of John's sister's, where they spent the night. Early the next morning they discussed what should be done when they reached Lyons, the next expected stop.

40

"The news broadcast says the Germans are nearing Paris," Pastor Meyer noted as they talked. "That means it is not safe to stay here much longer. From Lyons we can probably go to our college at Collonges and set up a temporary headquarters. If that is not advisable, we can go south to Anduze. Paul Badaut, one of our good friends, has offered us the use of his spacious home there. And in the countryside I'm sure we can direct the work of the church for quite some time without trouble from the Germans. But maybe we should wait until we get to Lyons to make a final decision."

En route to Lyons the next day, the group heard news which decided for them where they should go to set up the temporary church headquarters. Italy had entered the war as Germany's ally, and Italian troops stood poised to occupy all of the French-Italian border area. The little French-Swiss border town of Collonges, where the Seventh-day Adventist college was located, now lay exposed to a battle which could easily develop.

After traveling for several hours on the maze of back roads, John finally broke out onto Route Nationale No. 7. Although this was a major traffic artery to the south, it was not as heavily traveled as some of the roads leading directly out of Paris. Eight hours after leaving Lamotte-Beuvron they were in Lyons.

While Pastor Meyer visited his brother Paul, minister of the Lyons Seventh-day Adventist Church, Gabrielle and the others sought out their own friends. John set off for the home of Gilbert Beaujolin.

41

Weidner had always thought Gilbert was someone special from the first day he had seen him as a student on the campus of the college at Collonges. He was a brilliant, self-made man, yet possessed a sensitive character which was easily touched by the needs of others. Later, when John had gone to Lyons as a student religious-book salesman for the Seventh-day Adventists, he had unexpectedly met Beaujolin one day. Gilbert told him that he must stay at the Beaujolin home while he was selling in the city. There John also met Gilbert's lovely mother and older sister Annie. The four became close friends during the time young Weidner was a guest in the home.

John decided to enter the textile business in 1935, so he returned to Lyons to work as an apprentice in the trade. Beaujolin, already a success in textiles, gave him many pointers to help him learn the trade quickly. After John opened his own shop in Collonges in 1938, the two continued their friendship. Now they were together again at a time when the destinies of both might well be dramatically changed. With Gilbert when John arrived were his sister Annie and her husband, Joseph Langlade.

Lyons looked upon the war much as had Paris—the Germans would be stopped south of Paris. A counteroffensive would then push the invaders from the country. "How can we lose?" asked Gilbert as they sat talking in his home. "The English with their military power, and the Americans with their productive might. There is even talk the Russians will be in it with us soon. No, the Germans cannot get far in France. There is too much on our side!"

42

Through the evening hours the friends talked. By midnight they had agreed that whatever might happen, they would stay in close touch. Above all, they would not willingly accept life under German rule.

The next day John and his traveling companions debated whether to still try to go to Collonges or to travel on south to Anduze. Since the entry of the Italian forces into the war put Collonges near a second front, they decided on Anduze. Once the decision was made, John gave his new address to Beaujolin so that they could keep in contact. On the trip to the farming community the group heard on the car radio that the Germans had entered Paris and that their armored spearhead was aiming at Angoulême, 250 miles to the south.

Arriving in the small town on the evening of June 14, they located the attractive Badaut home on a hill overlooking the green vineyards which quilted the peaceful countryside. John found the contrast between the bustling, war-jittery Paris and peaceful, quiet Anduze most refreshing. The days ahead would be spent helping Pastor Meyer organize the new headquarters. He hoped there would also be time for hiking about the area and for leisurely visits with the country folk in the small town.

News on the radio told of an almost unmoving mass of French soldiers and civilians trying to flee south before the Germans. A fifty-mile jam of refugees was backed up northward from the Loire bridges, which had been dynamited by the retreating French army. German aircraft swept the roads clean so that their armored column could advance quickly.

Two days after the group arrived in Anduze, Gilbert Beaujolin's car roared up to the Badaut home. "John, it doesn't look as if the Germans are going to be stopped," Gilbert told his friend, his voice filled with emotion. "They've taken Paris! There is nothing to stop them from taking all of France! The French army is in a state of total collapse, from the reports I hear in Lyons. Why don't you and I see if we can get out of France ahead of the Germans? Maybe we can be of help to our countries from England."

John quickly agreed. He had already determined that he would try to get to England as soon as the new church headquarters had been established. The two friends began to lay out a plan.

"Gilbert and I are going to Sète, where we will try to get aboard an English ship," Weidner told Pastor Meyer and Gabrielle. "There should be an English vessel in the harbor, and I think we can persuade the captain to take us to England." John asked his sister to try to get word of the plan to their parents in Holland. "And Gabrielle," he counseled, "be careful wherever you go in the days ahead. Pray that God will lead me to do only those things which will be an honor to Him. I shall be praying, too, that He will guide and protect you."

In Beaujolin's car the two young men drove to Sète, a small Mediterranean port on the southern coast of France, and went immediately to the harbor. An air of tension gripped the little port city as they drove through the streets. It was as though everyone knew Sète had suddenly become one of the last doors of escape to freedom. French police were unusually numerous on the streets. Large numbers of people appeared to be waiting for the same opportunity John and Gilbert now sought.

At the waterfront they had little trouble locating a boat owner who was willing to take them about the harbor to look for an English ship. The large roll of francs John flashed convinced the boatman that it would be a rewarding trip. As they worked their way along the piers and anchorages among the ships, they spied the British Union Jack floating in the soft breeze from the stern of a large gray vessel.

"That is the one we're looking for," he said to the skipper of their little craft. "Take us over there and wait while we talk with the captain."

The tiny boat slid alongside the rope ladder hanging over the side of the ship, and John and Gilbert climbed aboard. A sailor pointed out the captain's cabin. At last they were knocking on the door of the man who could give them passage to England.

"I'm not so sure I can take you to England," the captain said. "There isn't much extra space on the ship since we're already heavily loaded, and I've had no instruction from England allowing me to pick up people like you in foreign ports. For all I know, you might be German spies."

Something, anything, John felt, had to be done to change the captain's thinking.

"But we have valid passports; furthermore we can pay well for the passage," John implored. "Money is no problem. We must get to England. And after all, you are an Englishman. You know our services can be of help to England. You would actually be doing a service to your country to see that we get there. The customs officials in England can investigate to determine if we are spies. You have nothing to lose."

The captain sat back in his chair thinking the matter over. "Well, Mr. Weidner, you say you are Dutch, so for you there isn't too much problem. But taking a Frenchman, like your friend here, I don't know." He paused for a long moment, then sighed and continued, "But you both seem like a decent sort—I'll take a chance. Come out to the ship again tomorrow morning. We'll be getting under way about noon. Don't be late though. The afternoon tide doesn't wait for you or me or anyone."

Back to their little boat went the two friends, now thoroughly relieved. "He'll take us!" Gilbert exclaimed as they started their short trip back to the dock. "Just think, John, we'll be in England in a week, and then we can begin doing something to help put the Nazis back where they belong."

They drove Gilbert's car to a garage and left it in the care of the owner. They locked the automobile, then mailed one set of keys and the car papers to Gabrielle in Anduze. A quick check of the hotels in town revealed that they would have to sleep on the beach for the night—every room in town was full.

As the two men were eating supper in a restaurant, the words of a radio newscast shocked them to immobility. "An armistice has just been signed between the French and German governments at Compiégne," the broadcast declared.

46

"Complete details of the cease-fire agreement are expected to be known shortly."

"So, it is done; we have capitulated!" exclaimed Gilbert when words finally returned after the shock of the news. "Everything will be different now. There will be trouble for everybody. Our decision to leave has been a wise one, John."

That night they slept very little. They were deeply troubled by the news that France had fallen to the invaders. Adding to the mental torment, the wind on the beach kept blowing sand in their faces. John could feel the salt from the humid sea air settling into his hair. Through the night as he came fitfully awake from time to time, he thought of the trip ahead. He wanted to get to England, where he felt he could serve his country; yet he felt remorse in leaving France. He loved the rich, rolling land which had been so good to him. But the decision to go had been made; and now that France had fallen, he knew it would be the best thing to do.

After a hasty breakfast near the beach the next morning, Gilbert and John sought the skipper of the little boat that had taken them out to the English ship the day before. As they rounded the corner where the small boat was tied up, they were startled to see not only the pudgy skipper but several blue-coated French policemen as well.

"What do you want here?" inquired one of the policemen as the two friends approached.

"To go out to the English vessel in the harbor," John replied, wondering why he was being questioned.

The gendarme's eyes swept the harbor quickly. "There is no English ship there now," he stated. "That ship left last night when the news of the armistice was received here. Now no one may leave the country until new regulations have been established by the government. If you try to contact other ship captains, you will be arrested. They are all being watched by our men. My advice to you is, Return to your home at once, and wait for further instructions from the new government."

This news added another shock. Only seconds before Weidner and Beaujolin had been expecting that their plans for reaching England were going to be successful. Now their hopes were shattered by the words of this policeman standing in front of them. As they looked across the harbor, they could see that their ship had, indeed, departed.

Sick at heart they went to the garage where they had left their car the night before and drove back to Anduze.

A few days later they heard of another escape possibility. "If you can get to Perpignan, they say the Spanish consul there is giving visas to cross into Spain," a friend told them. "From there you could go on into Portugal and catch a boat to England."

Early the next morning they set out for this French border city, located on the Mediterranean shore about one hundred kilometers west of Sète. They arrived in Perpignan late that evening.

At dawn the next day they went looking for the Spanish consulate. At last they found it, comfortably located in a better-than-average section of the city.

Its doors were bolted shut!

"Where is the Spanish consul?" John asked at a nearby store.

"You have business with the Spanish consul?" inquired the little Frenchman to whom they spoke. "So have hundreds of other people. They have been coming for the past two weeks, all wanting to get into Spain. Evidently the consul realized thousands would be coming. Anyway, yesterday morning he locked the place and headed for Spain. My guess is he won't be back for a month or more—at least not until the demand for passage through his country stops."

"You mean he just left without explaining to anyone?" asked John incredulously. "Surely he will be back soon. How can he run the affairs of his country here if he just closes up like that?"

Unimpressed by Weidner's concern, the little shopkeeper shrugged his shoulders and turned to his waiting customers.

"Well, John, let's face it, we've come to another dead end," sighed Beaujolin. "This time it looks as if we have no other place to turn. If all the ports are closed and the border is closed, we might just as well return to Lyons and develop some workable plan for escape from there."

Although he did not want to admit it, John had to agree with Gilbert—the way did seem closed. Had the two men been schooled in illegal activity, they might have given serious consideration to proceeding to the border anyway and trying to elude the few French and Spanish guards who kept watch in the area. And they probably would have succeeded in getting into Spain, too, for smugglers and other criminal types were making regular border crossings without being caught. But neither Weidner nor Beaujolin thought of such illegal activity now. They had been taught respect for the law, and their concept of right ruled out even thinking about illegally crossing the border. Had John known, standing there in the little store in Perpignan, that his future would involve crossing borders illegally not once but many times, his actions might have been different.

At that moment the war did seem to be over for the two young men. But, despite their discouragement, there was some consolation, however small. It was that the armistice left part of the country with some freedom. The French-Spanish border was still free, and a part of the French-Swiss border was also in the so-called Free Zone. The big seaport of Marseilles remained free; and, above all, the city of Lyons with its one million inhabitants was in the unoccupied zone. The French government was making its headquarters in the town of Vichy, and a demarcation line between the occupied and unoccupied zones ran northward from the western Pyrenees east of Bordeaux, then cut irregularly eastward south of Tours, dividing France.

As the two turned away from the little store in Perpignan, John had to agree with Gilbert that their best hope of doing anything constructive lay in going to Lyons. There was no possibility that John could return to his textile business in Paris; the Germans were there now!

"In Lyons we'll have to find some friends who can help us develop a plan that police or closed consulates cannot stop." John sighed. "Let's go back to Lyons."

III

the camps

IN LYONS, after their abortive attempts to escape to England, John and Gilbert turned their thoughts back to the immediate situation. They would need funds, they knew, if life was to go on successfully for them despite the changes that had come to the country. Hence they went back to the textile business. Gilbert, already established, merely took over the reins of his prosperous organization once again. For John, however, the process of getting back into business was an entirely new effort, since all of his inventory had been lost to the Germans in Paris.

Weidner was provided a rent-free office in the spacious Beaujolin enterprise. Then with Gilbert's help he began to contact friends he had known many years before when he had served an apprenticeship in France's largest textile-manufacturing center. Despite the increasing number of restrictions imposed by the newly created Vichy government, he was able to arrange for textile supplies and to find customers for his product. With the wartime restrictions on all "nonessential" commodities in France, many manufacturers of dresses and shirts and several department-store owners were eager to obtain quality goods, and John's business began to flourish.

The two friends continued to maintain close contact as the weeks stretched into months. John was offered use of the home of Annie and Joseph Langlade. Annie and Joseph often talked far into the night with John and Gilbert about their plans and hopes for the future. Being ardent patriots, the Langlades and Gilbert loved their country dearly. As Christians, they were vehemently opposed to the Nazi philosophy. They were also very much opposed to the armistice which France had signed, and to the Chef d'Etat of the new French government, Marshal Henri Philippe Pétain. They put their hope in the former tank-corps officer who had recently arrived in London—Charles de Gaulle. Their hearts swelled with pride when he spoke over the London radio:

"France has lost a battle.
But France has not lost the war!
Our country is in mortal peril.
Let us all fight to save her.
Vive la France!"

Many activities began to take up the time of the little group. Gilbert and his sister were becoming increasingly interested in the embryonic underground activities of Frenchmen who were determined to help their captive country. John also began new activities. He started visiting the offices of the Dutch consulate in Lyons to see if his services might be needed. There he became well acquainted with the consul, a man named Lambotte, and with the Dutch consul general for unoccupied France, Arie Sevenster, who came to Lyons frequently from his offices at Vichy.

The Germans continued to tighten their control in southern France through closer supervision of the Vichy government, and the help which the Dutch officials could give refugees diminished sharply.

Then further complications arose. Shortly after the armistice was signed, the Vichy government, under pressure of the Germans, severed diplomatic relations with the Dutch government in exile in London. Holland chose the neutral Swedish government to handle all matters pertaining to Dutch citizens in France. Not long after this action was taken, however, the Vichy government, again acting under even harder pressure from the Nazis, abolished the plan authorizing Sweden to handle Dutch matters in France. The function was transferred to the Vichy government's Bureau d'Administration des Neelandais.

These actions greatly impeded the effectiveness of such men as Sevenster and Lambotte in giving help to those in need. Not long after these oppressive actions were taken, Lambotte died, and his post in Lyons was filled by Maurice Jacquet, an enthusiastic Frenchman and tireless helper of the Dutch people.

As the months of 1941 went by, John's visits to the consulate became more frequent. In this way he kept himself informed on numerous aspects of the war. In one tragic facet he saw a pattern forming which bore no good for scores of his refugee countrymen in detention camps, or those arriving without help in the area. He developed an intense interest in their plight.

In 1941 the tide of refugees coming south increased as Nazi persecution of Jews in Belgium and Holland increased. The Dutch consulate in Lyons began to overflow with these homeless, driven people. They were in financial need, but the financial resources available to Sevenster were woefully small. The refugees were under constant threat of being sent to the detention camps. To escape this fate the incoming refugees wanted desperately to get into such safe countries as Switzerland and England.

To leave France they needed a *visa de sortie*. Because of German pressure these precious documents were extremely difficult to obtain.

"How many Dutch citizens are allowed to leave France?" John asked Sevenster as the two men talked together one day at the consul's office.

"Not nearly as many as we would like to see leaving, John," was the reply. "As diplomats, the only way we can help is through legal, diplomatic methods. But more and more we are seeing illegal roadblocks thrown in front of our efforts. Even as we proceed legally, there are frightening demands made of us for even the smallest requests. Most of these poor people are stranded here, and we simply do not know what to do for them. We must have money to help them live while in France and to pay for their passage out of France once we do obtain a visa, if that is possible."

John knew what the consul was talking about. Since the greater number of refugees were Jews, and because of the massive anti-Semitic program of the Germans, the collaborating Vichy government had already formed a special office, the Commission of Jewish Affairs. Xavier Vallat, who headed this new office, dealt out severe restrictions on all Jews, especially refugee Jews. Already the Gestapo and the Vichy government, working under a cloak of legality, were transferring refugees from French detention camps to German concentration camps.

The procedure was simple and varied little from day to day: The Gestapo would tell the Jewish Affairs office of the Vichy government that they needed a certain refugee in one of the camps—the purpose was really not too important. The Jewish Affairs office would then instruct the guards of the camp where the desired refugee was detained to bring him to the French-German border. There he would be turned over to the Gestapo.

Each day this pitiful tableau was enacted at the camps at Vernet-les-Bains, or Gurs, or Rivesaltes. The Dutch consuls, now stripped of all but the formality of their office, were helpless to prevent the merciless procession to death. Before the armistice the refugees who came to the camps in southern France were treated with some respect. In the aging enclosures, first built to care for prisoners of the Spanish Civil War, the refugees were given shelter and a small food ration. Many of them had traveled for days, sometimes weeks, to reach the comparative safety of unoccupied France. But after the armistice was signed with the Germans, this program of sometimes-kindness turned into nothing more than bare prison-camp care.

The camps were bad enough with their revolutionary and criminal elements already resident. When the attitude changed toward the "foreign" refugees, the situation turned quickly desperate. Before the armistice the Red Cross and other relief agencies were allowed to bring in food to supplement the meager ration doled out to the refugees. Afterward such agencies were more restricted, and fewer of their personnel were allowed to enter the gates. The camp guard was also increased. The regular gendarme force was supplemented by special government police, and the welfare of the refugees became entirely dependent upon whatever goodwill was shown them by the guards, the police, and the administration of the camp.

"Some of the prison officials are humane in their treatment of our people, but most are not," John was told by Sevenster on one of his visits to the consul's office. "A few camp chiefs are kind, but most follow closely the policy of the Vichy government to please the Germans. And the Germans obviously are aiming at complete liquidation of the Jews. Food supplies in the camps are very scarce, and there is no medical aid inside the prison walls.

"But the worst problem," Sevenster continued, "is that the Gestapo is dictating who shall be taken from the camps. We never hear from a refugee once the gendarmes take him away."

Arie Sevenster was a career diplomat for his country. Tall, strong both physically and morally, he was dedicated to duty. A real Dutch type, he came from the Frise, a highly conservative Protestant section of Holland. Sevenster felt deep sorrow for the Jews in their plight. From the first disappearance of a Jewish refugee, he had worked tirelessly to stop the horrible plan. Always outspoken, he forgot completely that his position and his life itself might be in jeopardy for the stand he was taking. His words and actions were setting him on a collision course with Vichy and the Germans, but he could not and would not stop.

"The government administration has asked me to forget the Jews and just take care of the Dutch people in France, and things will be much better for all of us," he told John. "But all the people I know from Holland are Dutch," he said passionately. "I know no Jews. All are Dutch to me, and I must help them—every one."

Sevenster worked long hours each day at the intricate task of obtaining visas for refugees to enter Spain. First he would appeal through the Dutch consulate in Spain for a Spanish transit visa to pass through the country. When such a document was in hand, he would then appeal to the French government for an exit visa from France. Once the diplomatic machinery had ground slowly to the point where this document was in hand, Sevenster sent the refugee on his way toward freedom. A trickle of refugees moved into Spain along this laborious route until November, 1942, when the Nazis occupied the southern part of France. From that time to D-Day it was impossible for a refugee to get out of France except through the underground.

During the worsening situation in 1941 Gilbert Beaujolin directed John's thoughts closer to action one day with a recommendation. "We need to do something to give aid to all these people who are facing death," he said. "We need an organization which can be more effective than one man working alone. We must have people working together who can devise ways to get around the many rules Vichy is using to stop the refugees from being freed from the camps."

Agreeing with Beaujolin's proposal, Weidner immediately began to help form such an organization. Gilbert explained that representatives of different religious faiths in the organization would be needed in order to do the most effective work. To achieve this goal they soon added to their board of directors Father P. Chaillet, a Jesuit priest who shared their desire to help, and Pastor Roland DePury, a warmhearted Protestant clergyman in Lyons. Gilbert became executive president of the new organization, which they called Les Amitiés Chrétiennes. The Catholic priest, the Protestant minister, and Weidner were members of the organization's board, along with Pastor Marc Boegner, chairman of the Federation of Protestants in France, and Cardinal Gerlier, of Lyons.

The group increased from four to six, then to ten and twelve members. Dedicated to helping persons of all faiths, or of no faith at all, who were being tormented or who faced deportation from the camps, this organization began a small-scale but important work.

At the same time John proposed an organization working exclusively for Dutch people in the camps. Maurice Jacquet, the consul, and Louis Assher, a famous Jewish diamond cutter, and other friends joined John in forming this group.

As the two groups began to function, John divided his days between his office, the consul headquarters, and visits to the camps.

The Dutch refugees, he noted, were generally treated better than were those from other countries. Most Dutch refugees were assigned to the camp at Chateauneuf-les-Bains near Vichy. Some were even assigned to hotels. Despite the assignment, the problems of the Dutch refugees were just as great as those of the other refugees—they might find their beds a bit softer, their meals a degree better, and their escape opportunities somewhat easier. But what was the advantage of escape when one had no valid papers and did not know what to do or where to go? On every French street corner there seemed to be a gendarme who was suspicious of anyone whose papers were not in order, or whose speech was not that of a Frenchman, or who did not seem to have a definite destination.

All of these things John Weidner learned through experience in the months that Les Amitiés Chrétiennes and the Dutch group were operating. He talked French officials into giving him papers as a social worker, which in turn gave him access to the camps. He put together a formula of foods to supplement the meager camp fare of the starving prisoners. He contacted friends who worked in government document offices where travel permits and identification papers were issued. He made friends with families living near the camps. They agreed to hire the prisoners John could get freed under the rules which allowed some "nonpolitical" detainees to live outside the prisons if their employment was assured. He engaged others who would aid in housing "political" prisoners who might be helped to escape. He contacted lawyers, talked with judges, worked with community and provincial officials, and sought financial help to supplement personal funds he was already spending on the operation.

Gradually John and his group began to classify the camp guards and members of the administrative groups of each camp according to their willingness to cooperate in freeing prisoners. Some guards, John discovered, were almost openly cooperative. Others were cooperative—for a price. Still others were "double men." They appeared to cooperate but were known to tell what they saw and heard to their leaders. Others, disgruntled because their nation had just lost a war, were inclined to practice brutality and low thinking of every sort.

Separating these various groups was a tedious but vital part of the organization's work. An approach made to a "double" guard could result in arrest. If a disgruntled guard was asked to help, he might arrest the requesting member or quickly turn him over to the administrators of the camp.

Among the hardest jobs was persuading Frenchmen living in the countryside around the camps to give jobs to prisoners Weidner knew would soon be taken from the camps by the Gestapo. Fearful of the many new regulations forced upon them, and having heard stories of Gestapo atrocities in other countries occupied by the Nazis, local citizens were naturally cautious about doing anything which would implicate them or cause their arrest by the invaders.

It was a hard and often thankless task into which Weidner put his entire strength and financial resources. During the months in which Les Amitiés Chrétiennes and his own small group were operating, John regularly gave twenty-five to thirty ten-pound parcels of food each week to prisoners closest to starvation. Legal fees which paid for the valuable arguments before judges to get certain prisoners out of the camps also came from the income of his textile business.

One day while Weidner was visiting in the camp at Chateauneuf-les-Bains, he found a detainee named Sidney Rosenthal, who had been recommended to him by the Dutch consulate. A Jew who could not leave the camp under any circumstances, Rosenthal, with his wife and child, seemed destined for certain deportation to a concentration camp. This was one person John decided should be helped.

Rosenthal appeared to be honest, he concluded, as the two talked at the camp. He realized what his fate would be unless help came soon from some source. The man said he would cooperate in whatever plan could be worked out for his escape.

Back in Lyons John formulated this plan: He would have the prisoner request permission to go for dental work to Clermont-Ferrand, a town about twenty miles from the camp. There Weidner would meet him, and they would travel to Lyons, where further plans for his safety could be made. Since camp restrictions were not applied with the same force to women and children as to men, Mrs. Rosenthal would request permission to visit a nearby friend. She would be met by a member of John's organization at the little train station in Royat, from which point she would travel toward Vichy, then swing south again and meet her husband when he and Weidner arrived in Lyons from a completely different route.

On the morning of the planned escape Rosenthal was met at the camp checkout point by a gendarme about whom John's organization knew nothing. Weidner's plans, however, were not dependent upon the particular political beliefs of the gendarme. Together the prisoner and guard set off by bus for Clermont-Ferrand.

John had chosen Rosenthal's dentist with great care. He was a foe of the Germans, willing to cooperate to save lives and to free France from the invaders. Perhaps the dentist's most important asset was that his office opened on two streets which met at the point of a triangle. Patients could enter from either street and leave either way. This was unknown to the guard accompanying Rosenthal. Given only one address for the dentist's office, he was completely unaware that the building fronted on two streets.

At the address given Rosenthal and his guard, John waited to make sure no problem had delayed or postponed the trip. When he saw Rosenthal enter the building with the guard, Weidner hurried around to the other entrance.

Inside the building, in the waiting room, Rosenthal and the guard sat down to wait for the dental appointment. In about ten minutes the prisoner asked permission to visit the restroom, which was down the long corridor connecting the two entrances of the dentist's office. The guard, sitting to one side in the waiting room, could not see down the corridor, nor did he suspect any unusual move on Rosenthal's part. He readily granted the prisoner's request.

Rosenthal, having been told every move he should make by Weidner several days earlier, entered the restroom and immediately popped out again and checked the hallway toward the waiting room. When he noted that all was clear, he hurried to the entrance at which John was waiting.

Outside, the prisoner breathed, "My friend, you have kept your word. You are here! How can I thank you?"

"Don't thank me, at least not yet," said John. "We have a long way to go, and we must hurry. Here are your papers. If we are stopped, act as though you have had these papers a million years and that you belong in this part of France. Whatever happens, keep up your confidence; and we will get away with this. If either of us is apprehended and questioned, however, neither you nor I must indicate that we know each other. That way at least one of us will go free. Follow me closely, and let's move as if we know exactly what we are doing."

"I understand perfectly. If you are ready, I am," Rosenthal replied.

John had set Rosenthal's dental appointment for thirty minutes before a bus left Clermont-Ferrand for the little city of Thiers. The route to Thiers was not the well-traveled way to go to Lyons from Clermont-Ferrand. He hoped this fact, plus their travel by bus instead of by train, would give them an advantage in their escape. The train station would be the first place the gendarme and local police would go looking for Rosenthal, Weidner knew.

The two men hurried to the bus station. There they found the bus practically loaded. With tickets already purchased by John, they slipped on unnoticed. As the vehicle roared out of the station in Clermont-Ferrand, John breathed more easily. No gendarmes had been at the station, and no one seemed to take any interest in the two men.

As they traveled, John reviewed the rest of the route to himself. "We are on our way to Thiers first," he mused. "From there we will go by bus southeastward to St. Etienne. There we will catch another bus for Lyons. Rosenthal's wife will probably be there waiting for us. I'm sure she left the camp for Royat ahead of him this morning."

The bus began to slow down as it entered Thiers. "I hope he acts just as he did at Clermont-Ferrand," John thought to himself. "There may be gendarmes here, but they won't ask for papers unless they feel there is something suspicious about us. If Rosenthal will act confident, then all will go well."

Weidner and Rosenthal dismounted from the bus when it reached the station and went through the process of boarding another bus bound for St. Etienne with no difficulty. At St. Etienne their change to a bus for Lyons was made without a hitch. A short time later the Rosenthals had a joyous reunion in Lyons. When further arrangements had been made, John took the family on to Switzerland and freedom.

Every time John completed the escape of refugees such as the Rosenthals, he dug a little deeper into his conscience to ask, "Am I doing what is right in this work? We are saving people from certain death, but we are using illegal means to gain their freedom. We forge identification and travel papers; we ask guards to renounce their appointed job when they help us. We elude, falsify, evade, and outwit. As a Christian, am I doing right in this?"

Throughout his years of underground leadership John continued to apply these questions and thoughts to the work he was doing. But each time he found resolution in prayer and a deep inward searching of his life to make sure neither hatred nor personal gain was the motive that drove him day and night. "I feel the hand of God leading me onward," he admitted to himself on one such occasion. "These countless refugees need the help of a compassionate friend. They need the love of God demonstrated amid the torment and terror of this awful war. I believe the work our organization is doing will show the love that only He can give."

IV

the BORDER

ONE MORNING early in 1942 John Weidner awakened with an idea that brought a turning point to his work of helping refugees. "We are doing much to get prisoners out of the camps and to find places for them to work or hide," he reflected, "but that is only half a solution. Everywhere the gendarmes stand ready to arrest these people and turn them back to the camps. They can never be safe here in France, even if we find places for them to stay out in the countryside. The only safe place is across the border in Switzerland or in Spain, where the Gestapo cannot order their seizure. We are doing only half a job unless we get them not only out of the camps but out of the country as well."

John realized that he was in a particularly good position to help the refugees out of France and into Switzerland. Few people knew the French-Swiss border of the St. Julien-Collonges-Annemasse area as well as he did. He had spent a dozen years at the college in Collonges, and hardly a day had passed without his taking a hike either across the border itself or up onto the Saleve Mountain, which towered along the border just off the college campus.

The college was one mile from the border, and a road led directly from the campus to the customshouse located astride the boundary line. The Saleve rose steeply behind the campus. The little village of Collonges (population, 2,000) was stretched out along the road leading to the border. Usually about two hundred students from numerous European countries were attending the college, which was operated by the Southern European Division of Seventh-day Adventists. On Saturday afternoons John, his brother François, his sisters Gabrielle and Annette, and their parents would take walks along the road through Collonges and into Switzerland. They were joyful walks, he remembered, as the family would cross the border and stroll through the beautiful Swiss countryside toward Geneva three miles away.

Weidner had also learned to know the border during hundreds of trips to the University of Geneva, which he attended while living in Collonges, and on numerous trips into Geneva to sessions of the League of Nations. An avid student of history and political science, he would sit through the long sessions of the League as it deliberated and debated great issues. When the fiery oratory ended, he would rush to talk with the noted men who had participated in the discussions. During these years he met Aristide Briand, the peppery, eloquent French representative to the League. And he met Litvinov, the Russian representative; Dr. Gustav Stresemann, from Germany; and Neville Chamberlain, of Great Britain. He heard Haile Selassie's impassioned plea before the League in 1937 when Italian troops invaded the little emperor's country. John sat in on meetings of the great disarmament conference in 1936 and heard leaders predict that if a solution to the armament race could not be found, Europe would be in the flames of war within a few years.

"Why, I could take refugees across the border with a blindfold on if I needed to," reasoned Weidner as he thought more about guiding them across the French-Swiss line. "But some problems must be solved before I can begin doing it."

The biggest obstruction to establishing any systematic escape route into Switzerland, John knew, was the new regulation requiring special travel permits for movement within fifty miles of the border. Weidner knew he could not continue to get special travel papers for use in the border area time after time without some logical reason.

"There is an answer," he concluded after studying the problem for some time. "I'll open another textile store at Annecy; then I'll have a perfectly good reason to be near the border at any time I choose."

Annecy was a pleasant, thriving resort city of twenty thousand persons lying along the northern end of beautiful Lake Annecy, just thirty miles from the Swiss border. Connections by rail were easily made from Annecy to Lyons or to the south toward Marseilles. The city was ideally situated to serve as a staging point near the border where refugees could be brought from several points throughout France. Its hum of business also promised Weidner a prosperous front for his underground activities.

Within a few days he found a suitable building in the city for his new store and hired personnel to run the office and to help in contacting customers in the Savoy area in which Annecy is located. Weidner obtained the papers and other documents which would allow him unlimited freedom of travel into the general border sector. As he made the three-hour train trip back to Lyons after setting up the new business in Annecy, he realized that he doubtless would make the trip many times in the future. "I probably won't be as relaxed on some of those trips as I am today," he thought as he leaned back in his seat and watched the peaceful French countryside.

A week later he led his first refugees from Lyons to Annecy. Three times the gendarmes came through the train cars checking the papers of passengers. Weidner's friends at the documents office in Lyons had done a careful job, and there was no difficulty.

"Your papers have been made in the same way and marked with the same stamps given every day to those who apply," John had quietly told the refugees before they boarded the train for Annecy. "The only difference is that your papers were made after working hours when the documents director had gone home. It took only twenty-four hours to get them. Our friends are very efficient in providing us with false documents."

John quickly learned the tricks of guiding refugees. All identification papers of Dutch, Belgian, or other foreign refugees, he discovered, had to specify that the refugees were from the Alsace area of France. In that area the

French spoke a language very similar to that of the Germans who lived just across the Rhine River in Germany. When a guard, checking identification papers, saw an Alsace address, he would not question the language of the holder of the papers since he could not understand the broken French of the Alsace area anyway. Weidner always warned refugees that they were to travel as though they were alone—that the person sitting next to them on the seat was merely an acquaintance of that journey. Following this plan, only one person had to worry about convincing the guards. When several people admitted knowing each other, the gendarmes could pit one against another to obtain confessions.

At the Annecy train station was a crucial checkpoint through which all incoming passengers had to pass. Many refugees had already made attempts to cross the border, and they naturally went through Annecy on the way. This made the guards at the checkpoint in the Annecy station unusually thorough with even slightly suspicious persons. Shortly after he began traveling to Annecy regularly, however, John noticed several ways in which he might bypass the close scrutiny of the guards. The station restaurant opened onto the street; and although a guard was stationed outside the restaurant door, he occasionally slipped away to smoke a cigarette or for other purposes. This, then, became a route by which John sometimes took refugees when he did not want them to have to undergo the rigid examination of the guards at the main checkpoint located in the station entrance.

A second method involved the main exit from the station. The ticket collector's cubicle and that of the guard stood side by side at this exit. After a train had been in the station for some time and it seemed that all its passengers had left the station, the ticket collector would close his gate and leave to relax until the next train arrived. The guard often left at the same time. Watching carefully, Weidner would see the ticket collector linger near his booth a few moments after the guard had strolled away. He would then hurry to the ticket collector, his group of refugees trailing him, and ask the man to take their tickets so that they could be on their way into the city. Concerned only about the fares, the collector would lift the bar, take the tickets, and the group would walk out of the station.

At other times John sent refugees, one at a time, walking slowly down the station platform toward an open area paralleling the railroad tracks. The refugees were instructed to stroll along this open area until they reached the first street that crossed the tracks. There they were to turn onto the street and walk until they were out of sight of the station. They would wait then until Weidner came along. This latter procedure was used very seldom because it was such a bold scheme for leaving the station illegally.

When he did take refugees through the checkpoints, John always explained to them in advance that they should be confident in front of the guards. "Your papers are the very best," he would point out. "There is no reason why you should be questioned any more than other persons making this same trip, unless you do something out of the ordinary. Be calm, answer all questions as honestly as you can, and never act afraid or be in a hurry to get away from the guards." Such instruction paid off, for no refugee he accompanied was ever arrested on any of the scores of train trips he made from Lyons to Annecy.

John sometimes had the help of a brave Alsatian gendarme named Dupont when he moved refugees from one point to another. Dupont worked effectively until arrested by the Nazis for his underground work. He later died in a concentration camp.

In Annecy, Weidner usually took the refugees to his store, where they stayed overnight. Sometimes, however, there would be too many to stay at the store. He found an answer to this problem in a small, quiet woman who operated a gift shop several blocks away. Her name, she said, was Marie-Louise Meunier; and she burned with a deep passion to help people in need. The little middle-aged woman responded quickly to John's request for help.

"Bring them to me," she directed. "Bring all you want. I'll make sure they remain hidden until they are ready to move on. The back of my store has plenty of room in it. No one comes there unless I know about it first. They will be safe with me."

Weidner often left Annecy early in the morning by bus with refugees he was guiding to the border. Sometimes, however, he borrowed a car from friends, especially if he wanted to bypass the control station at the village of Cruseilles, between Annecy and St. Julien at the border. He skirted the village by traveling over back roads to the west. At Annecy he would have to make a decision as to which method he wanted to use in traveling to the border.

He could travel by bus to a point a mile or two before the control station in Cruseilles. There he could take the refugees to a friend's farmhouse on the pretense of making a visit. The group would leave the farmhouse through the back door and travel through the fields which bordered the Saleve Mountain. This route took them across the top of the mountain and down the other side at a point about two miles from the barbed wire of the border itself. The route across the Saleve was physically the most difficult to use, but it afforded less chance of contact with gendarmes and Italian or German guards manning the control stations.

The second route was by bus through all the control stations between Annecy, Cruseilles, St. Julien, and the border point at which Weidner decided to make the crossing attempt. This involved scrutiny by guards at the control station in Cruseilles, at another just south of St. Julien, and at yet another located east of St. Julien. The St. Julien-Collonges-Annemasse road which ran east from the border town was parallel and very close to the barbed strands marking the actual border. This route John took whenever he received word from friends that the guards at the control stations were making routine checks of travelers.

At other times, when high German officials were inspecting the area, for example, the checking at the control stations became very thorough. Any remotely suspicious act was enough to set the guards off on an hours-long siege of questioning. A refugee qualification for travel on the "all stations" route also included complete confidence in Weidner's leadership.

A third route closely paralleled the one by bus to the border, with the exception that John usually used a car. Just below the control station in Cruseilles he turned off the main Annecy-Cruseilles-St. Julien highway onto one of three or four small side roads which angled northwestward around the control station, rejoining the highway some miles farther on. This route avoided the usually tricky checkpoint near Cruseilles and helped cut down the odds that the group might be caught.

Once Weidner reached the border, he became dependent upon a considerable group of friends for the completion of his tasks. Farmers, faculty members at the Adventist college at Collonges, government officials favorable to the underground, storekeepers, and others, each with firsthand knowledge of the immediate situation on the border, were of prime importance as he reached the area in which they lived. These friends could tell him if new guards had been assigned to the area, if patrols along the border were being increased, or if there had been an unusual amount of questioning of the local citizenry by the Germans. Most important of all, they knew which sections of the barbed wire on the border were charged with electricity! These friends also provided wire cutters, ladders, and other implements needed to get through or over the wire near their home, no matter what the condition of the strands. Since they lived in the escape areas, they were free to move about and serve as scouts while John and the refugees hid in their homes.

In the first months of 1942 there were only the French police to worry about as border crossings were made in the

74

Savoy area of the French-Swiss border. After the German occupation of southern France in November, 1942, however, first the Italian and then the German troops had to be contended with. In addition there were the Gardes Mobiles (government riot troops) and the customs service. After this date, control along the escape areas of the French-Swiss border increased sharply.

When the Italians were on the border, security was sometimes not too great, for many of them did not seem to take the war very seriously. This attitude was reflected in the often lackadaisical way in which they carried out their duties. Though the treaties of Benito Mussolini, the Italian dictator, with Hitler's government stipulated that the Italians should treat the French as enemies, it was hard for some Italian guards who had lived on the French-Italian border before the war to regard the fun-loving French people as enemies. On several occasions when he had a group of refugees to take across the border, John sent an attractive young lady ahead to engage the Italian guard in conversation. Inevitably the guard would become so interested in the girl that he paid little attention to refugees crossing the border. At all times, however, top control of the border was directed by the Germans; and when their inspectors were about, security was tightened accordingly.

The difficult task of classifying guards as to their attitude toward the underground continued to be an important part of border crossing. It was a hard job because of the complex control which operated for everyone. If a gendarme on the border let a refugee escape in his sector, he never knew if the refugee would turn back and reveal himself as a member of the Gestapo, sent to check on the integrity of the gendarmes. Similarly, an Italian guard never knew if the gendarme on duty with him at a control point might be telling the German command everything he did to help the refugees or others who might want to cross the border. In this nerve-fraying game of double agentry it was hard for John and his friends to put their trust in any guard.

More deeply involved in the strange, terror-filled task of border crossing each passing day, John realized more than ever that his life needed constant divine direction. He attended church on Saturday mornings whenever possible, and more and more he turned to prayer for comfort and strength. "My Father," John often prayed, "help me to be kind to those I try to help. Where they have known only hatred, help me to be loving. And give me confidence that this work will accomplish what You have placed me in the world to do."

V

eaRly contacts

At FIVE O'CLOCK each morning a sealed
freight train left the little railroad station at Annemasse,
France, en route to Geneva. It was as regular as the sunrise,
always keeping to its schedule, never varying more than a
few minutes, for its trip was only a few miles in length. The
shortness of the trip, however, was not an indication of the
train's importance—at least not to the French and Swiss
guards who had to check it thoroughly each time it crossed
the border. It was one of those leftover fragments of peace
remaining in the war. The Swiss needed some "nonessential"
items which France was happy to supply. France found use,
too, for products from Switzerland, despite the war which
had raised a barrier between the two nations.

The daily ritual of the sealed freight train meant absolutely nothing to John Weidner as he sat pondering a particularly difficult problem one day in Lyons. He needed to
get into Switzerland and to go on to Bern without being
caught. Previously he had been leading Jewish refugees
across the French-Swiss border only, not on into the coun-

try. To get across the border into Switzerland was only one problem. Another was not to get caught by the Swiss guards, for they had orders to return certain categories of escapees from France. Only the very old and families with young children found refuge in Switzerland. John, as a single person, would be returned to France if he were caught trying to enter Switzerland. The reason for his desire to travel to Bern now was his need to obtain permission not only to enter the country without restriction but also to set up a system whereby he could return safely to France after completing his work.

As he sat thinking about the problem, he decided that a letter to a close friend in Geneva who had contacts with the French consulate there might help. The coded message which came back was helpful, and it sparked John's interest in the little freight train that ran between Annemasse and Geneva.

The letter reported that the train carried only freight and that since it was searched and sealed at the Annemasse station, it was impossible to get aboard there. "But the engineer of the train is a friend of the Resistance movement. He has agreed to move the train very slowly across a bridge about a mile out of Annemasse. You should be on the girders of the bridge on the date given above; and as the train passes, you can drop from the bridge into the coal car. The engineer will help you, so there should be no difficulty in making this jump. As the railroad at the border is usually not manned by French and German guards, you will probably be able to proceed into Switzerland without any inspection of the train. After the train has reached Switzerland, it will be slowed again so that you can get off before reaching Eaux-Vives, where there is a Swiss customs checkpoint. Then you can probably get to Bern to work out your plans for regular entry into Switzerland without difficulty."

The plan sounded good to Weidner with one exception: it was a very tricky idea. He didn't know the engineer, had never been on the bridge from which he was to jump, and didn't know where he would be dropped off in Switzerland. But even in those days of intrigue and terror a close friend such as John had in Geneva could be trusted. Everything depended upon the trust of friends if progress in saving lives was to be made.

The Swiss checkpoint was three miles inside Switzerland, so there was plenty of distance for the engineer to drop him off unseen in the hilly Swiss countryside. The more he studied the plan, the more he became convinced it would work. His underground companions had recently brought word that Dr. W. A. Visser 't Hooft, General Secretary of the World Council of Churches, whose headquarters were in Geneva, was ready to aid John's work if needed. And Johan Bosch Van Rosenthal, Dutch minister in Bern, had also offered help.

Dr. Visser 't Hooft had heard about Weidner's refugee work from several escapees whom John had helped. Among these was Nico Gazan, whom he had taken over the Saleve, along with Gazan's wife, and then into Switzerland. From Gazan the World Council official had obtained a full and enthusiastic report of Weidner's activities. Gazan had sent word to John that Dr. Visser 't Hooft was ready to help him.

With the situation in France worsening daily and with problems—especially a lack of money—piling up, John decided to try to go to Switzerland and then return to France after conferences with the officials. The return from Switzerland was considered very risky, and without some kind of extra help Weidner knew he could not expect to make the trip more than a few times without being caught.

It was from the grateful Gazan that he got his answer. If he could get to Geneva and Bern without being taken by Swiss authorities, Van Rosenthal would then arrange for him to obtain special papers which would help solve the border-crossing problem. Gazan let John know he had also arranged a conference in Geneva with a Mr. Demierre, a security officer of the Swiss government, who could also give assistance.

At dawn John scaled the girders of the bridge where he was to meet the train. He settled down on a cold metal beam directly above the train tracks; and while he waited there in the chilly morning air, he began asking himself questions: How slowly would the train be going? What if there were guards at the border? Would they come into the engine cab where he would be hiding?

His thoughts were interrupted by the sound of the approaching train. In a few minutes it rounded a curve about a mile away, the cars snaking along behind the smoke-belching engine. As the freight cars loomed closer, John threw his feet over the side of the steel crossarm and prepared to let go. His eyes strained through the early light for the dimensions of the coal car and for the engineer who was somehow supposed to help him.

"Where is that fellow?" John gritted his teeth as he hung from the girder. Suddenly he saw him standing in one corner of the coal car behind the approaching engine. He was gesturing to Weidner. The train had slowed down considerably, and the jump now seemed reasonable. Just as the roof of the engine passed beneath his feet, he dropped onto the coal. Then the engineer's powerful arm was around him, pulling him out of the coal and into the cab of the engine.

"A good jump," he shouted above the din of the engine. "You might have landed on your face, but you haven't even gotten your clothes dirty. Come on up here with me, and we'll get this train moving again."

As they moved along, rapidly now, John fell silent, watching the engineer. The trainman didn't offer information about himself, and Weidner didn't ask for any. Both men had jobs to do, and silence was helpful to them both. Weidner suddenly noticed that the train was losing speed and attempted to look out the window to see what was wrong.

"Get back! Get down!" the engineer warned him quickly. "This is our unlucky day. There are guards at the border ahead. They usually aren't there. We'll go past them, but they will probably come to the engine after they have checked the cars. That closet there," he said, pointing to a small cubicle at the corner of the cab, "get in there if I tell you to, and be very still. It's where I hang my clothes. They won't think of looking there. They'll probably poke around in the coal and then leave."

4

John crouched out of sight as the engineer brought the hissing engine to a halt about two hundred feet beyond the guards. As he pulled the train to a stop, he stuck his head far out of the cab window so that he could see what the guards were doing.

"They're checking the cars very carefully this morning," he said quietly as he watched the rear of the train from his seat at the window. "Hey, they've got two fellows," he added in startled excitement. "They must have been hiding between the cars back there all the way from Annemasse. Now the guards are coming up this way; they're coming to the cab."

He ducked his head back into the cab and leaped for the little closet. "Quick! Get in there and don't move. I'll make sure they don't look inside. But stay quiet if you hear them coming into the cab."

John slipped into the little wooden closet, and the engineer stepped quickly out of the cab onto the ground to meet the guards.

Beside the cab the engineer greeted the German guards. He started to engage them in conversation, but they cut him short with directions to show them aboard the engine. Without a word the engineer led the way up the ladder into the cab. The guards looked about, then with long poles they had brought with them poked into the coal for several minutes until they were satisfied that no one was hiding there. Muttering about the two prisoners who stood manacled beside the cab steps, the guards left the engine. The engineer stepped down with them. "May I proceed?" he asked.

"Yes, you may go," one of the guards snapped.

The engineer mounted to the engine again, sat down in his seat, and pushed the levers. The train began to move slowly away from the border. "You can come out now," he shouted to John as the freight picked up speed.

"What did they say?" Weidner asked as he came out of the closet. "It was so tight in there I couldn't hear what you were saying."

"They just wanted to know if I had seen the two men they caught get on at Annemasse. I told them I hadn't seen anything, which was the truth. They'll probably be taken back to Annemasse and jailed. They're the first we've had try to get across between the cars for several months now. That is no way to cross the border, between the cars."

As the train swung slowly around a long curve that climbed gently into a cut in the hills, the engineer signaled John to get over to the door of the cab again. "We'll be losing speed on this grade, and when we come out of the cut, we won't be traveling more than fifteen miles an hour. You jump far out from the cab when we reach the end of the cut, and you'll have no trouble. Good luck!"

As the engineer turned back to his work, Weidner shouted his thanks for the help he had given. He eased his way down the cab's two steps and stood on the bottom rung. When the engine reached the end of the cut, he leaped out, landing upright on the run on level ground. Within a few steps he had complete control again and was able to stop well away from the moving train. The engineer looked back from the cab window toward the spot where Weidner had leaped, and when he saw that he had landed safely, he raised his thumb in a gesture of victory.

Weidner left the railroad and headed toward a nearby road. Walking at a steady pace, he soon reached the Geneva suburbs, where he caught a streetcar which took him to the home of the friend whose letter had outlined the border-crossing method for him.

"I need some Swiss money so that I can go to Bern for a permit to stay in the country," Weidner told his friend. "There are several people I need to see in both Geneva and Bern; but Bern must come first, since government head-quarters there is the only place I can get the permit I need." John's friend handed him the funds, and he left for the train station at Cornavin, arriving three hours later in Bern. Although there had been Swiss guards aboard the train between the two cities, they had not asked for his papers.

The office of Johan Bosch Van Rosenthal, minister of the Dutch legation in Bern, was John's first stop in the Swiss capital. There he met the Dutch government official for the first time and gave him a complete report of the work his Dutch relief organization had been carrying on for Jews and other refugees. Weidner also brought news about the activities of Jacquet, the Dutch consul at Lyons, and Arie Sevenster, consul general at Vichy. Rosenthal carefully noted the information and encouraged him to continue his refugee work. He provided John with a travel permit good for one week and gave him funds for use in Switzerland. Then Weidner left for Geneva.

A Dutchman himself, Dr. W. A. Visser 't Hooft greeted John cordially at the World Council of Churches headquarters in Geneva. As Weidner explained the escape work he had been doing, the distinguished clergyman listened with more than usual interest.

"I want to help you with whatever aid we can give—money or recommendations or whatever. I am sure your work will increase in importance as the war goes on, and we will have opportunity to work together in many ways. We have some funds here we want to turn over to you if you feel they can be put to good use at this time," Dr. Visser 't Hooft said. He gave Weidner 200,000 French francs. "I shall be expecting to hear from you regularly. If I am not available at any time, you can contact Nico Gazan. He will see that I hear of your needs promptly. The next time you come to Switzerland we will have much more to discuss. You are doing a good work, John. I hope you will be guided safely in the days ahead," Dr. Visser 't Hooft said.

That afternoon Weidner again went to Bern, this time to see friends at the Southern European Division headquarters of the Seventh-day Adventist Church, and to discuss with Pastors A. V. Olson and Walter R. Beach the activities of the Adventist Church in France. Communications between the division headquarters and France were difficult, and these church leaders were eager for all the firsthand information that could be brought to them. Through the week Weidner traveled from Bern to Geneva several times, visiting Dr. Visser 't Hooft at his home on several occasions. He was careful not to visit the World Council of Churches headquarters afterward, except on rare occasions. He did not want the large network of spies operating in Geneva to tab him as an unusual visitor and begin to investigate his activities.

At the end of the week when he had completed his visits, Weidner made preparations to return to France. Arrangements had been made with the Swiss authorities through his friend in Geneva for him to be taken to the Cropettes detention camp, into which all illegal entrants from France were placed.

"You will be put into the camp as though you had illegally entered Switzerland from France," his friend said. "Then early in the morning you will be taken to the border with other illegal entrants and sent back into France. We are sure you know how to avoid the border guards as you make your way home. Our men will help you as best they can."

That evening he entered the detention camp, where he found a strange mixture of refugees and criminals. For the refugees, now facing serious consequences, he could feel great sorrow. But for the criminals, who ran contraband supplies across the border, John had little sympathy. They caused nothing but hardship for those whose lives depended upon border crossing. Guards, however, made little distinction between the criminals and the refugees.

At about four o'clock the next morning the Swiss guards roused the prisoners and hustled them toward the border in a truck. Once there, they opened the back of the vehicle. The prisoners jumped out, immediately scattering like chickens. Each was hoping to avoid the guards they knew were patrolling the border in France. Some in their haste stumbled directly into the guards and were marched off to unknown fates. But John worked with a skill born of numerous encounters with danger. He moved carefully toward the nearest growth of trees. From their protective shelter he surveyed the border area around him with care. Pausing often to catch any movement around him, he was soon through the barbed wire, across the border road, and into the trees of France beyond. With a sigh of relief he finally came to the familiar road that led toward the campus of the college at Collonges.

VI

GENEVA ARREST

WITH the financial help he was getting from Geneva, John Weidner's underground activities widened in scope. The store at Annecy was now serving as a hiding place for greater numbers of Jewish and other refugees fleeing from France into Switzerland. Some of these people were destined ultimately to escape from the Nazi terror through Spain. But Switzerland would serve as their staging area, where plans would be made for their flight through France to Spain, then into Portugal, and eventually on to England.

With the growth of activity, however, came also a corresponding increase in problems of operation. Primarily, John needed more money for his operations, a smoother functioning connection for the reception of news which would aid his activities, and better arrangements for the passage of refugees over the border. One day, with these problems mounting and a lack of counsel on which he could rely, he decided to make another trip to Geneva and Bern to talk there with supporters of his work.

"I will be in Geneva for a few days," he told Raymonde Pillot, his secretary, when he had completed plans for the trip. "Arrangements have been made in Switzerland so that all I need to do at the border is to let the guards know who I am, and they will let me go on about my business. This will make it much easier for me to make future trips.

"Be sure to check with the consul while I am gone in case there is some special help they need," John told the girl. As she noted his instructions, he realized how valuable Raymonde had become to his underground work. A member of the Seventh-day Adventist church in Lyons, where John was also a member, she was efficient, clever, and tight-lipped about the secrets they shared. She knew all about John's business in Lyons and Annecy, and she was equally knowledgeable about the underground organization he was perfecting. Already she had carried messages to members of his group in Annecy, and she could be relied on at any time John needed her help for some mission he could not attempt himself.

On the train from Lyons to the border the underground leader thought over the available escape routes which had been established in the Savoy area. Recently he had added a small culvert which ran under the road on the border near St. Julien to his list of possibilities. The little under-the-road route lay near the customshouse at St. Julien, where he had found a new, important friend of the organization. He was Arthur Charroin, a police inspector at the customshouse, who began using his official position to help Weidner lead people to freedom. He and Charroin were constantly seeking new methods for crossing the border because German patrols were especially trained to detect places most often used for escape in the past.

"I will do anything I can to help you, John," Charroin had said when Weidner came to him on the recommendation of a close friend. "In my position I can help you very much, so do not hesitate to contact me." Little did Arthur Charroin realize as he talked with John that this offer would be paid for with his life.

Charroin closely watched the Germans who maintained control around the St. Julien customshouse. He studied every move they made and became familiar with the blind spots in their network of border surveillance. One day he demonstrated to Weidner in a dramatic way how well he knew the Germans.

"You come to the customshouse tomorrow morning and ask for me," he told John when he learned that Weidner needed to get into Switzerland again. The next day, as directed, Weidner walked to the customshouse. Outside stood the French and German guards on the French side of the border. Down the road John could see the Swiss guards policing the road on their side of the barrier. The customshouse, built beside the road, contained offices of both the French and Swiss customs personnel—both units were combined in one long building running along the road. John asked for Inspector Charroin.

When the inspector appeared, he took Weidner to one side of the room where he could talk with him privately. "Now, John, I want you to follow me outside. But we will not be going out the front door. We'll go out the back door. When we are outside, you watch me closely. If I point toward Switzerland, you start walking along behind the building toward Geneva. Keep walking behind the building and in the trees, but stay away from the road for at least a mile. Then you can come back toward the road. Keep a sharp eye for any sign of guards as you move, though. It sounds simple, and it is; but make sure you stay in the trees away from the road until you are far enough away that the guards here at the border won't see you when you return to the road."

Outside John watched Charroin attentively. When the customs official had surveyed the area carefully, he pointed his finger toward Geneva. Weidner quickly walked away into the platane trees which surrounded the customshouse and the countryside of that area.

Each crackle of dead leaves and twigs seemed to John like explosions which could be heard a mile away as he hurried along in the heavy growth. To his right was the barbed wire of the border, which executed a gentle curve near the customshouse. He didn't want to veer too far that way for fear of being seen by a guard. At the same time he had to stay out of sight of the road from the customshouse until well away from the border checkpoint. John walked quickly, counting his steps until he felt certain he had gone far enough. Then, slowing his pace, he moved gently back toward the road. Through the trees he could make out the cut which was the roadway. Then he saw a stop which the Geneva bus used. He headed for it cautiously. Breaking into the sunlight of the roadway, he found it completely deserted except for a lone farmer trudging back toward France.

In less than ten minutes the Geneva-bound bus pulled to a stop and Weidner stepped aboard. Within the hour, thanks to Inspector Charroin's unorthodox border-crossing method, he was in Geneva.

Another route to Switzerland John sometimes used lay farther to the east near the city of Thonon. He occasionally sent a few refugees into Switzerland by boat across Lake Geneva from a spot near Thonon, but this was a dangerous route because both French and Swiss police boats patrolled the lake. But under the cover of night skilled boatmen could get the refugees through. A small border river, the Arve, also served as an escape crossing. Sometimes its waters were neck-deep; but as it was a singularly unlikely spot to try to cross the border, the patrols did not check the small stream very often.

Now riding in the train from Lyons en route to see Dr. Visser 't Hooft and other officials in Switzerland, John reached Annecy without incident. After checking in at his store, he left for the border area, which he reached that evening near Collonges. A friend confirmed that the barbed wire had not yet been electrified, and Weidner passed through the strands and ran across the cleared stretch of land into Switzerland.

"It is good that they have arranged it so that I won't have to elude the Swiss guards anymore," he mused as he slowed to a walk near the edge of the cleared area. "It is too much pressure having to get to Bern for a special permit each time I need to be in the country for any length of time. The new arrangement will be a welcome relief."

A figure loomed out of the night ahead of John. "Halt where you are!"

Weidner stopped as the figure came closer, taking the shape of a Swiss sentry.

"What are you doing here?" asked the soldier.

"I am going to Geneva," John replied. "My name is John Weidner. I was told that if I gave my name, I could proceed to Geneva to do the business I have come for."

"I know nothing about such an arrangement," the guard said, keeping his gun leveled at John's head. "No one told me about it. I'll have to take you to Camp des Cropettes."

"But that was what I was told," protested Weidner. "Why don't you call to your officer in charge. I'm sure he will say it is all right."

"That may be, but it also may not be. Anyway, it's too late to do anything tonight. We'll see about it in the morning. You are going to the camp for the night. Now, let's go!"

With the bayoneted gun pointed at his back John did not protest further. He felt sure he would be directed to Dr. Visser 't Hooft when he saw the officer in the morning. After all, there could be administrative slips when the word did not get down to the soldiers who had to carry out orders.

Next morning John's guard reappeared at his cell. "Come along now. We'll see what the officer has to say this morning," he said as they went to camp headquarters.

"I don't know anything about such an agreement," the officer stated when John was brought before him. "Are you sure you aren't trying to cover up something with your story? We get plenty of fellows like you through here. They have one story one time, another the next."

"Absolutely not," countered the now irritated Weidner. "I was told on the best authority that this arrangement had been made, and that it was an honorable one. The only thing you should do is to take me to Dr. Visser 't Hooft's office and straighten the matter out."

The officer and the guard left John alone while they had a private conversation. "You may be right," said the officer when they had finished talking together, "but we must check your story."

From the way the officer spoke John knew that his story was not believed. He knew, too, that his stay at Cropettes could be lengthy if he did not do something personally to try to get out of the camp. As the guard took him back to his cell, his mind churned over ideas to get out of the camp. He became more and more nervous about his situation. He had thought when he crossed the border that he would be in Switzerland only a few days at most. But now he was in jail with no way of knowing how long he must remain. Back in France there were refugees who were depending on his help in obtaining their freedom. The more he thought about his situation the more frustrated he became.

John stuck his hand absentmindedly into a pocket, fingering some franc notes there. Suddenly he knew what he would do. He pulled out several notes.

Taking a piece of paper from a small notebook which he was carrying, he scribbled a note to a close friend who lived in Geneva. It was a simple message: "Please inform Dr. Visser 't Hooft that I am in Camp des Cropettes." He signed the note, then wrapped the francs around the paper, tied the little package with a piece of string he had found, and heaved it through a window in his cell onto the busy street outside. He could only hope and pray that someone who believed in doing good deeds would pick it up.

Early the next morning John's guard reappeared. "You're going to get your wish," he said, unlocking the cell. "We're on our way to see Dr. Visser 't Hooft."

As Weidner and the guard walked along the streets of Geneva, John mentioned that they were about to pass St. Antoine Prison, a well-known place of confinement.

"You know about St. Antoine?" asked the guard with a puzzled look on his face.

"Of course I do," replied John. "I have lived at Collonges much of my life. My father and I have been past this prison many times. I know Geneva as well as I do any city in France."

The two were abreast of the prison's entrance now. Without warning the guard suddenly grabbed Weidner and shoved him brutally through the prison gate and quickly placed the underground leader in confinement.

Startled at the sudden turn of events, John protested vigorously. "Why are you doing this? You are supposed to be taking me to Dr. Visser 't Hooft's office. You told me we were going to see him. Why have you lied? I can't prove anything here in St. Antoine. What kind of justice is this anyway?"

Unmoved by the protests, the guard walked away. Becoming more dejected, Weidner sat down in the tiny cell to contemplate his strange treatment. "It must be that the note was not picked up," he thought, as he tried to plan what his next move would be. "As long as they hold me here, I'll never be able to prove my story."

But John's little money-bound note had not been neglected. A passerby had found it, removed the money, and carried the note to John's Geneva friend. The friend had gone to Camp des Cropettes to speak in John's behalf after notifying Dr. Visser 't Hooft's office. But Weidner had already been removed to St. Antoine.

That afternoon a Swiss official arrived at St. Antoine. "I'll take Mr. Weidner with me," he said to the prison commander. "His case is being handled by other authorities. The matter does not need further inquiry here."

John was taken to the office of Lieut. Paul Rochat, of the Swiss army. "It is unfortunate that you have been detained like this," said the officer. "There was, of course, a misunderstanding. We have these difficulties because one section of the army, which has control over the border, has known that you are helping refugees over the border. That, of course, is forbidden. But here in the intelligence section we know that you are doing your work to help others without taking money, as most do. We have told the border control section about your work. They know now that you are under our protection, and arrangements have been made with them so that you can enter and leave Switzerland when you need to. But be quiet about it and don't attract attention, because spies are everywhere. And even if our sympathies are with the Allies and the type of work you are doing, we still have to safeguard our official neutrality."

John thanked the Swiss army official. Then he went on his way to see the head of the World Council of Churches. The two men, meeting at Dr. Visser 't Hooft's home, discussed developments in France and the exact role Weidner would have in helping World Council member groups obtain information from Council headquarters.

Weidner also visited the Dutch legation in Bern. There he handed over a letter from Dr. Jonkheer Loudon, head of the Dutch legation in Paris before the war. Since hostilities began, he had been forced into inactivity in Cannes on the Riviera. The letter, an appeal for financial assistance from the Dutch government in exile in London, was to be coded and dispatched to Great Britain.

"Helping refugees now has to be done almost entirely by illegal methods," John explained to the Dutch minister. "The consuls are being arrested, and even those who can still operate find new difficulties each day. Security is being tightened everywhere. The consuls' lives are in danger every time they attempt to help the refugees."

Van Rosenthal said, "We have spoken to the Dutch government in exile in London about your work, John. They are impressed by your faithful efforts to help your country. You can count on assistance from this office in the future. With the situation tightening throughout France, we will welcome any help you can give to Dutch citizens who come to your attention. We will give specific aid as funds become available. We shall be watching your work with great interest."

Back John went to the border, then to Annecy and Lyons, where a visitor was waiting. His name, he said, was Benno Nykerk, and he was a Jewish businessman working in Brussels. He gave the names of several mutual friends so that Weidner would know he was trustworthy.

"I have been wondering if it would be possible to establish a complete escape line running from Holland through Brussels to Paris, and then to Lyons and Switzerland, or Toulouse and Spain," said Nykerk. "We have heard of your work, and you might be able to develop such a route. I could cooperate with you in bringing people from Brussels to Paris. I know many others who could help us get from Holland to Brussels."

After several hours of discussion, John was convinced both of Nykerk's reliability and of the feasibility of such an escape line. "I will go to work on the plan," he told his visitor. "You should tell your friends they will be contacted soon to give their help. Make sure of one thing, though. Discuss this only with those you would trust with your life, for that is what it amounts to, you know—your very life. I want you to go to Switzerland before you return to Brussels and talk with Dr. Visser 't Hooft so that you will understand the full extent of the work we must do."

When he was alone again, John reviewed the growing outreach of his underground organization. Despite a multitude of activities and some involvement of others, he was still doing practically all the work, taking all the chances himself. But with the Germans operating in southern France more often now, and with the tightening of regulations everywhere, he would have to rely more upon his friends.

One day they will arrest me, he thought. That day may not be far away. But when it comes, I want to have those around me who can carry on the work without any break. These poor refugee people *have* to get through to freedom. Their freedom should not depend on one man alone. The organization must have a solid footing, with many people contributing to its operation.

As he sat there pondering the future, John's thought that he might soon be arrested a second time was strangely prophetic. Indeed, it wasn't long in coming.

VII

a family

JOSEPH SMIT on a warm day in July, 1942, was a very worried man. He was a Jew living in Rotterdam. He had already been arrested once by the Gestapo, and more of his friends were being arrested every day. Although wealthy like himself, many of them did not return to their homes from the Gestapo headquarters after they were taken away. His day was coming, Smit knew; and if he didn't do something quickly, he would not return either.

Smit had more than himself to think about, of course. There were his wife, his daughter Selma, and his teen-age son Max. There were also two other children, both tiny babies. Gray-haired Grandmother Smit was part of the family, too.

"If it were just myself, I might survive," Joseph thought. "But all of us cannot expect to stay here, with the Gestapo making more arrests each day and with new names being added to the execution lists every hour."

So Joseph Smit acted like the businessman he was. He went to see someone he felt could help him with the problem at hand—escape. He called on David, a friend who had information about escaping.

"Yes, yes; I know a 'passer' who will get you out of the country," David assured him. "But, Joseph, it will cost so much, very much! These men are demanding high prices to take people across the borders."

"It doesn't matter," Smit replied. "Our lives are in danger here. No price can be too high. Tell me where to find the man."

In less than an hour Joseph Smit met the passer, whose price, $500 per person, was, as David had said, very high. But Smit was a desperate man, and the passer knew it.

"I will take you to Switzerland for this price," he agreed with Smit. "First we will cross the border into Belgium, then go on to Paris. From there we will go into the southern part of France, and then arrange to get into Switzerland. It will take several days, and it will be dangerous. But I will get you there, you can count on that. You will have to pay me in cash before we leave, of course."

Three days later they began the journey. The group walked over back roads during the afternoon. That evening they arrived at a farmhouse near the Dutch-Belgian border. The passer made arrangements for the Smits to spend the night at the farmhouse while he went to see people who, he said, would help them continue their journey.

"I'll be back early in the morning. We will move along quickly then," he assured the family.

But Joseph Smit was suspicious of the passer. And he was scared. He spent a sleepless night in the farmhouse, with fears mounting about the escape undertaking. Why, Smit wondered, should the passer have to contact others when they had traveled only a short distance from Rotterdam? The border area where the farmhouse was located, he imagined, was in a very dangerous place. Perhaps the passer was abandoning them because he knew the farmhouse would be raided during the night. Smit thought about one of his friends who had recently tried to escape in this same area. He had died with a bullet in his back.

When dawn finally came, Smit's fears had grown until he was nearly hysterical. Seven o'clock came—then eight, nine, and ten. Still the passer hadn't returned for them. Then, when the family's panic had reached epic proportions, the passer returned.

"I've got everything arranged," he announced confidently. "In Brussels my contact will meet us and take charge of you. He will accompany you on toward the border of France, then to Paris. Things are going just fine, completely according to schedule."

Joseph protested when he heard that the passer was turning them over to another man. "I thought you would be taking us all the way to Switzerland. Now you tell us you are stopping in Brussels. How do we know we can trust this new man you have in mind?"

"You could not expect me to take you all the way myself," the passer answered. "I've got to stay close to Holland, or the Gestapo will pick me up. Don't worry about the new man—he is a good guide. He will see that you go safely along the route. You will arrive in Switzerland as I promised you. It isn't really important whether I go with you, just as long as you get there."

After the exchange between the two men, the passer led Smit and his family across the border during the night without incident and moved on toward Brussels. In the morning they boarded one of the interurban cars which run throughout Belgium. Rolling along through the little country Joseph Smit had a moment of relaxation. They might be successful in their escape after all, he thought, if things went as smoothly as they had thus far. But a few moments later the streetcar jerked to a halt, and two German guards entered. The unexpected entry of the guards all but paralyzed Smit with fear because their passer had not provided them with travel papers or identification books. Luckily though, after making a quick check through the car without asking for any papers, the guards left. Two hours later the group entered Brussels. They went to a café in the Place de la Bourse, where, according to their passer, they would meet the man who would take them across the Franco-Belgian border and to Paris.

In the café another wave of fear engulfed Joseph Smit. Three hours went by, and still the new guide had not arrived. At five o'clock the passer got up from the table where the family was sitting. "I'm going out to look for the guide," he said. "Something may have happened to him. If that is the case, we'll have to make other arrangements. I'll be back within an hour."

Smit, in the strange and frightening situation, begged the passer not to leave them. But the passer insisted he must look for the other guide. In about an hour he returned with news that the guide had been arrested.

"I hadn't counted on this, of course," the passer said, "but we will work something out in the morning. Everything will be fine. I've already contacted another friend here who will put me up for the night. I want you and your family to go to a hotel near here," he explained to Joseph. "I will meet you here in the café early in the morning."

Joseph led his family to the nearest hotel, where they registered under false names. Another sleepless night dragged by as he worried about what would happen to them the next day. Early in the morning, as they had arranged, he found the passer at the café. The man did have identification papers for them, but they had been hastily and poorly made.

"I know they aren't too good," the guide admitted as they sat down at the table, "but they were all I could get overnight. You must have papers to travel from here on. Anyway, they will do. Now, about going to Switzerland. I told you last night that my helper has been arrested. But I've found another man. The trouble is that he must have more money if he is to take you with him."

"But we paid you all the money you said was required for the entire trip," Smit complained. "You said that was all I would have to pay."

"Yes, but I did not count on my helper's being arrested. It is unfortunate, but that's the way it goes sometimes. There really is no choice. Either you pay more or there will be no one to lead you from here on!"

A FAMILY

Joseph Smit, as he listened to the passer's new demand, concluded that he was dealing with a completely dishonest man. But what was the choice? As far as Smit could tell, there was none. He was in a foreign land, entirely dependent upon the crooked passer who sat beside him. The passer knew Smit had more money, for he had taken special care to inquire in advance about every possession the family would carry with them. Finally the demand for more money was met. When Smit finished paying, he was a poor man. "But if I can gain freedom, it will be worth everything," he thought as he handed over the money.

That afternoon Joseph met the new guide. By nightfall they were on their way to the Franco-Belgian border, where the guide got in touch with the French underground, who provided new papers so that the family could travel in France. In Paris they were taken to a small convent and given shelter for the night. The next morning the guide returned with another set of papers which would allow the Smits to cross from occupied into unoccupied France. Then he took them to the train station and got them settled for the trip to Lyons.

Shortly before the train was to leave, he turned to Joseph. "I'm going to step off the train for a few minutes to get some things I forgot," he said. "But I'll be back before the train leaves. It is still fifteen minutes before departure, so I'll have plenty of time to get back."

Without waiting for an answer from the protesting Smit he hurried off the coach. Joseph felt that one of his last hopes for escape was rushing away as he watched the guide go quickly down the steps of the coach and hurry back into the station.

The guide never came back.

As the train pulled out of the station without the guide, terrible fear gripped Joseph Smit. Ahead on the route to Lyons lay the strong control point between occupied and unoccupied France, where they would face inspection by both the French and the Germans. There were also gendarmes and German guards on the train who might question them. And Joseph had no place to go when he got to Lyons —if he did get there! For Joseph Smit it was a train ride filled with terror, and the best he could do was to clutch close to his trembling body the prized Ausweis passes needed for his family to cross the demarcation line into unoccupied France.

But the Smits arrived in Lyons. They had not been suspected in any of the several contacts with officials along the way. Now, as they stepped from the train in Lyons, Joseph forced himself to conquer the fear which had gripped him for the past few days. This enabled him to make a rational decision.

"We shall go to the Dutch consul here in Lyons," he announced to his family. "They can certainly help us if anyone can."

At the consul's office they got the name of someone who might help: John Weidner.

"The Smits have just arrived in Lyons without anything," Jacquet, the consul, informed Weidner. "They have been robbed of all their funds by dishonest passers. They have no money to continue their journey to the border. In Holland they are now wanted by the Gestapo, so we must give them what help we can. We put them up in a local hotel last night, but it would be better if they could have a safer place until they are on their way to the border."

A better hiding place was easy for Weidner to arrange. He had recently rented a small apartment in Lyons to which refugees could be taken for shelter overnight. Although apartments were extremely hard to find, John had learned of the place from friends in Lyons who knew he needed such a shelter for refugees.

When they reached the apartment, John outlined to Smit what he could expect in the next few days. "This evening some of our men will come here to take pictures of you and your family," he explained. "These pictures will be used to prepare new documents so that you can get into the French-Swiss border area through Annecy. By tomorrow afternoon the papers should be complete. We can leave for Annecy early the next morning. It is important that we go to Annecy then because that will be market day. Many people from the countryside will be in town, and the trains will be so full that the guards won't be checking the passengers too closely. Market day is always the best time to go through Annecy."

"You are doing all this for no money?" asked the unbelieving Joseph Smit. "All the others have wanted money and more money. Then when they got our money, they left us stranded and in danger. But you do not ask for money. I don't have any money left; but if I did, I would give it to you, for you have not asked for my money first."

107

"It is true that it costs money to help people get across the border," John admitted, "but often there is no money. When we find people like you, we do what we can with funds that have come from others."

Weidner left the apartment to make plans for the Smit trip to the border. First he contacted the French underground members who would be preparing the documents to see if the papers could be ready for the Smits to leave Lyons on Annecy market day. Then he went to see his secretary, Raymonde Pillot. She knew the exact status of refugees who were now ready for travel to the border.

"Are there others we could take along with the Smits?" John asked Raymonde.

"Yes, there are Nico Gazan and his wife, Mary; and Armand Lap, whose father was recently killed by the Gestapo," answered the girl. "They all have documents, and their names have been cleared by the immigration office in Geneva for entry into Switzerland. They can leave any time you are ready."

"Then we will go day after tomorrow. With seven in the Smit family and the other three, we should go in two groups, though," John said. "I will take part of them in one section of the train. You can bring the others in another coach. But be sure, Raymonde, when you check with the people from the French underground, that they make out the papers for the Smits as though they are from Alsace. Their French is very poor, and without documents stating they come from Alsace, they will arouse the gendarmes' suspicions if they talk with them on the train."

A FAMILY

Confident that Raymonde would do an efficient job, John set to work on matters pertaining to his textile business. His life had recently become a jumble of run-together days and nights. His underground activities seemed strangely blended with those of his business life. He had to guard himself constantly so that he did not let underground secrets slip into his business conversations when he met clients in his office. It was a fearful life he led, and only one slip in conversation with the wrong person could result in his immediate arrest.

In those days, when sleep came fitfully because of the pressure he was under, Weidner found increasing solace in the inner knowledge that he was trying to do what he believed God would have him do. "He hath sent me to bind up the brokenhearted, to proclaim liberty to the captives, and the opening of the prison to them that are bound," was a passage of Scripture John frequently quoted to himself.

Two days later John and Raymonde met the Smits, the Gazans, and Lap at the train station in Lyons. Weidner took Armand Lap, Mr. and Mrs. Gazan, who spoke fluent French in spite of the fact that they were Dutch, and the two older Smit children with him. Joseph Smit, his wife, Grandmother Smit, and the two babies went with Raymonde. Each refugee had excellent identification and travel papers prepared during the night by underground members who were employees in the Lyons' government documents office.

The train made good time as the two groups traveled toward Annecy, John's group in the forward part of the train, Raymonde's well to the rear. When they reached the Annecy station, John looked at the refugees sitting around him in the coach. He wanted to reassure them at this rough checkpoint. But the rule could not be broken—no talking between the guide and the refugees. Too many arrests of others had occurred because a gendarme or German guard had overheard a conversation in a foreign language between guide and refugees.

"They will be all right," John said to himself. "The Smit youngsters are alert enough. The others have been told just what to do. There will be no trouble."

He reasoned correctly—there were no problems at the checkpoint. Almost before he realized it, they were entering the familiar street that led to his Annecy store. A few minutes after his group arrived, Raymonde came in with the others. Without speaking to his workers in the front part of the store, John led the refugees to the back of the building and hid them.

"We will stay here through the afternoon," he said. "There is not enough room for all of you to spend the night here. Some will have to go to another store nearby. But rest here among the boxes, and we will get some food soon. Whatever you do, don't go to the front of the store or outside the building. I'll be checking on the business and will return in a little while."

When darkness had fallen over the city, John took part of the group along the darkened streets to Marie-Louise Meunier's store.

"Ah, John," she said, smiling at him, "you have brought some more of them. Of course they can stay here tonight.

A FAMILY

Any time you want to you can bring refugees here. The Germans and the French are not watching my store. It is safe to bring refugees here."

Miss Meunier, it seemed to John, had an almost child-like innocence about the consequences of discovery that she was hiding refugees in her store.

When the seven o'clock bus left Annecy for St. Julien the next morning, John and his little band of refugees were aboard, Raymonde and the others were to follow about an hour later. If anything went wrong for the first group, the hour interval would allow time for one of his group to get back to warn Raymonde. They planned to meet at a farmhouse outside Cruseilles near the Saleve.

John and Raymonde had discussed all the possibilities for the escape after the others had gone to bed the night before. Finally they had decided that the safest route would be across the Saleve Mountain. Such a large number of refugees might arouse suspicion at the control stations on the roads leading to the border.

Now, as the bus roared through the brisk, clear morning toward the control station near Cruseilles, John kept close watch ahead so that he wouldn't miss the place where he wanted to get off. It was about six miles from Annecy to the first control point, and he wanted to leave the bus before it reached the checkpoint.

Soon he saw the familiar landmarks that told him they were nearing the little dirt road leading to the farmhouse. "You can let us off there," he told the driver, pointing to the road.

111

The group left the bus and quickly covered the half mile to the farmhouse. Soon they were sitting relaxed in the welcome shelter of the farmer's living room.

"We can expect Raymonde's group in about an hour," John told his friend. "When they get here, we will start immediately for the mountain. If we expect to get to the border this evening, we will have to move right along."

When the other group arrived, John sent Raymonde back to Annecy. Then he took the ten refugees out the back door of the farmhouse. Weidner set a steady pace, with the refugees strung out behind him on the little path leading upward to the mountain. He slowed a bit as he realized that most of them were from the flatlands of Holland, with no mountain experience such as he had. Then, too, there was Grandmother Smit. John knew her age would not let her keep up a fast pace too long.

Walking steadily, with only brief rest periods, they reached the top of the mountain by noontime. They paused only for a moment to admire the grand sweep of Switzerland which John loved so much. If they were to be at the border by nightfall, they would have to keep moving.

But as they started through the series of vales and hillocks atop the great mountain, Grandmother Smit began to lag behind. "I can't keep up," she gasped. "I'm just an old woman. I don't think I can make it."

"Sure you can," John assured her. "You've been doing fine so far. We've already come a great distance. Just keep walking steadily without trying to speed up or slow down. A steady pace will get us there much more quickly."

They walked another fifteen minutes. Then suddenly John realized that Grandmother Smit wasn't in the group. Looking back, he saw her several hundred feet away.

"I'll never make it," she said when he reached her. "I'm too old. You and the others go ahead. Leave me here; leave me here! I'd rather die on the mountain. Just leave me and go ahead."

"We couldn't do that. You are part of our group. We won't get to the border if *you* don't. Now come on; just lean on me, and I'll help you along. We'll be going down the mountain soon. Then it will be much easier."

Weidner had already been taking turns with the other men carrying the Smit babies. Now the tottering grandmother became a real task. He tried everything he could think of to keep her going. Nothing seemed to work.

"Let me die," she pleaded. "It is *my* life. Just let me lie down here and die. You can go on without me; it won't make any difference."

But to Weidner it did make a difference. His philosophy of life rebelled at leaving an old woman to die alone in the mountains—no matter how useless she might feel. So he pushed her ahead of him; and when that didn't seem to work, he placed her arm around his neck and carried her along. She was slowing the pace considerably, he realized; and as he saw the sun sinking in the western sky, he began to worry whether they would still have enough light to get safely down the mountain to the house near Collonges where he wanted to stop. He took another grip on Grandmother Smit's arm and stepped up the pace.

Despite the added problem, the group made good progress once they got onto the trail leading down the mountainside. As twilight settled over the border area, they were only a half mile from the house where the refugees would wait while John checked the border.

"We'll be able to make it over the border tonight if there aren't any special patrols. Before midnight you will be inside Switzerland," he announced as they came in sight of the farmhouse.

When he had settled his charges for rest and food, John struck off toward Collonges, where he expected to get help from Roger Fasnacht, the administrator of the college, who never hesitated to help Weidner whenever he was asked.

"I have ten people who need to get across the border tonight, Roger," he told his friend when they met on the college campus. "We'll need your help as lookout for the crossing. Can you come back with me and help us?"

"I'll come, John. This is a good night for crossing. The border has been very quiet lately. Those living along the barbed wire tell me the patrols seem less frequent now than they have been for many weeks."

"I hope to get these refugees into Switzerland quickly," John confided as the two set out for the farmhouse. "There is so much activity going on right now that I can't afford to stay away from Lyons too long. I'll come back with you and spend the night in Collonges. Then I'll take a bus to Annecy in the morning."

The refugees were eager to start for the border when the two men returned to the farmhouse. Even Grandmother

114

Smit, having rested and eaten a good meal, seemed happy at the prospects of getting into Switzerland in a short time.

"It has been hard, this journey," she remarked to Weidner with a smile. "But, young man, you have brought us safely this far. Now take us the rest of the way!"

As the group walked around the edge of a field behind the farmhouse and started into the woods through which the border ran, John outlined the way they would make the crossing.

In another ten minutes they reached the spot at the border where they were to cross. Roger's skill at finding precise spots on the border even in the blackest of nights was at its best. He led the group the last two hundred yards to the edge of the highway running parallel to the two fences of barbed wire.

"You should cross here," he said as they crawled through the undergrowth to the edge of the roadway. "Go across the road one at a time rather than in a group. If you bunch up, some will have to wait at the wire. If a patrol comes, you don't want several people standing by the wire waiting to get through."

Silently John nodded agreement. He looked both ways along the road. "I'll go on across and unhook the wires from the posts," he said. "When I'm done, I'll whistle. Then you can start sending them across. Send the babies across early so that they can be gotten away from the road quickly. Then if they cry, they'll be far enough away that they won't be heard. If something goes wrong, I'll whistle twice, and you'll know that I won't be able to get back tonight."

Weidner hunched low and sprinted across the road to the first set of wires. Working rapidly, he unhooked the lower strands, then crawled to the second fence and began to work. When the strands were loose, he went back to the first fence to check along the highway. Then he whistled for Roger to start sending the refugees across.

Out of the black night Armand Lap scurried toward John. Pulling hard on the lower strands, Weidner raised them so Lap could crawl through. Next came Smit carrying one of the babies. John took the child and handed it to Lap, who stood inside Switzerland, then returned to help Smit through the first fence. Then came Mrs. Smit with the other baby. The others came rapidly, and in a few minutes all were through the first fence.

As John started to turn from the strands to give final instructions to the refugees who now waited just inside the second fence, his ears picked up a sound. It was a motor, and it was rapidly approaching. He gave two short, sharp whistles to warn Roger. Then he scrambled for the second series of barbed wires and pushed through them quickly. "Be very quiet," he warned the group. To the left through the trees there was a clearing which gave a limited view of the road for about half a mile. He watched that spot intently.

When lights broke through the trees, John had the answer to the sound he had heard. Only German patrol trucks carried the pattern of the approaching blackout lights.

"Let's go," he said, preparing to run into the cleared area. "When I drop to the ground, you drop beside me. Keep flattened out. Now run!"

116

A FAMILY

They had about three or four minutes, John knew, before the truck would come abreast of them. Although they were safely into Switzerland, still he didn't want the patrol to know they had passed through the border at that place. If they saw the group in the cleared Swiss area they would stop, examine, and rehook the loosened strands, and then they would strengthen the patrol greatly in the days ahead. Weidner wanted to use that spot again if possible. The only way to do that would be to keep the Germans from knowing someone had gone through the wires.

John dived into the clearing, and the others dropped quickly. He snaked his way around so that he could watch the spot where the vehicle would pass on the road. The noise of the truck was loud now. Suddenly he saw the tiny slits of light go flashing past the spot.

"They've kept going," he whispered to the group. "They didn't spot anything unusual. You can relax now."

Although the group could relax, Weidner couldn't. That patrol truck would be returning sometime within the next hour. John's problem was that he did not know exactly when.

"I'll have to go on into Switzerland, then return tomorrow by some other route," he said to the band of refugees. "It's not according to our plans, but it will be good to have a peaceful night's sleep in Switzerland again. No bombers, no blackout, no Gestapo. Yes, it will be a good night to sleep!"

117

VIII

the problems

IN EARLY 1942 the Nazis began a systematic annihilation of Jews throughout the Netherlands. The death decree sent additional thousands of stricken people fleeing through Belgium and across France. They came to a fear-ridden land in which many of their race were already confined to camps, where they awaited the will of their captors.

At Lyons requests for help from John Weidner began to pile up. His escape organization was now operating efficiently on several routes, and he often found himself working far into the night on plans for moving the various refugee groups.

Around him he drew an enlarging circle of friends whom he could trust. In Berthy Albrecht, a blustery but exceedingly kindhearted resident of Lyons, he found someone who would provide a safe shelter for those who fled. David Verloop and Paul Van Cleeff in Belgium were friends he knew he could count on. He found several young girls who developed a special romantic approach to helping others escape. There were Jacqueline, Anita, Simone, Andree, and Okkie, who, under John's direction, often strolled through the mountains near the border on the arm of an escaping refugee or airman. To passersby, and to the border guards, they appeared to be simply young lovers seeking the quiet beauty of the mountains. But when darkness fell, the girls would return to the shelter of a farmhouse or a waiting car near the border, and their "boyfriend" would slip through the barbed wire into Switzerland.

Quiet, efficient Marie-France could take refugees or fliers carefully along the routes southward from Paris. Herman Laatsman, head of the organization in Paris, sent along a girl who had escaped from Holland. Laatsman recommended her highly as a courier, and with a minimum of training she became highly valuable to the organization. Her name was Suzy Kraay.

During the stepped-up activities of the growing organization American airmen being passed along from one trusted member of the group to the next would often ask, "What is your name? What organization are you? We want to tell those in charge in London of your good work."

John knew that the surest way to become a victim of the Gestapo was for a name of one of the undergrounders to slip from the wrong tongue at the wrong time. But the name of an organization did seem likely to bind the loyalty and efforts of all members of the group, and using an organization name would give airmen-escapees who wanted one a name to report on in London.

Laatsman, discussing the subject one day with Weidner, suggested, "Our primary work is with the Dutch people.

119

Paris is the central point in our escape system. Why not combine the two and call our group 'Dutch-Paris'?"

So the group was named, and the organization went into the official book and records of Resistance groups as "*reseau* [network] Dutch-Paris."

The underground organization operated smoothly, but some peculiar problems often threatened to spoil its usefulness. For example, the people passed along the routes were not always above selfishness or above using the hard-won underground machinery for a "lark."

Sometimes refugee boys, many of them in no particular or immediate danger, appealed to members of John's underground group to take them to Switzerland. Their reasons for needing to get out of the country were often fabricated lies to cover a craving for adventure. This practice led to strict screening methods by the underground after Weidner's group had taken one or two of these youngsters across the border and later found them back in the area from which they had departed, bragging about their adventure and passing out Swiss chocolates.

One day John was asked by a minister to help a Dutch teen-ager get into Spain. The clergyman said the boy had arrived the day before, asking for help, but he did not know anything else about him. By now keenly aware of the youthful adventurers who had tricked his organization a few times already, Weidner was far from ready to send the boy through his Pyrenees escape route without thorough checking. He took the boy into the street in front of the minister's house.

120

"Well, my friend, you want to go to Spain, do you?" he asked as he sized up the boy.

"Yes, I do. I want to get to England, where I can help win the war. I have no money and no friends, but I must get to England. My family has been mistreated by the Germans. We must drive them from our land."

John listened carefully to the boy's story. He noted that he had said he had no friends or money. "If he is a spy," thought Weidner to himself, "he will slip up somewhere. With this story I don't think he is just out for adventure. If I tell him it costs money to get to England and he answers that he may be able to get some, then I'll know he's lying, because he has already said he has no money or friends in this area. If he says he'll meet me with money sometime tomorrow, I had better not be here tomorrow. Chances are he will return with the Gestapo."

"It takes money to get to Spain. Don't you know that?" John pressed the young man. "It will cost ten thousand francs just to get across the Pyrenees."

Mouth agape at the huge cost of the project, the boy became pale and silent.

Watching him, John still clung to the suspicion that he might be a German spy planted to trap him. The minister had admitted he did not know him—he was only trying to do him a favor.

"Well," thought Weidner as he watched the boy closely, "the next few minutes will tell whether he is a spy."

But the boy did not leave. In a whispered effort he said, "But I've got to get to England. That is the only place I can help. I have a trunk of clothes here with me. Do you think I could get enough money from them?"

"Of course not," snapped John. "It looks as though you'll never get to Spain." And he spun on his heel to walk back to the minister's house.

As he left the boy, he did not look back. Once inside the minister's house he moved to the window and peered out from behind the shutters. What he saw made him turn back toward the door. The youngster had fallen to his knees in the street and was sobbing out his sorrow there on the cobblestones.

"You want to go to England very much, don't you?" John said as he stood over the youth. "Well, you shall go. Anyone whose heart nearly breaks because he can't help his country deserves to go where he can help. Come along with me. We will get you started to Spain, and England."

Often when young men asked Weidner to lead them to Switzerland, he told them he was taking only those who would, after reaching that country, immediately restage for the trip back through southeastern France to Spain, Portugal, and then England, where they would join their country's forces. Such rules separated the armchair adventurers from those who wanted to serve.

A Jewish family was once recommended to John as in much need. They were in immediate danger from the Germans, he was told, and they needed to get out of France.

"We are poor people," the father explained. "We have heard that it costs considerable money to cross the border, but we have almost nothing."

Seeing their obvious plight, Weidner arranged for their escape. He paid all expenses of their lodging, transportation, and other necessities from his own pocket and saw them safely into Switzerland.

A few days later he received a jolt from one of his underground companions. "You know the family you sent over to Switzerland the other day?" his friend asked. "Do you remember that they had some loaves of bread with them?"

John said he remembered the loaves.

"Well, those loaves of bread contained bars of gold. The family cashed the gold in when they got over the border. Actually they were very rich people!"

Such incidents in which Weidner's group was fooled by dishonesty were few, but there were enough to make the underground band lean toward strict questioning of those who asked for help.

As the war progressed, Allied bombing of the occupied countries of Europe increased. A large number of Allied fliers, whose planes had been crippled by the Germans, parachuted to safety in the countryside. Once down, however, they faced the harrowing task of trying to return to England. Some of these fliers filtered along the escape routes established by Weidner. Extra precaution had to be taken in protecting them and passing them to freedom again.

As the first of the downed airmen came to John's attention, he saw that a procedure must be established to guide them through the occupied countries. Fliers from America and other countries ate differently than did the French people. The American and the Frenchman, for example, both ate with the fork in the right hand, but the Frenchman almost always used a piece of bread in his left hand to assist in putting food on his fork. This habit had to be taught to American escapees.

This was one of many small but important differences which were often big factors for the escaping airmen. Well-trained members of the German SS and even an untrained member of the Waffen SS could quickly pick out an escapee who made even the smallest of mistakes. Sharp-eyed French gendarmes or German soldiers could spot the unusual eating habit of the foreign escapee easily. So Weidner made sure all escaping airmen learned the French way of eating before giving them much public exposure.

It was easy, too, for German spies to disguise themselves as Allied airmen to obtain information about underground activities. John's group laid plans to determine whether the airmen who came to their attention were really genuine. One method involved disguising two undergrounders as members of the German Gestapo. Their uniforms, language, and bearing were strictly Gestapo, despite the fact that they were actually members of John's group. An airman suspected of being a spy was led into a room in which John or another underground member began explaining plans for the projected escape.

Suddenly the two "Gestapo" officers would burst into the room and arrest the member of the underground and the airman. The underground member would be led outside for immediate execution. Then the disguised officers would attack the flier. "You are attempting to escape," they would charge. "We have orders to shoot all of your kind. We are going to carry out those orders outside this very room. Come on now; we'll get this thing over quickly!"

If the airman was a member of the Allied forces, all he could do when confronted with such a situation would be to protest the action and give his name, rank, and military serial number. A German spy, however, had another choice. He could identify himself as a German spy, cite his organization's name, and ask the "Gestapo" officers to verify the information he was giving.

With frightening regularity the Germans sent spies through the various underground organizations. Some of them had been to America and had studied English until they spoke it perfectly, with the latest American slang and expressions. They took the name and identification papers of an airman being held in a German prison, learned his background, and were extremely clever in their moves. Many times other Allied airmen, being escorted with these spies, believed them to be the men they claimed to be.

Among the refugees passed through the escape routes set up by Weidner, there came one day a man who had already been tagged as a spy before John saw him. Knowing that they had a spy on their hands, without the spy's awareness that he had been identified, presented a unique situation. Through underground friends, advice was obtained from London about the spy.

"Send him through the regular route," John was advised. "Act as though he is genuine in every way. This man is known to us also. When he reaches England, we will take over from there."

The spy was escorted through France to Spain, then to Portugal and on to England. Every move he made, however, was watched. When he had been operating in England for about three months and had made many contacts with other spies, he was arrested along with the contacts he had visited.

Passing American airmen through the escape routes was often a mixture of hilarity and horror. In Paris, John and his friends once picked up an entire ten-man air crew of a bomber which had been shot down by the Germans. The group was to be led to Toulouse, then over the Pyrenees to Spain. He divided the airmen into three groups for the trip. Each group was to travel separately and rendezvous in Toulouse to make further plans for the climb over the Pyrenees. On the morning of the rendezvous John was leading his airmen along the street when another of the groups happened to pass along the opposite side of the street. Suddenly one of the airmen in John's company shouted, "Hello, Joe, old buddy!" at a friend he recognized. The shout, in English, instantly turned scores of heads along the crowded street.

"Shut up!" hissed Weidner at the airman. "If there are Germans around, they'll be here in a minute!" Luckily neither Germans nor gendarmes showed up. Evidently no collaborators heard the shout either, for John was able to lead the men to the rendezvous without further incident.

The large number of heavy smokers among the fliers was another source of trouble to John's organization. Since their supply never seemed to be exhausted, they smoked their cigarettes only half through before throwing the unsmoked portion away.

"No Frenchman would think of leaving that much cigarette unsmoked," John explained to one of the fliers. "If you have to smoke, be sure to use up practically all of the cigarette before throwing it away. Such an obviously foreign habit will bring the Germans after us quickly."

Despite the difficulties in evading regular police and special guards while traveling through the country with escaping airmen and refugees, the greatest single problem was finding homes in which the escapees could stay. The penalty for hiding them was death. To relieve this problem John made contacts with the owners of hotels in several French towns. If he found hotel managers who were sympathetic to the Resistance movement, he asked them to keep refugees or airmen overnight without placing their names in the hotel registry. The Gestapo and the gendarmes constantly checked hotels for the names of persons they wanted. They also checked rooms against the record in the registry to see if hotel managers were keeping truthful records of guests. The penalty for hotel managers housing escapees was the same as for private homeowners—death.

"I will give you extra money for each person you allow to stay without entering his name in the registry until after we leave," John told one cooperative hotel manager. "You can enter false names for them on slips of paper—names which correspond with their false papers—which you can hold through the night. If the Gestapo finds there are rooms occupied with no name on the registry, you can tell them that because you were rushed at the time you asked your guests to sign their names on slips of paper rather than in registry to help get them to their rooms quicker. Tell them you were going to transcribe the information later to the registry. If they don't search the rooms, then the chances of evasion for the night are very good. If they do search, you will be cleared by having names on the slips of paper to match names of your guests. Even if arrests are made, you can say you had no way of knowing false papers were involved. You will be clear."

Several hotels, like the Ibis in Paris, the Panier Fleuri in Toulouse, and the Novelty in Lyons, were giving this valuable aid to John's underground unit at the height of its activities, and hundreds of escapees were kept overnight by these loyal hotelmen.

Among the refugees Weidner occasionally found either ignorance or ungratefulness for the help his group was trying to give. In his store in Annecy he once showed a German-Jewish refugee couple the thin mattress which was to serve as their resting place for the night.

"Is *that* the only thing you can offer me?" snipped the wife as she viewed the makeshift bed. "Why, I've never slept on anything like that before in my life!"

"If it does not please you, you are perfectly free to walk down the street to the local hotel," John said. "They have nicer beds than we do. But they also have special visitors each night. They come without warning, and they wear shirts of dark green or black. They carry pistols, too. And they have a nasty habit of taking people like you off to jail. If you want a visit from them tonight, feel free to go to the hotel."

The woman had a sound night's sleep on the thin mattress in his store.

Another refugee woman was surprised when John said he would be taking her family from Annecy to the border by several modes of transportation, including walking for a considerable distance.

"But I thought we would be taking a taxi from Annecy to Geneva!" she exclaimed. "Do we have to use such a primitive method of escaping?"

Naturally talkative, John found it easy to approach people as he sought to perfect the escape organization he was directing. His confident manner won many valuable helpers to his group who, had they been approached by someone less definite than Weidner, might not have helped the refugees. With the underground unit's activities increasing rapidly in 1943, John moved about more often to check on the various escape operations. He went back, not long after it had been organized, to the Pyrenees escape line to see if that route was functioning smoothly.

From Toulouse John went south toward St. Gaudens, then on to the little spa town of Barbazan, where he was to meet a group of refugees bound for the Pyrenees.

In the escapee group were four American airmen, several other refugees, a Catholic priest, and two guides. The hours of waiting after John arrived passed in uneventful conversation until one o'clock in the morning.

From his observations throughout the evening John could see that the guides and the other underground members were handling their duties efficiently. This was one route, he felt, that would be extremely valuable in the days ahead when the routes into Switzerland would be filled with difficulties. His organization preferred not to take airmen to Switzerland anyway, since there was no way for them to reach England from there unless they came back across southeastern France via the Annecy-Avignon-Toulouse escape line.

Shortly after 1 A.M. the group set off toward the towering mountains which were still some distance away. By six o'clock, just as daylight was breaking, they reached the home of a sheepherder, where they paused for rest before attempting the rugged heights ahead. As they sat in the little hut, one of the guides suddenly stuck his head through the doorway and shouted, "Get out; get out quick! A German patrol is coming!"

The group bolted outside, running in frantic pursuit of the guide. When they had gone over a small rise a few hundred feet from the hut, the guide signaled them to get down while he went to see what the patrol was doing. Soon he returned. "They have gone on up the mountain toward the west," he told them. "They checked at the sheepherder's hut, but they weren't suspicious of anything."

At the next stop on the upward trek, John decided to turn back toward Barbazan. The others could go on now without him. The snow level was down to three thousand feet, and it was biting cold as John left the group. He knew he would have to travel fast, but with great caution, as he descended toward Barbazan again. The entire return hike would have to be made in broad daylight. Weidner was rankled with himself because he had not given enough thought to this return.

"It was silly to come this far with the group," he muttered to himself. "If I had continued only a couple of hours with them, I could have made the return in darkness. Now I'll have to keep sharp eyes for all sorts of guards and police."

Within two hours he saw several German border patrols. With each descending step his chances of detection were increasing. Although he had valid identification papers, he knew it would not do for the guards to stop him here in the mountains. He could give no local address; and even if he did, the local citizenry would not recognize him if they were questioned by the guards.

Several hours later he saw a small village ahead. Surrounding it was a large stand of trees, and he decided to stay in the trees during daylight, then travel to Barbazan that night.

Through the day the underground leader shivered as the cold mountain winds whistled through the trees where he huddled. At nightfall he slipped out of the trees and strode off toward Barbazan. The next night he spent in warmth and safety with members of his organization in Toulouse.

IX

BORDER INCIDENT

THERE ARE two of them, the man and his wife," said Jacquet. "They are Mr. and Mrs. Tony Vogel. They must get into Switzerland, because Tony has just escaped from a German slave labor gang working on the Atlantic wall along the French coast. Our legal ways of helping them are exhausted. Will you help them, John?"

"Of course," said John, who was visiting the Dutch consul in Lyons.

First he arranged for false papers. Then he took the Vogels to Annecy. By the time they arrived there John knew how he would get them across the border.

"We will rent a taxi here," he said as they left the Annecy train station. "I have a friend here, a taxi driver, whose eyes are blind when I tell him to make them that way. We will travel with him to a farmhouse on the border east of St. Julien. If all goes well, you should be over the border tonight, safe in Switzerland."

Arrangements made, the group headed for St. Julien. John had told friends in Annecy that he expected to return

132

in about two hours. That was the time it normally took to make the trip from Annecy through Cruseilles to St. Julien and then on to Collonges and Annemasse and back to Annecy. The route made a complete circle of the Saleve Mountain. For several miles between St. Julien and Annemasse the road ran parallel to, and just a few feet from, the border.

At the control station at Le Chable, between Cruseilles and St. Julien, the taxi had to stop for inspection by the French gendarmes. The guards that day seemed unusually thorough in their work, but the Vogels' false papers passed inspection, and the taxi driver continued to St. Julien, then swung onto the border highway leading through Collonges to Annemasse. A few miles east of the town John asked him to stop.

"See that line of trees running along the other side of the road," he said to the Vogels. "That is where the border passes. Only a short distance through the trees is Switzerland, and the way has been cleared for you to cross the border here. The barbed wire has been cut directly opposite where we are now. If there is some reason why you cannot cross, however, come back to the taxi and wait for me. I'm going to the farmhouse over there to talk with a friend. Keep a sharp watch both ways along the road if you have to come back. Make sure there are no cars coming before you cross the road. Get back into the trees if someone comes along."

John and the Vogels stepped out of the taxi. The couple walked swiftly across the road toward the spot Weidner

133

had indicated. "I should be back in about ten minutes," John said to his friend in the taxi. "If they can't make it, they will be back by then also. Just pray that no gendarmes come along while we are gone. If they do, you better get out quick and start acting like something is wrong with the motor."

Having given the word of caution to the cabbie, Weidner went to the farmhouse, where he talked with Mr. Lavergnat, an underground member, about plans for a group of refugees who would be using the same escape point as the Vogels the next day.

When John got back to the taxi, only the driver was there.

"They must have gotten through safely," he said. "I've heard or seen nothing since they disappeared into the trees."

Traveling rapidly in the taxi, they soon came to the control station between Collonges and Annemasse. John had given little thought to this checkpoint since his own papers were in order and his friend, the driver, was a reliable man.

When they pulled to a stop at the control station, the guard poked his head inside the cab. "Where are the others?" he asked, looking angrily at Weidner.

"The others—what others do you mean?" John replied, wondering how the guard would know there had been others with them.

"The man and woman who were with you when you went through the control station below St. Julien. The guards there gave us a call and said there was a taxi with four people in it bound for Annemasse. Now, where are the others?"

John had not counted on the guards at the other control station calling ahead. The only hope he had was to be as honest and confident as possible.

"I stepped out of the taxi to see a friend. When I came back, they had gone," he declared.

"That doesn't sound right to me," the guard replied. "You probably let them out so that they could sneak across the border. Come on out, both of you. We want to have a talk with you."

The guard collected their identification and travel papers and ordered them into the control office. The driver was led to one room, Weidner to another, where he was told to sit down.

"Now let's have the truth about what happened to those other people," said the French police officer. "They were with you when you passed the control station below St. Julien. You said all four of you were going to Annemasse. You have not yet reached Annemasse, but now there are only two of you in the car. Where are the others?"

"I left the taxi to see my friend, Mr. Lavergnat; and when I returned to the taxi, they were not there. That is the way it happened," John repeated.

"But why didn't you wait for them? Why didn't you tell the guards below St. Julien they would be leaving the taxi? Why didn't you tell the guards you were going to help them escape over the border? You are telling lies, nothing but lies," the officer stated.

135

The questioning had gone on for about two hours when one of the guards suddenly grabbed John about the throat and began choking him. "You'd better tell us about those people. If you don't, we'll do this until you can't breathe anymore." His fingers tightened about Weidner's throat. "Now talk! Give us the information we want!"

"But I have told you the truth," Weidner gasped when the guard's grip on his neck relaxed. "They left the taxi; they were gone when I came back. I didn't take them across the border. I have nothing more to say."

Another guard entered the room. "The taxi driver says this guy got out and went off to a farmhouse," he said, pointing at John. "He says the couple got out, too, and walked across the road into the trees. He says he didn't know where they were going, and he didn't ask. He couldn't see anything this guy did while he was in the house. When he came back to the taxi, the cabbie says he was ordered to proceed to Annemasse."

"That still doesn't tell us what is behind all this," declared the officer. "Now let's start again. Why did you get out at that farmhouse? Why did the couple leave the car? What were they anyway, smugglers? Or maybe they were Gestapo agents checking how well we watch the border, huh? Is that what you are, part of a plan to see if we are watching our border sector well enough?"

The questioning dragged on through another hour. Under the ceaseless pressure weariness began to dog Weidner, but his mind remained alert. He stuck to his story. He could see that the officer was greatly worried that he might be part of a smuggling operation, or a member of a Gestapo spy team checking on border security of the French gendarmes. Finally John decided to take a chance.

"Look," he told the officer, "the couple are Dutch. They are being mistreated by the Germans. If they went across the border to Switzerland, I am glad. As you can see from my papers, I too am a Dutchman. How could I help but wish them well? Even if I had helped them, what harm could they do to the French?"

"So you are a member of the underground, are you?" asked the officer. "Is that why you say you are Dutch, so we will think you are not under our rules? Well, I can tell you that story won't work either. You have to abide by the rules of France even if you are a foreigner."

The police officer scowled furiously, but his voice took on a different tone as John stated his concern for his fellow countrymen. He stood up, turned toward the guards who waited nearby, and motioned them to another room, leaving Weidner sitting alone with his thoughts. The minutes dragged along as John considered his dilemma.

His desperate mind tried to fathom the taxi driver's response to his captors, and he began to regret that he had involved the poor fellow. He was thankful that he told the same story about stopping at the farmhouse. How could he convince the French guard that his story was true, that he was not a smuggler or an undercover agent of the Gestapo sent to check on their border security? Why had he been so stupid as to have failed to realize the guards at the roadblocks would check on the movements of the taxi?

After an hour the officer came back from his conference with the guards. "O.K., my friend, you can get up now. We have what we need from you. I'm sure you are a member of the underground, but of what underground I still don't know. But it doesn't matter. Sometimes in this crazy war we try to find out too many things from everybody and wind up not knowing anything about anybody." He led John to the door.

"There is your taxi awaiting your pleasure." He smiled. "Good-bye and good luck."

Surprised, Weidner climbed into the taxi and sank back thankfully into the soft seat. "Let's go," he said to his friend who was waiting at the wheel. As they pulled away from the control station, John turned toward the officer who still stood watching from the door. Weidner threw him a salute. *"Au revoir, mon capitaine,"* he murmured. *"Au revoir et merci beaucoup."*

Rolling along the highway leading to Annemasse, John and his friend recounted their experiences to each other. "I told them you were part of the underground, but that your work was only to help people," admitted the taxi driver. "The officer came in with the guards when they left you; and when he heard that, he seemed greatly impressed. He is a patriotic Frenchman, I believe."

John arrived back in Annecy at 1 A.M. exhausted, but he called his worried associates. Then before retiring he knelt by his bed to offer a prayer of thanksgiving.

X

JAIL IN CRUSEILLES

IT WAS WARM on the bus, and very peaceful as the big machine droned along the Annecy-St. Julien highway. Weidner sat content and relaxed in a seat about halfway back in the bus. He felt especially good on this July day. Things had been going well for the underground lately as it assisted Jewish refugees across the border into Switzerland.

John was on his way to Switzerland again, this time to arrange for another group to be received and cared for once they got across the border. He had left the bus station in Annecy a short time earlier, expecting to travel through Cruseilles and St. Julien, then on to Collonges, where he would cross the border near the town during the night. It wasn't exactly a routine trip, however, because there was some danger of being caught even under the best of conditions. But this did not promise to be a trip of spectacular problems, either.

He was only half aware of the slower motion of the bus as it now came into the small country town of Cruseilles. "Just another bus station, another control point—little

139

things to make life interesting," he mused. The great vehicle turned from the highway toward the little station, then turned again and came to a stop. Peasants, carrying big bags of produce, began to crowd the aisle, their large bundles and bags poking people who remained aboard. Finally the exodus was complete, and the boarding of new passengers began. There would be a full bus to St. Julien.

When the new passengers had settled into their seats, two French gendarmes entered. They began checking travel and identification papers of everyone on the bus. One on each side of the aisle, they worked their way from front to back.

"This is just another of the many annoyances we've inherited from the war," John told himself as he watched the approaching police.

"Well, at least I won't have trouble with them. My papers are in order. They show clearly that I am a Dutchman, that my store is in Annecy, and that I am authorized to travel anywhere in the border area."

The police had now come to the row of seats in which John sat. He handed over his documents and settled back to wait for the scrutiny the gendarmes always seemed to give his papers because they identified him as a Dutch citizen.

"Where are you going, Mr. Weidner?" asked the gendarme, leaning across the seats toward him.

"To Collonges."

"And your business there, what is it to be?"

"I am in the textile business; I am often in Collonges in my work."

140

"Is that where your offices are?" asked the French policeman.

"No, my store is in Annecy, but I have business in Collonges."

"I'm afraid we will need to talk with you a bit further about your business, Mr. Weidner. Please step off the bus with me."

"But that will make me late for my appointments in Collonges. My papers are all in order—you can see that."

"There are some things we need to discuss with you," insisted the gendarme. "Now, come along with me!"

For some reason the policeman was not satisfied with his papers—or with his story. Which it was Weidner could not tell. As he got up from his seat to follow the gendarme off the bus, his mind searched over all the possibilities that could have caused the policeman to suspect him.

As they stepped down from the bus, the second gendarme joined them. One on each side they led him through the station and along the streets to the small Cruseilles prison. At the prison office they confronted him again.

"You say you are a Dutchman, yet you speak perfect French," one of the gendarmes said. "That seems very strange to us."

"It isn't strange at all," Weidner replied. "I've been living in France for the past twelve years. I've learned the language well in that time."

"But it is strange anyway. And you are on your way toward the border. It would be easy for you to slip across the border at Collonges, wouldn't it?"

"It might be, but I have friends at Collonges who can identify me, and there is business I wish to do there, also. This matter can be cleared up quickly enough. If you doubt my word just call the prefecture's office in Annecy. That is where my papers were made out. If I were someone trying to slip across the border, I certainly wouldn't use such a nearby prefecture office, would I? I would have had my papers made out in Bordeaux or Le Mans, some faraway place like that which would be hard to check on."

Ignoring his answer, both gendarmes suddenly stepped up the questioning, asking about numerous matters, many of which had nothing to do with the immediate situation. Not satisfied by his calm answers, they resorted to violence.

"We'll get the truth out of you if we are here all day. We want truth, not lies!"

Without warning one of the policemen smashed his fist into the side of John's head, nearly toppling him from his chair. The second gendarme joined in as the pair used fists and rifle butts in mercilessly battering their prisoner. In a snarling rage they stripped off his clothes, then continued the beating even as they shot question after question at him. Fists, boots, and rifle butts struck Weidner's body, but he was determined not to give them any information, even if it meant death. They jumped on his bare feet with their heavy boots and smashed his head until blood streamed down his body. They shouted curses and insults at him.

"When will you tell us the truth?" one demanded. "We'll keep this up until you tell us the truth. We don't want to hear any more of your lies."

"Telephone to the prefecture in Annecy and ask him if the records there do not confirm my story," John pleaded. "The records are at Annecy; they will tell the truth if you don't believe me."

"That's just another of your tales, not the truth," one of the policemen yelled again. "You are not John Weidner. Who are you? You won't get out of this alive if you don't give the right answers."

Finally, tired of their bloody work, they dragged Weidner to a cell. Bleeding, barely conscious, he lay in a heap on the flat piece of wood which served as a bed in the bare cell. Three hours later the policemen returned. They took Weidner from the cell and began beating him again. This time they added new methods of torture. In addition to beating and kicking, they twisted Weidner's arms behind his back, telling him both would be broken if he did not give them satisfactory answers.

"Tell us why you were trying to escape to Switzerland," they shouted. "Tell us you are a Dutchman trying to escape from France. You know that is right. When we are done with you, you'll wish you had told the truth!"

"My name is John Weidner. I am going to Collonges, where I have studied at the seminary of the college for many years," John repeated once again to the gendarmes.

Convinced that John wanted to escape to Switzerland as a refugee, they became even more enraged because Weidner wouldn't admit to them what they now believed. They were not so much infuriated that he might be trying to escape as they were that he wouldn't admit such a fact to them.

But now they no longer took down his answers in the notebooks they had used earlier. Their anger had steadily risen with their increasing brutality. They were not even listening to his answers. They seemed obsessed by the brutal tactics they were using on their prisoner.

Finally they ended their inquisition, picked Weidner up from the floor, and dragged him back to the cell. Hardly conscious of what was going on around him, John received another blow as the policemen threw him down on the board that served as a bed.

It was becoming dark on this summer day which had started out so peacefully for John. Through the night he frequently awakened in spasms of terror. His body was a mass of pain, and his bloody head hurt fiercely. In those waking moments thoughts raced through his brain, but the answer to his dilemma would not come.

"I've got to find some way to get out of this situation," he told himself as he lay back on the hard board. "If I don't think of something soon, they might kill me."

In his pain he remembered to ask for divine help. Through the night he prayed even as he planned for what he might do when the gendarmes returned the next day.

When he awakened again, sunshine filtered into the cell from a tiny slitlike window above his head. He lay on the hard board contemplating the stream of light. Somehow it seemed to be an omen that things would go better this day than they had before. But when he raised himself from the floor, he knew it would be many days before the pain of the beating he had suffered would leave his body.

144

"I must exercise to try to keep my muscles from becoming cramped," he thought as he struggled to an upright position. "The pain will go away quicker if I exercise."

He walked slowly about the cell, pausing now and then to rub an especially painful spot on his body. He could stand or walk about the cubicle, or he could lie down on the board on the floor. But there was no chair on which he could sit. He could also view a narrow scene in the prison garden from the little slit window.

On one of these painful trips about the cell he glanced through the little slit. In the garden he could see a woman whom he believed was one of the guards' wives. As he watched her working, a plan took shape in his mind.

"Madame, madame, I am here in this cell," John called softly to the woman. She turned to look at the prison wall. "I'm right here," John called again, this time waving his hand so that she could see which window his voice was coming from. She gazed toward his cell for some time, then took a few steps closer.

"My name is John Weidner, and I need to let my uncle know I am here. Would you telephone Mr. Normand at the farm on the St. Julien highway for me and tell him John Weidner is in this prison? He will know what to do."

The woman continued to gaze toward John's cell, saying nothing. Then abruptly she turned away, and Weidner couldn't see her anymore.

What would she do? She didn't say she would make the call. But she didn't say she wouldn't. All he could do was wait and see—and hope.

6 145

Again he lay down on the board. His bones ached, and now his stomach began to hurt from hunger. He continued to turn over in his mind the possibilities of the unexpected contact with the woman in the garden. He felt certain that if she would only contact Mr. Normand, things would change. He was influential in town, and if the gendarmes were aware that someone else knew about his being in jail, they would perhaps begin to listen to reason.

John didn't have to wait long for an answer. Within half an hour after his monologue with the woman in the garden he heard the telephone ring in the prison office. A long conversation followed, but he couldn't hear the words distinctly. A few minutes later the key rattled in the lock of his cell door.

"Won't you please come out into the office, Mr. Weidner? There are some things we would like to discuss with you," said one of the two gendarmes who had beaten him so mercilessly the day before. The policeman spoke in a mild, pleasant voice.

Puzzled by the friendly tone, John crawled from his hard bed and limped toward the door. "What tactic is this?" he asked himself. "Are they just trying to be nice until they get me in the office so that they can start beating me again?" He kept a distance between himself and the policeman, who now backed into the little prison office.

"Sit here in this chair; it is the most comfortable one," the gendarme offered. "We have a few things yet to discuss, but it should not take too long. I want to be sure you are comfortable, though. Does the chair feel all right?"

146

Nodding, John watched the gendarme closely. "He's leading up to something worse than yesterday, or else someone higher up has told him my story is the truth. If that is so, they know they have no real case against me," John thought. "This fellow is just too nice not to have some motive behind his actions."

The other gendarme entered the office, and they began their questioning again; but this time everything was different. They were polite and obviously eager to make a good impression on their prisoner. He was given time to answer, and they continued to be overly solicitous of his comfort.

"Now we have the story about your trip to Collonges cleared up," they admitted after a few minutes of questioning. "There remains only the matter of the large number of food ration tickets you had when we took you from the bus. You undoubtedly have a good story about them, just as you did about your travels. But we should review that matter a bit; don't you think so, Mr. Weidner?"

As the questioning progressed, John knew at last that the gendarmes were not going to beat him again. "They've been told that my story is true; now they are trying to make me feel good so that I won't report their dirty work to the higher authorities," he said to himself. "If I want to get out of this jail, I'll have to plead guilty to having those extra ration tickets and take my chances with a judge. But at least that will get me out of jail. The judge probably won't do more than fine me for carrying the tickets."

So Weidner admitted the ration tickets were his. He asked that he be taken before a judge who would decide what should be done. The extra tickets were to have been used to buy food for the increasing number of Jewish refugees he and his friends were passing from Lyons to the Swiss border.

"If the judge appears friendly, I may even be able to tell him something of the plight of the refugees, and he might let me keep the tickets," John reasoned.

Weidner's request seemed to please the now completely affable gendarmes. "Fine, fine," one of them said. "That is the right decision. We'll set up a hearing with the judge in St. Julien tomorrow. In the meantime we will want to make sure you are comfortable in your cell. You'll need a better bed, some blankets, and some food. Of course you'll need some good food!"

Through the afternoon and evening Weidner became a special prisoner in the Cruseilles jail. He received all the courtesies he had been denied the previous day. He was given tasty soups and other excellent vegetarian food, since John had told the gendarmes he was a vegetarian. When he went to sleep that night, he realized fully that the police were trying hard not to lose face and also to find an excuse for having arrested him. They had hit upon the extra ration cards as the excuse they needed.

At St. Julien on the following day they took Weidner in handcuffs to the office of the judge. As the proceeding began, the gendarmes told of the prisoner's arrest, stumbling vaguely over the time they had spent beating him. They dwelt at length on the subject of the extra ration tickets. Then John was asked to tell his own story. He told of his arrest, but he did not go into detail about the beatings he had received. He wanted to be set free to go about his business. If he accused the police of brutal treatment, he knew he would have to spend considerable time waiting for a trial.

When he had finished, the judge looked up from his papers. "You admit having the extra ration tickets, do you, Mr. Weidner? That is an offense we do not pass lightly over in wartime, you know. There is just so much food, and it has to go around for all. If there were many people like you, we would soon run short of food."

Weidner admitted he realized the seriousness of the matter.

"You say you were on your way to Collonges," the judge said. "I have many friends there myself. Perhaps we have some mutual friends."

The informal conversation that followed between the judge and prisoner disclosed that they did, indeed, have mutual friends in the town.

"It is good that we have so many friends," the judge agreed. "I know people on the border as well as others in Geneva. The consul of France in Geneva, Mr. Mondon, is a good friend of mine also."

"You know Mr. Mondon?" John asked the judge. "He is a friend of mine, too. You might even want to telephone him for a recommendation for me. He has known me for a number of years."

"So you know Mondon? Of course, I'll call him right now, and we'll see what he has to say about you."

Reaching for the telephone, the judge placed a call to the consul's office. As he spoke, John could hear that he was getting a good recommendation.

"Yes, he knows you," the judge said to John as he laid the telephone down. "He says you are working with the refugees, and that is probably why you had the extra ration tickets. That is a good work you are doing. And as far as the charge of carrying extra ration tickets is concerned, just forget it.

"Now, guards," the judge rasped at the gendarmes, "take those handcuffs off this man."

An hour later John and the gendarmes were aboard a bus heading for Cruseilles. But this time he was a passenger again, en route to Annecy to recuperate from the beating he had suffered. The police, returning to their posts at the prison, were obviously grateful to him for not exposing their cruel treatment. Weidner thought about their brutal treatment, but he could not hate them.

XI

ROUTE TO SPAIN

IN NOVEMBER, 1942, American armed forces swept past Gibraltar into the Mediterranean in a great invasion armada. From hundreds of ships the troops swarmed onto the beaches of North Africa. The size of the force and its speed startled the Germans, who sent military units racing through unoccupied France to the southern French coast. For days the rumble of Nazi tanks, troop transports, and supply trucks echoed through the countryside of southern France.

With the army came a complete intelligence and counter-intelligence network to supplement the already considerable complex of Nazi-directed anti-Resistance activity. At every street corner, it seemed, a German soldier now stood—and in the middle of the block a Gestapo headquarters manned by the dreaded blackshirts. Now throughout what had been unoccupied France there roamed the Abwehr (German army intelligence-counterintelligence), the French police, the gendarmerie, the Gardes Mobiles (government riot troops), and the hated Milice (French Gestapo). Each group had a part to play in seeking out members of the Resistance; each employed its own special methods of torture and cruelty.

As the Nazis slashed through southern France toward the Mediterranean coast, Weidner knew his work would become much more difficult than when the southern zone was at least partially free of full-scale anti-Resistance operations. He realized that Dutch-Paris would now have to operate much more secretly than when only an occasional Nazi watched over the work of the French police. He could no longer expect the occasional protection of the French which he once enjoyed. No longer would there be a possibility of obtaining transit visas for Dutchmen in Switzerland who wanted to cross through southeastern France into Spain in order to go on to England. The last vestiges of diplomacy were destroyed. Every problem would now be ten times more difficult to overcome than before the German army entered southern France.

As he watched the armored columns roar southward past Lyons, John knew he must take his organization deep underground if it was to survive and continue to operate effectively. Now the feeling that perhaps he should not travel to the northern part of the country because it was illegal was replaced by the feeling that the lives of scores of people fully depended on such travel. Though once he had felt that using a false name was strictly illegal, he now knew that the only way he could possibly continue to save Jewish lives and others threatened by the Nazis was to travel under any name which would permit him to move about at all.

Southern France had become an armed German camp with a deadly complex of secret and semisecret organizations whose only purpose was to suppress all efforts to save the lives of Jews, escaping Allied airmen, and others.

Where Weidner had previously made every attempt at legality in his work, he now realized that the standard once called illegality did not actually apply to the horrendous Nazi organization, whose standards began at a subhuman level and from there went downward.

Even as the dust of the fast-moving motorized columns still hung in the air, John made plans to travel to any point —Toulouse, Paris, Brussels, or anywhere—if it would speed the escape of refugees. To send others was to risk their lives, perhaps unnecessarily, especially when so many decisions had to be made by him as an underground leader. So Weidner began to travel across the face of France as he knit his organization more closely together.

From Annecy he received a request for help that sent him to southeastern France. A young Dutch citizen, bound from temporary shelter in Switzerland to England via the French-Spanish border near Perpignan, was informed that he could find help at the home of Pastor Chapal, a Calvinist minister in the city. When he told Pastor Chapal that others were planning to make a similar attempt to cross southeastern France to Spain and then go on to England, the clergyman, realizing the help these young people needed, called John Weidner.

"I can feed them and perhaps keep one or two overnight, but I can't help them get all the way across France," Pastor

Chapal said to Weidner when he arrived. "They need places to stay and directions for getting through France. When they leave my home, they are on their own. I know some of them will be arrested along the way because they don't know how to avoid the Gestapo. I have minister friends in other cities who might help, but they must be contacted, and I cannot do that."

Weidner took the list of possible contacts the minister offered. "In a few days I should have a route arranged. When plans are completed, I'll let you know. You can send these boys along with more safety then."

Several days later he had completed the dangerous task of contacting other ministers and friends in several towns. At Avignon he arranged overnight shelter for the escapees. Near the Spanish border he found Gabriel Nahas, a young medical student, who agreed to help in caring for the new route at its southern end. Nahas took the alias Georges Brantes in John's group for identification purposes.

When he was in Annecy again, Weidner reported to Pastor Chapal that the new route had been completed. As he explained procedures of the route, John's own desire to escape to England and join his countrymen working against the Nazis returned. But he couldn't think only of himself. Maurice Jacquet, the new consul in Lyons who had taken Lambotte's place, had been forthright about it.

"You are doing work which we are no longer allowed to do openly at the consul office, John," he said. "Your services are needed here in France; there are many persons who will not live if you leave. Much as you might want to

154

go to England, your greatest service to your country at this time is to stay here in France."

Weidner could not dispute the official's words.

Not only was his situation changed, but so was that of his close friend, Gilbert Beaujolin. Although the two still worked closely together and continued to relax together whenever time permitted, Gilbert had found other interests, too. In recent months he had become one of the leaders of a rapidly developing underground organization called "Alliance." Because Weidner and Beaujolin were close friends, Alliance now began giving help to John's underground unit.

As the young Dutch escapees used the new route through France to Spain, John saw that this line would become more important in the future. Valuable as it was to get people into Switzerland, it was not a satisfactory situation for those who wanted to help against the invaders in an active way. Completely surrounded by nations at war, Switzerland could absorb escapees and give them shelter, but it could not transport them to Allied countries. Allied airmen shot down in occupied countries naturally wanted to return to England, where they could again serve in the defense of freedom. Officials in governments and potential fighting men of countries occupied by the Germans likewise found escape to Switzerland unacceptable. They wanted to join the forces of their own governments in exile in England.

Weidner realized that a route to Spain should be organized to move all types of escapees. This would be difficult. But crossing the Pyrenees into Spain was the only practical route along which all types of persons could successfully be moved. The Nazis were increasing their patrols in the lowland areas of the border, where many young Dutchmen were trying to escape en route to Spain, and that escape route would soon be impossible.

One of John's worst fears concerning the German arrival in southern France came true shortly after they made their sweep southward in November, 1942. Word reached him that Arie Sevenster, representative of the Netherlands in Vichy, had been arrested. That left only Mario Janse, the chancellor, in Vichy, and even his position was so shaky that it was next to impossible for him to help refugees.

Then word came that Testers, the French consul in Toulouse, and Kolkman, the consul in Perpignan, had also been arrested by the Gestapo. This news was shocking because Kolkman, especially, had been largely responsible for the successful crossings by the Dutch nationals using the Annecy-Avignon-Perpignan escape line.

The noose seemed to be tightening a little bit every day. It would be only a matter of days until all the consuls were taken. When that happened, every diplomatic move, however slight, to help the refugees would have to be carried on solely through the underground.

In December, 1942, John went to Toulouse to explore possibilities for the new route into Spain. Before he left Lyons, however, he took the precaution of arranging to make sales contacts for a friend who managed a large textile factory. This was to ensure that Weidner, if questioned by the Nazis while in the border area south of Toulouse, would have a logical, and truthful, reason for his presence there.

In Toulouse he went to see Mrs. Sevenster, who, having been told she could visit her imprisoned husband from time to time, had moved to that city with her two daughters.

"Our courage is good," she told John when they met at her tiny apartment. "Arie is in the prison at Evaux-les-Bains with many other prominent French people, including President Herriot. They are treating him fairly well. Of course, things are not as good for him as I would like, but it is a prison. I guess everything is all right."

That evening John went to see a man named Aarts who had been appointed Dutch consul in Toulouse after the arrest of Testers. He discussed with Aarts the disorganized situation of the Kolkman escape route near Perpignan and told the consul he wanted to establish a new escape line which would cross through the Pyrenees.

"When I have the arrangements completed, I'll contact you again," John said. "You can then begin referring refugees or other escapees to our guides here in Toulouse. We will take care of the guides both financially and technically, so there will be no problems after the route is established."

From Aarts's house he went back into the city, where he met Eric Ter Raa, a young Dutchman who wanted to cross the Pyrenees to escape to England. Together they went to the home of Mrs. Lil Van Wyhe, a Frenchwoman who had been married to a Dutchman. Her husband had died, but Mrs. Van Wyhe had valuable information about conditions in the Pyrenees. She also gave them the address of a guide who had crossed the mountains many times.

When they found the guide, John said he needed his help to cross the Pyrenees. "My friend here will be going to Spain to stay, but I will be returning to Toulouse. We need to know what your price is for such a trip. I am not carrying much money with me right now, but perhaps you would be more interested in something else anyway." John held up his arm. "This wristwatch, for example, is one of the best Swiss makes on the market. This ought to take us quite a distance."

The guide reached out his hand for the watch John had slipped from his arm. "It is a good watch," he acknowledged. "I will take it, but it is not enough. I saw a cigarette lighter in your pocket. If you give them both to me, I'll take you over and bring you back."

Cigarette lighters, as the war cut off civilian uses of metal, had become very precious and extremely hard to get. Each time John crossed the border into Switzerland, he purchased several lighters which he used as bribes to get out of difficult situations.

"All right, it is a deal," Weidner agreed. "You take the cigarette lighter now. The watch I will wear until you have returned me safely to Toulouse. That way I know we will complete the trip quickly, eh?"

"The trip will go quickly, be sure of that. We will stretch your Dutch legs on the passes. But that comes later. You have to worry about papers now. There is the Zone Interdite, the forbidden place, you know. Frenchmen must have special papers to go there. And for foreigners it is even more difficult."

The forbidden zone would be a problem, John knew. But when he returned to Mrs. Van Wyhe's home, he found that the problem could be worked out.

"Yes, they do require special papers," she told him. "But I have a good friend in the government documents office here which prepares those papers. Tonight I will see that he prepares a set for you."

"And for my friend, Eric—what can we get for him?" John asked. "He arrived here in Toulouse illegally. He wants to get to England. What can you do for him?"

"We'll take care of him, too. He'll need complete identification and travel papers, and a *laissez-passer* document for the Zone Interdite."

"But he doesn't speak French, remember that. French papers won't do," John pointed out.

"That's right; he can't use French papers," Mrs. Van Wyhe said. "But my friend will know what to do. He has arranged many false papers. He'll have the answer."

A few hours later she came back with the precious papers. "Your friend has just become a member of the Organization Todt," she declared. "That's a group of skilled people from throughout the occupied countries the Germans are sending to different areas to help in their war effort. Your friend will become Mr. Van Ryn, and his papers show he is to be a worker at a chemical plant near the border. The Nazis should believe these papers, and certainly the French gendarmes will not question them."

The next day Weidner, Van Ryn, and André, the guide, set out for the mountains. Of the three main routes to the border, they chose the route through Foix. Several prewar customers of his textile business lived in that city; and if he was stopped, he could use their names. He felt sure they would tell the Germans that he was, in fact, a textile merchant in the city on business.

The three arrived at the Foix railroad station in the evening and started through the French control point at the exit. John and the guide showed their documents and passed through the checkpoint without incident. Eric, however, didn't make it.

"What kind of papers are these?" snapped the French guard. "Organization Todt—I've never heard of that. You come along with me to the German headquarters down the street. They'll know about it—if it really exists."

With the guard close at his heels, Eric went through the checkpoint and out onto the street. John and André trailed behind, keeping plenty of distance, so that they would not be identified with the escapee. Then they waited across the street as the guard led Eric into the German headquarters.

"We'll wait here for an hour. If he doesn't come out by then, we'll have to leave," Weidner said to the guide. "I just hope he can convince the Germans that his papers are authentic. Otherwise he'll be on his way to prison shortly."

John glanced at the watch he would be giving the guide when they got back to Toulouse—if they ever got back. It had been a half hour since Eric went into the building. Suddenly the door opened, and out walked the young Dutchman. John wanted to race across the street and hug him, but he knew better. There would be time for emotion later. They followed along behind Eric until he turned a corner, then quickened their pace until they came abreast of him.

"What did they do?" Weidner asked.

"It's not safe to talk here on the street. Let's go to the hotel as we were planning," broke in André. "We can talk there."

The trio quickly found the hotel, registered, and then Eric told them of his ordeal with the Germans.

"They hadn't seen anyone from the Organization Todt before," he said. "But as it was listed in their book of governmental agencies, they didn't doubt its existence. Since I've done engineering in Holland, I was able to convince them with technical language that I was a professional man. They stamped my papers to show that they had checked them. Now I can travel without trouble at the checkpoints. It actually was a help having them pick me up."

When Eric had finished telling his experience, André left to talk with friends in Foix about crossing the mountains. He returned with bad news.

"The regulations for the Zone Interdite have been changed," he said. "Now only those living in the Zone can go into it. All others must get a special paper given only by the Germans themselves. You wouldn't stand a chance with them. Neither would I. Only Eric can go into the Zone, since his papers have now been stamped by the Germans."

"Maybe I ought to return to Carcassonne and try to get Organization Todt papers also," John suggested. "That might help me get the special Zone papers." But then he realized such a solution wouldn't help his guide, who spoke

161

only French. "No, that wouldn't do at all. We must find another way to get through," he told the others. "It may be dangerous, but we've got to get this new route established for the refugees. We've got to go on."

"Well, if we are going ahead, I have an idea that might work," ventured the guide. "The driver of the bus that runs from Foix to Ax-les-Thermes near the mountains is a good friend of mine. I think he will give us help. If we can manage it, I'm sure he will let us ride on the top of his bus. He will hide us among the baggage. He has done that for others I know. The Zone Interdite starts at Ussat-les-Bains only ten miles from here. There are also several German checkpoints. If we went by train, we would have to pass through the checkpoints openly. They would see that we don't have proper papers for the Zone. But riding on the bus will be different, because they don't usually check the baggage area on top. Eric will have no problem. He can ride inside in safety."

"It may work," John agreed. "We can travel to Tarascon on the roof of the bus. From there we can easily reach the mountains. Yes, I think it will work."

That night the three men went to the Foix station to board the bus—John and the guide on top, Eric inside. But when they saw French gendarmes and German soldiers all about the station, they knew it would be impossible to climb on top of the bus without being seen.

"We'll have to wait until tomorrow and then see if we can't find some other way to get aboard," Weidner said, and they turned back toward the hotel. "If we come back early enough in the afternoon, we might be able to hide among the baggage before the bus is brought into the station passenger area."

About three o'clock the next afternoon John and André met the bus driver in the garage where the buses were serviced, and the driver helped them onto the luggage carrier on top of the vehicle, then piled boxes of merchandise about them so that they would not be seen. Two hours later he returned to move the bus to the passenger area for the run to Ax-les-Thermes.

As the passengers boarded, the driver brought other pieces of luggage, including a crate of chickens, to add to the boxes he had already piled around the two men. He whispered encouragement to John and André, who lay huddled among the boxes, as he tied a canvas over the load. In a few minutes the bus rumbled out of the Foix station.

About half an hour later the big vehicle pulled to a stop at a German checkpoint. The two men on top of the bus, realizing that the stop was for a German inspection, steeled themselves into absolute immobility. But the chickens in the cage nearby raised a great cackling chorus. John could hear the driver talking with the German police. As the conversation continued, the two stowaways also heard someone start up the metal ladder on the side of the bus. They stretched themselves flat against the roof behind the big cage of chickens. Suddenly the canvas was thrown back, and a German policeman shouted in laughter at the squawking chickens in the cage. Behind the chickens John and the guide lay silent, frightened, scarcely breathing. The guard gave the cage a playful nudge with his rifle butt to stir the chickens to their squawking symphony again, then flipped the canvas back over the luggage carrier and retied it.

Again the bus roared away toward the mountains. Two hours and many stops later the driver came up the ladder and threw the canvas back.

"This is the place you wanted to get off," he said. "I had quite a time with the Germans back there. They couldn't understand what I was telling them about the chickens, so they had to go up and look for themselves."

"Lucky for you, luckier for us," John said. "Thanks for the ride."

Quickly the men got down from the bus and joined Eric. That night they stayed in the attic of the home of one of André's friends.

At three o'clock the next morning they left for the mountains, which were only a short distance away. But Weidner knew it would take at least eighteen to twenty hours with little rest to reach Andorra, the little neutral country separating France and Spain. There they planned to arrange for the regular passage of escapees to Spain.

Although it was dark during the early hours of the trip, André seemed to know exactly which way to go; and when daylight finally broke, they were already climbing the steeper ridges of the towering mountains. As they stopped to rest a moment, John suddenly felt the bitter cold. On the peaks ahead he could see heavy snow.

After climbing for nearly four hours the guide called a halt so that they could eat some food they had brought with them. As they ate, he searched the slopes below with a telescope. Suddenly he handed the instrument to John. "Look down there on that long, smooth slope leading toward Ax-les-Thermes. Tell me what you see."

Peering through the glass Weidner could make out three tiny figures climbing up the slope. As he studied them more carefully, he saw rifles slung over their shoulders. "They're German soldiers!" Weidner exclaimed. "They must be patrols—and they are coming this way!"

"That's right; they are coming this way," André confirmed. "We'll have to step up our pace for the next couple of hours if we want to outdistance them. And we'll have to keep a sharp watch ahead. Often one patrol will come down from the border of Andorra and another patrol, just like the one down there, will come up to take its place. Let's shove off now. I don't want to tangle with them."

The climb was now becoming more demanding. John and the guide, both experienced mountaineers, were meeting the test, but Eric, accustomed only to the lowlands of Holland, was already beginning to tire.

Patches of snow soon added to their difficulties. André led John and Eric around the snow whenever he could, but at times they were forced to tramp through drifts several feet deep, which left them cold and wet.

After about twenty minutes of stiff hiking André stopped in a depression in the rocks. He took another look toward the German patrol with his telescope.

"They are about the same distance from us, but they are taking a different route," he said. "I think we can slow down now, because they are heading in a direction almost parallel with us."

That news was comforting to Eric, who had become exhausted. André picked up the young Dutchman's rucksack and slung it over his shoulder.

"We'll go more slowly, Eric. You can make it if you use your hiking stick more and don't try to go too fast. Just keep a steady pace."

In an hour they had reached a jagged ridge which looked down on many of the sharp peaks around them. As André again surveyed the boulder-strewn terrain, he dropped down quickly beside John and Eric, who were sitting on the ground.

"There is another patrol, and this one is much closer," he said. "They are looking this way with their telescope. I'm not sure whether they saw me. They must have been in that cabin we passed about half an hour ago. We'd better stay here under cover until we see what they are going to do. If they come this way, we'll have to get out fast."

"I could never make it if they came this way," moaned Eric. "If they come up here, just go on. Leave me behind. I'll hide somewhere. I can't make it anymore; I'm not used to these mountains."

"You'll make it, Eric," insisted John. "Besides, they may not come this way at all. Even if they do, we aren't going to leave you here alone. We are going to get to Andorra today—together!"

The problem was solved a few minutes later when André saw the German patrol moving in an opposite direction from the course the three were traveling. "Just a few more ridges, and we'll be at the home of a friend where we can spend the night," he said.

Darkness had settled on the cold, snow-covered Pyrenees when the three men who had been climbing for more than fifteen hours finally sighted a house about two miles inside Andorra, not far from the town which served as the little country's business center.

When they reached the house, John and Eric waited in the freezing cold while André went inside to make arrangements for lodging. At last he called his two weary companions in to a warm fire. That night the three slept in a barn near the house, their teeth chattering under thin blankets.

"Anyway, this is better than being on the mountains with the patrols moving about," John said during one fretful session when the harsh cold robbed them of sleep. "We couldn't have a fire if we were out there, and we wouldn't have these blankets. Out there both the Spanish and the Germans are keeping watch—the Spanish for smugglers, the Germans for people trying to escape. And don't forget the French police—they're looking for smugglers, too. Cold as it is, I'm glad I'm here in the barn!"

With the sun warming the barn next morning, John, André, and Eric made plans for the day.

"There are two ways to get to Barcelona, Eric," André explained. "You can walk across the Spanish border on the other side of Andorra, then catch the bus that runs to the interior. Or you can go into Andorra with us this morning and take your chances on riding the bus from the town. Either way you'll probably be taken to the Spanish refugee camp and from there after a time you will get to the Netherlands consul in Barcelona. But if the Spanish guards are nasty, they can have you sent back to France, where the Gestapo can get at you. That is very seldom done, but it is a possibility."

Eric, his muscles aching from the previous day's experience, decided to take the bus leaving from the town in Andorra. "I couldn't walk another day if it meant my life," he said. "I'll take my chances by going from the town."

John asked André to obtain Spanish money from his friend for Eric to use to buy a bus ticket and for other expenses in getting to Barcelona. When they had the money, the three walked down the mountain path to the picturesque town. At the edge of the little village John and the guide said good-bye to Eric.

"I shall pray for your safety on the trip, Eric," John said. "We have done all we can for you now, but God can do things we cannot. I believe He will guide you safely."

Eric walked stiffly down the village street toward the bus station, and two hours later, as they toured the town, John and André saw the bus going up the mountain road in a cloud of dust toward the Spanish border.

That night the two men stopped at the home of a Spanish peasant. Through the day they had studied the various roads and trails André said could be used through Andorra to Spain. Now John had all the information he needed to successfully operate the Pyrenees escape route, although he wouldn't be leading the escapees himself. He was not familiar enough with the rugged mountains and the problems which could be encountered to act intelligently if a crisis came.

In the peasant's home they found five Spanish smugglers preparing to leave for France. After considerable haggling, André persuaded the Spaniards to include John and him in their group. The smugglers knew every trick of evading the various patrols in the mountains, and travel with them would be safer than going alone. About three o'clock the next morning they set out for Foix, hiking steadily until they were well down from the highest peaks by midday. Another few hours of rough climbing brought them to the outskirts of Tarascon.

Earlier, because of the large number of German and French patrols in the mountains, the smugglers had divided into three groups, each taking a slightly different route. Now, as the group John and André were with came into full view of Tarascon, they heard rifle fire to their left. The nearby shots sent them rushing downward across the ridges and through the defiles. Soon they sighted the road leading into the town. From their vantage point on a ridge, the smugglers could see two German soldiers manning a road-block near the first houses of the village.

"We can't get past them," John whispered to André. "We should go around the town and then come in from the other side. They certainly aren't guarding the other side."

The guide agreed, and they left the smugglers, who had plans of their own for the large sacks of hard-to-get items they carried. Weidner and André slowly circled the town, keeping behind hills and trees. Several times they met villagers, whom they engaged in conversation in an attempt to find out what the situation in the town was. When they located the road on the opposite side of the town, they walked along it into the village without difficulty. In a café they discovered why so many patrols were in the mountains.

"Thirty Frenchmen are on the mountains this afternoon trying to get into Spain," one of the men in the café said. "The Germans are determined to catch them before nightfall so that they can't get into Andorra. With the patrols everywhere it looks as if they will catch them, too."

Late that evening they rode a bus to Foix, returning the same way they had gone to Ax-les-Thermes—on top among the baggage. The next morning they took a train to Toulouse, where Weidner contacted Gabriel Nahas, directing him to take charge of the Pyrenees escape line. Nahas was a skillful young patriot who knew the rugged mountain area well. He had many contacts with guides who regularly crossed the peaks and was capable of making fast and accurate decisions, a quality necessary in operating an escape route. He arranged with Nahas to run the new escape line in cooperation with Aarts in Toulouse.

When he left for Lyons a few days later, John could take satisfaction in the new route he had established. In the hands of Aarts, Nahas, and other members of the organization in Toulouse, the new line would save many refugees and an increasing number of Allied airmen. Although it had nearly cost him his life on several occasions, he had punched another hole to freedom through the border curtain.

XII

the count escapes

ANNIE LANGLADE, at whose home he had stayed for many months, introduced John one day to Count François de Menthon.

"He is a brave man who has already done much for France in the war," she told Weidner. "The count is considered a pioneer of the Resistance movement, and he is hated by the enemy."

In 1942 the count had been publicly humiliated by a group of pro-Nazi French youth. They threw him into the central water fountain of Annecy as an expression of their dislike of his activities. In 1939, while in the French army, he had been wounded in the early days of the battle against the Germans. He was captured, but he escaped and fled to southern France. There, in Lyons, which was known in all of France as the "capital of the Resistance movement," he began laying plans to harass and drive the invaders from French soil.

Count de Menthon lived with his wife and six children in a medieval castle high in the forest overlooking beautiful

171

Lake Annecy. He was a respected professor of law at the University of Lyons and was well liked by the populace of the Savoy, which touches the Swiss border. He was also a leader of the Catholic Association of French Youth. A militant patriot, he began underground work shortly after fleeing to southern France, and within a few months he became the leader of the underground organization called Liberte.

In the midst of heightening underground activity in 1943, the count called on Weidner one day.

"Annie tells me you are familiar with the Swiss border and that you cross it yourself rather regularly," he said. "You are the man I need to help me. I must see the representatives of General de Gaulle to make arrangements to visit the general himself in London. There are many matters connected with my trip that I am not at liberty to discuss now, but I assure you my journey is an important one for France."

John told the count it would be a privilege to help him.

The next day he began the complicated process of arranging for the count's escape. His first contact was made with the Swiss government in Geneva through couriers of his underground group. He wanted to be sure the count would meet no difficulties, once inside Switzerland, in meeting the de Gaulle representatives. Then Weidner talked with the men who were to guide de Menthon across the border.

"This man is very important to the future of France," Weidner told the two men he had chosen to help the count. "We must make sure no harm comes to him on the way to

172

his contact. General de Gaulle is personally interested in having the count become part of his staff. And he must talk with de Gaulle's representative in Switzerland to arrange for his trip to England."

Near the little border village of Archamps, on the road between St. Julien and Annemasse, a stream ran under the roadway. The Germans had tangled the large pipe which carried the stream with barbed wire because at that point there was no other barrier between France and Switzerland.

"We will use the pipe for the count's escape," Weidner said. "He will be brought to Archamps by bus. Then you can take him to the stream during the night. When the road is clear, you move into the stream and cut the wire just enough to get through. You will also have to dam the stream temporarily so that you can wade through the culvert; otherwise the water will be too high in the pipe for you to get through. Be sure you put the strands back exactly as they were. The dam, if you construct it of mud and small rocks, will wash away quickly and won't be noticed."

A few days later Count de Menthon arrived at the little village and met the passers who were to see him across the border. In the darkness of night they proceeded to the pipe. They inched their way along the bank of the little stream, and then one of the passers cut the coils of barbed wire.

While the man worked at the coils, his companion and the count shoved rocks into the stream and piled dirt around them. Finally the level of the stream below their dam began to drop. The count and one passer then shoved themselves through the small hole that the third member of the group had cut in the wires. Quickly the man with the cutters jerked the wires back into place to hide the hole. The count slogged through muddy water in the pipe toward the safety of Switzerland. The danger was past, and Geneva lay only a few miles away.

After several days of meetings in Switzerland, the count slipped back into France. Some days later at Ambérieu, fifty miles from Annecy, an Allied plane landed at night and took him to England. In London he joined the provisional government of General de Gaulle as minister of justice. After the liberation of France, Count de Menthon was the official French representative at the famed Nuremberg war crimes trials.

For the count's family, living in relative peace in the picturesque castle in the forest above the beautiful lake, the months slipped by in almost monotonous regularity. Monotonous, that is, until one day the Nazis, in a typically senseless move to terrorize the prospering new government of de Gaulle, declared that they would arrest and imprison the members of all families of Frenchmen serving in the de Gaulle government.

That announcement uprooted scores of families and sent them in all directions in an effort to avoid capture. Among them was Mrs. de Menthon, the count's wife. With her as she fled from the castle were several of her children. But the youngest, a boy only five, she could not take because of the furious pace and hazards of the escape. The youngster was hidden with friends, but his mother knew she could not bear to leave him behind for any long period of time. Then she

174

remembered the man who had helped her husband escape.

"Won't you bring him to me in Switzerland?" Mrs. de Menthon asked John. "I know you can bring him through safely. You have helped so many already. He is my youngest—and my dearest!"

"I will bring him," Weidner assured the anxious mother. Then, thinking about the approaching Christmas season, he added, "I will bring him to you for Christmas!"

A few days of planning were required to map an escape route that would be best for the youngster. They arrived at the border area in cold, wet weather which extended all along the French-Swiss boundary. The rain fell steadily; and when they reached the point where he wanted to cross with the child between St. Julien and Collonges, the little creek running through no-man's-land was swollen and angry looking.

"This is the best place, the only place that can be considered safe right now," he thought as he viewed the murky waters of the stream. "The guards are watching everywhere else along the border. The only reason this place is open is that they don't think a person would walk through so much water in such cold weather. It doesn't look too promising, but I'll have to give it a try in the morning anyway."

Just before dawn John roused the youngster from his bed in the farmhouse where they had spent the night. After a hasty breakfast they stumbled out into the wet, cold dawn. "We will stay close together as we walk; and when you get tired, I can carry you," John told the boy as they set off toward the stream.

The barbed wire barrier was no problem to Weidner, but the creek looked even wider than the day before.

"We're going to cross the stream now," he explained. "It seems deep from here, but I have been across before. The water has never come above my waist. I'll put you on my shoulders so that you will be high above the water. Then in just a little while we'll be in Switzerland. You will see your mother again very soon. How does that strike you?"

The boy answered with a vigorous nod and a wide smile, and Weidner scooped him up and swung him to his shoulders. The little fellow grasped John's hair tightly and held on.

Slowly, feeling carefully to put his feet on level places among the rocks, John stepped into the water. Although the current was not very swift, the coldness of the water numbed him as he moved deeper into the stream. Soon the water was at waist level, and they were still some distance from the middle of the stream. Then it rose to mid-chest, touching the small legs of the little boy. The chilling coldness of the water made it hard for John to move steadily. If he could have plunged his entire body into the stream at once, it would have been easier; but to move slowly, feeling carefully for each foothold, made the cold even more painful.

Now the water was just below his shoulders, and they were still not in midstream. Suddenly John was struck by the thought that if the water came over his head at midstream, he would have to swim and care for the youngster too. Could he do it? He took another step, and the water swirled over his shoulders and then to his chin. In midstream at last, John slowly took another step—again the water was

176

just at chin level. Then another step, and it was halfway down his neck. Another step brought the water to his shoulders!

"We've made it!" he whispered. "A few more steps, and we'll be out. Hang on tight now; we'll make it."

The youngster tightened his grip on John's hair, causing him to flinch despite the numbing cold. "Easy, go easy," he told the boy. "That hair does come out, you know, if you pull too hard."

The boy giggled, then loosened his hold as they climbed out of the stream.

When the winter sun broke through the clouds over Switzerland later that day, Weidner and the youngest son of Count de Menthon were warm and comfortable in a car driving through the streets of Geneva on the way to a happy Christmas reunion for the boy and his mother.

When the car finally stopped, the boy's mother had the door open and was clasping the child in her arms. "You're here! You're here! You're here!" she said, as though repetition would assure her that it was no dream. Tears streamed down her face, and she pulled the boy even closer.

As he watched the joyous reunion, John was struck suddenly by the enormity of the trust this woman had placed in him. "Thank God, I didn't fail," he said silently.

Holding her child close, Mrs. de Menthon turned to John. "You have done more for us than we can ever repay. Now I want to hear all about the trip."

Some months after he had taken the count's son to Switzerland, Weidner received a message from Charles

Guillon, head of de Gaulle's French Red Cross in Geneva. Weidner had met the official during one of his trips to Dr. Visser 't Hooft's office, and the two quickly became friends. Now Guillon wanted to know if John would help guide Xavier de Gaulle, the brother of General de Gaulle, from his home in Normandy across the border to Switzerland. Like the members of the families of other officials in the French government in exile, Xavier de Gaulle was slated for arrest by the Nazis.

John sent a member of his underground group to the de Gaulle home, but within a short time his guide was back. "De Gaulle wasn't there," the guide said. "He must have been afraid he was about to be arrested. I was told he should be somewhere in the Savoy area by now, but no one seems to know exactly where he is staying. Everyone is keeping his whereabouts secret."

Back John went to Guillon, to see if he might know where de Gaulle had gone and if he still needed help in escaping.

"Yes, he still needs your help," the Red Cross official reported. "Xavier left before your man got there because the Gestapo was coming to jail him. You will find him staying near a border village right here," Guillon said, pointing to a wall map. "He doesn't know how to get across the border, so he is counting on your help very much, John."

Weidner dispatched another member of his group to the address Guillon had indicated. This time Xavier de Gaulle was located and given instructions for the escape attempt. Several days later another guide met de Gaulle at the border and took him safely across to Switzerland.

During the winter of 1943, the routes across the border in the St. Julien-to-Annemasse area became almost impossible to use because of the unusually cold weather. Heavy snow often fell on the countryside, making it both difficult and dangerous to cross through the barbed-wire barricades.

One evening as he traveled from Lyons to Annecy on another border-crossing mission, John sat in his train compartment looking out at the dismal, winter-barren countryside. As the train moved farther eastward, he noticed that the snow which covered the ground was becoming deeper. Soon the train began to slow; then it stopped altogether. Finally word came back that heavy snow was blocking the tracks—and no snowplow was available. The train soon began to back slowly toward Lyons. As it picked up speed, John realized that he wouldn't be going to Switzerland through his familiar crossing routes this time. If the snow was so heavy it stopped trains west of Annecy, it would certainly be too deep to cross in the St. Julien-Annemasse area.

As he rode the train speeding back to Lyons, Weidner resolved that he would try a new route across the border, one he had thought of for just such a time as this. It lay to the north, through a small village high in the mountains near the French-Swiss border. A friend named Fred lived there. He knew the mountains and could serve as a guide.

Arriving back in Lyons, John caught another train going north. About noon the next day he arrived at the mountain village and met his friend, who was an excellent skier, and who, Weidner was sure, could take him safely across the mountains that lay between the village and Switzerland.

"The trains are not running to Annecy because of the heavy snow," John told his friend. "I must get to Switzerland to obtain clearance for a new group of refugees who will be leaving Paris later this week. If you will guide me, I'm sure we can ski through the mountains. I can reach Geneva from the northwest." An experienced skier himself, John knew that this new route would be longer and more exhausting than his regular routes. But there was not much choice; he had to get to Switzerland with the list of refugees.

His plan was to cross over the Col de la Faucille and then to pass near Ferney-Voltaire, crossing the border near that point. At Bossy, Switzerland, a bus would take him the ten miles into Geneva.

The village of Ferney-Voltaire had a special attraction to Weidner, for it was here that the famed philosopher Voltaire had lived from 1758 to 1778. During those years Voltaire had made his brilliant defense of conscience in behalf of John Calas, the last Protestant martyr who had been wrongly accused because of his faith. Since the time of that great defense, religious liberty has been well established in France.

"We'll travel very lightly," Fred said as they prepared to cross the mountains. "The snow is fairly good for skiing now, but the trip is a long one. We should stay fairly close together, too. The German alpine troops are watching the mountains closely these days. If they spot us, we'll have the run of our lives!"

180

Soon they were moving out of the village on the snow which lay deep in the mountains.

After pausing to eat a small lunch, they pushed off again. Glancing to the left as they started down another hill, John caught sight of several tiny figures on a ridge about a mile away. Instantly he shouted to Fred.

"Do you think they are Germans?" he asked. "I can't make them out clearly."

Fred swung sharply to the left and pulled up behind a little rise. He studied the distant figures.

"Yes, they're Germans," he answered. "If you look closely, you can see the tips of their rifles above their helmets. Those are German helmets. They may not see us, but we'll know soon enough. Let's wait here and see if they make any move our way."

After only a few seconds the German patrol went into action, skiing single file straight toward John and Fred.

"They've seen us," shouted Fred. "Let's go, fast! The border is still about five miles away."

The two men were straining hard. On downhill runs they took fantastic chances in turns and jumps. As they topped the ridges, they could see that the Germans were gaining on them. Once or twice they heard rifle shots behind them, but the terrific speed at which both groups were moving made accuracy impossible.

The German patrol continued to gain on Weidner and his guide despite their best efforts to keep ahead. John began to lose the rhythm of arms, body, and legs so necessary to skiing and several times almost crashed into the snow. Fred

181

was ahead of Weidner, but was holding back a bit from his top speed to stay near his friend. As they shot across the snow, he shouted encouragement to John to keep his spirits up.

"We may never see the border wires; they are probably buried far below us in the snow somewhere around here. If we can just keep ahead of them for another few minutes, they will stop when we get over the border," Fred yelled. "The Swiss are watching the border, too, you know."

Confident that they were now near the border marker, John dug desperately with his poles as he plunged over the snow. His face was raw from the frigid air. The inside of his nose and throat burned from the huge gulps of air he had been taking in the exertion.

The German patrol suddenly began firing rapidly at the fugitives; and, glancing back, Fred saw a sight that made him shout with joy. "We're across! We've made it across the border!" he exclaimed to John. "They are drawn up to fire more accurately, but they wouldn't do that unless they knew we had crossed the border. Keep going just a little longer till we are out of rifle range."

In a minute or two they were out of range and thankfully stopped to rest.

XIII

the Gestapo

YOU ARE John Henry Weidner?"

"Yes."

"We are the Gestapo. You will come with us. There are questions you must answer."

"But what have I done?"

"You will come with us—now. Get your coat."

It had been that simple. They had come to John's apartment in Lyons and told him he was under arrest. The charge? There was no charge really, the plain-clothed Gestapo officers said. There were simply questions he needed to answer. That was reason enough for arrest in southern France in 1943.

So they had gone, John and the officers, to the Gestapo headquarters in Lyons. There the frightening, time-consuming ritual began. He was fingerprinted. Then pictures were made—many pictures. Then his life history was taken.

"Where were you born, Weidner?" they asked. "How long have you been in France? What is your religion? What is your business here? What are your political feelings?"

The questioning seemed endless. The strain increased as the hours dragged by.

"Now, Weidner, we are most interested in the nature of your activities in the past few months. It is known that you have been helping your people—the Dutch—in their illegal movements, and that you have given them assistance forbidden by the present government. We are interested in hearing your story about these activities," said the officer.

"I have helped some of my people," John conceded as he sat before the bored-looking, black-clad officer at Gestapo headquarters. "There are many here in southern France who are without income; they are starving, and I have always tried to help those in need."

"And you have been giving 'assistance' to your Dutch consulate here in Lyons also. What of this? Can't the consulate help itself without your assistance?"

"Certain work of the consulate in helping Dutchmen in France has been made more difficult through many new government regulations," John replied in a steady voice. "I have been asked to give some assistance to our people by the consul, Mr. Jacquet, merely as an easier way for the consulate to render its legal services."

"Blockhead!" the Gestapo officer shouted angrily. "Do you expect me to believe such stupid talk? You have been giving illegal aid to Jews, and your consulate has also been giving such aid. Don't expect me to believe your stupid lies!"

"I can only tell you the truth," John continued as he sat on the hard chair facing the officer. "Mr. Jacquet will tell the truth, also. He is a good and honorable man."

"We shall see about that," said the furious officer. "We shall know quickly all about the activities in which you have been engaged. Now we are also interested in your relationship with a Dr. Magnus. You recall some 'assistance' you gave him? Do you deny, Weidner, that you have seen Dr. Magnus?"

Yes, John thought as the name was mentioned, he knew Dr. Magnus. He had found the refugee physician at the Dutch consulate, penniless, desperate to escape, and in need of a friend. Weidner had given him food, found him a place to stay, and, if everything went well, he would help the doctor cross the border into Switzerland soon. Why, though, were the Gestapo interested in Dr. Magnus?

"Yes, I know him," Weidner acknowledged, choosing his words carefully.

"You gave him money?"

"Yes."

"And where is Dr. Magnus now?"

"I am not sure—somewhere in southern France, I believe. I have not seen him for a number of days."

"You knew he was a Jew?" the officer snapped.

"He never told me he was a Jew."

"How did he come to France? Perhaps you can tell us that."

"I met him at the Dutch consulate. He said he was without work or means. I didn't ask how he came to France. I gave him some money at that time."

"The money, was it a loan or a gift?"

"It was a gift, as far as I was concerned."

"And you did not ask Dr. Magnus for a receipt?"

"No; I gave the money to him as a gift. He said he needed help."

"Let's forget about Dr. Magnus for a few minutes. You are a very active man, it seems. Are you in contact with members of the underground, the Resistance movement, in southern France?"

"I know a lot of French people," said John. "Some of them have said they do not like the Germans. But so many have said that—it doesn't mean these people are members of the underground. You know as I do that there is discontent in the country."

"You are very clever in your answers, aren't you?" the officer said as he got up from the desk. "But cleverness will not help you in the long run. Our methods are thorough, very thorough—you can be assured of that. I advise you to be simple and direct in answering me. Don't attempt to be clever, because my patience is running short. There are, as you know, considerable underground activities of the Dutch in Paris. What do you know about those activities?"

"I know absolutely nothing of the type of underground activities of which you speak."

"These names: Jacques Faber, Jules Vandame, Michael Ranault, Annette Pigot, Edmond Janzen, Helene Durand— do you recognize any of them?"

"I have not heard of or known any of those people."

"Ah-h, now you are trying to cooperate with us, aren't you, Mr. Weidner?" The officer smiled. "To every question I ask you give a negative answer—or a smart one! All you have told is stupid lies, and that's too bad for you. You will be sorry soon, very soon, that you have not told me the truth." Glaring at Weidner, the Gestapo officer hammered his fist on the desk and left the room.

About twenty minutes later two other officers came in. They began the questioning all over again: John's history, Dr. Magnus, the money, John's work at the consulate, his participation in underground activities, his knowledge of a list of people who were supposed to be underground members in Paris. The questioning went on far into the night. John defended himself by sticking with his story that he had done nothing against the Germans, only that he gave help to those in need. Finally the Gestapo officers ordered Weidner taken to the torture room. He was stripped, his hands were tied behind his back, and he was thrown into a tub filled with cold water. A guard shoved John's head under the water and held it against the bottom of the tub until Weidner, beginning to drown, thrashed violently against the strong grip of the guard. Then his head was jerked out of the water.

"Now, blockhead, will you answer our questions?" shouted one of the officers.

"No," John said as he gasped for air.

The guard slammed Weidner's head under the water again, jerking it up just as he was about to drown.

"The group in Paris, you know about them?"

"No," gasped Weidner.

A third time his head was pushed under the water. Between lapses into semiconsciousness, John alternated between prayer and a discipline of mind which refused to let him tell anything about his own organization. He had been truthful thus far in answering questions; he did not want to betray his friends even if he had to die.

The torture went on. One hour, two, then three.

Finally he was pulled from the tub and half dragged to another area of the torture chamber. There he was kicked about by the officers. Several times he tried to stand, only to be sent sprawling by a vicious kick from behind. He was slapped, kicked, and beaten in a senseless demonstration. Then he was led to yet another part of the chamber, and all the while the questioning continued.

"This is something you will enjoy very much, Mr. Weidner. It is designed to make your legs feel more comfortable."

The officers standing nearby grinned as the guards brought John to the new area. On the floor were what appeared to be large steel rulers set on edge.

"Kneel down," the guard rasped. "Kneel right here!" As Weidner's knees came down on the floor, the steel rulers pressed deeply into both legs just below the knees. The pain was excruciating.

"There, doesn't that feel comfortable? That is the comfort we give people like you who will not give us the information we want. We have other comforts that you will enjoy, too—if you live long enough to get to them!"

Waves of pain rolled over John. He was dimly aware that the Gestapo did not know too much about him, but they did sense that he had some connection with the underground, and this drove them on.

Weidner knew they would also ask Jacquet questions about his work, but he felt that Jacquet would not say anything to give him away. Nor did he want to say anything that would hurt Jacquet, and in answering the Gestapo he gave hazy, general replies, always careful to avoid telling outright lies. But he realized that misleading answers could help avoid bigger problems.

It was near three o'clock the next morning when the torture and the questioning ended. Most of the time John was hardly aware of what was going on around him. He could hear the questions, but they sounded far away. Each new pain was agonizing; but after what he had already been through, the new pains didn't seem to matter. His greatest fear was that he would lose control and give information which would implicate the many friends who were part of his organization. He prayed almost continually now, not that God would deliver him, but that He would help him be faithful to the trust others had placed in him.

When he was thrown into a cell with other prisoners, John huddled in the corner, in too much pain to sleep. In his trouble he appealed to divine agencies again.

John prayed, "Be with me for what is coming tomorrow. You know the ending of things from the beginning, and You can see the motives of every man's heart. Help me, I pray, that my motives will be right no matter what happens tomorrow. And if it be in Thy will, help me to survive this ordeal."

Confident that his prayer would be answered, Weidner finally slipped off to sleep just before dawn.

At ten o'clock a guard brought water and some bread. A few minutes later Weidner was taken back into the small room where the officer who had originally questioned him waited.

"So here we are again, Weidner," the officer said as he and the prisoner sat down facing each other. "But you don't look as bright today as you did yesterday. I told you that clever answers would only bring you harm. Now maybe we can proceed with the questioning along more fruitful lines."

Through the morning and into the afternoon the monotony of questions which he had answered many times fell upon John. Although still badly hurt from the hours of torture, he now had relatively good control of himself. The answers he gave were much as they had been the day before. By midafternoon, however, he was becoming extremely groggy. Nausea, the need for sleep, and deep pain from the beatings and the steel rulers made him lose track of the questions, which often had to be repeated before he could respond. Suddenly, without any warning, the officer stood up.

"Enough!" he shouted. "I've heard enough from you. Get out of here!"

The guards led the trembling Weidner back to his cell, where he collapsed, his mind racing to try and focus on what would happen in the future.

Just before nightfall a guard reappeared at the cell door.

"John Weidner," he said.

Weidner crawled slowly to his feet.

"Come with me."

Moving slowly, John plodded along behind the guard to the prison office. There, without explanation, he was handed his papers, money, and watch. The front door of the office opened.

"We are through with you, Weidner," snapped the guard. "You can go."

Hardly able to believe his ears, he stumbled into the street and reeled back to his tiny apartment.

Shortly after his ordeal, Weidner learned that Maurice Jacquet had also been arrested and released by the Gestapo. He went to see the consul.

"You remember Dr. Magnus, John?" Maurice asked. "He was arrested; and while being questioned, he gave your name and mine. After he was released, he reached Switzerland through the work of your organization; but, of course, the soldiers who questioned him passed the answers along to their administrative superiors. The report finally came to the Gestapo. When the Gestapo saw the name Magnus, they issued orders for his arrest because their files showed that he was Jewish; but by that time the doctor was already in Switzerland. When they couldn't find Magnus, they came looking for you and me.

"It was certainly foolish of the fellow to give our names," Jacquet continued. "He was evidently thinking only about his own safety, for he must have known they would come looking for us if we were connected in any way with him. He was thinking only about his own freedom.

"I was not tortured while they held me, probably because I am a diplomatic official. In all my answers, though,

191

I was careful not to say anything that would throw suspicion on you or reveal anything about the work you are doing. We can both be sure now, though, that there is a file for each of us in the Gestapo offices. We must be very careful in the future, because next time it will not be so easy."

Not long after his experience with the Gestapo, John was on a streetcar rumbling through the streets of Nancy. Some thirty-five other persons were also aboard, traveling to various destinations. But for several passengers their destinations became a common one when the car ground to a sudden stop near the center of the city.

Up the aisle trooped a contingent of German soldiers. "All men under the age of thirty-five will get off," one of them shouted along the aisle. "Outside you will wait quietly for further orders."

Under thirty-five included Weidner, so he stepped off the car with the others. There the "further orders" consisted of one word. "March," said the officer in charge.

Despite his plans to make several contacts in the Nancy area with people who needed to get to Switzerland, John spent the night in a German detention camp. And still he didn't know what was to happen!

Early the next morning the picture became clearer. The young men were taken from the camp and marched off to the Nancy railway station. As they shuffled along, Weidner quietly asked one of those near him what was happening.

"We are being sent to Germany as forced laborers," the young fellow whispered. "They are rounding up all the young guys to work in war production so that more Germans can be sent to the front lines. Nobody knows how long we will be gone or exactly where we are being sent yet."

The prisoners moved onto the train. Soon they were speeding eastward through the French countryside. Watching the green hills roll by outside the train, John felt a great weight of frustration sweep over him. What could be done he didn't know at that moment, but he felt sure there would be some others aboard the train who would join him in an escape attempt of some kind. The train was racing southward through France, bearing toward the east, and it wasn't far to Basel in Switzerland.

"Escape from this train! That's impossible!" said the first fellow John spoke to about it. "The guards would shoot us down so quick . . . we just wouldn't have a chance. If you want to escape, you escape alone!"

The answer was the same all along the car. Nobody wanted to take the chance. The guards, they said, would kill anyone who tried to escape.

But their answers did not satisfy Weidner. He wanted to get on with his work. Their answers might be good enough for his fellow prisoners, but they weren't good enough for John. He had to at least try.

His try came a few minutes later. He had edged his way toward one of the doors of the coach, hoping that the train might slow down as it rounded one of the curving embankments which served as the rail roadbed between the hills.

Sure enough, the train began to slow on an upgrade curve. As they approached the long fill between the hills,

193

John could see that the embankment dropped off sharply from the railway—exactly what he wanted! How far it was to the bottom he couldn't know. But this was the time to go.

He stood up quickly, took a few steps to the door, opened it, and without pausing leaped. He fell through the air—then the world went black!

When he regained consciousness, the world was still black. But it was the black of night. He rolled over from the sprawl in which he had landed, and every inch of the move was painful. But as he sat up, he realized that although he hurt everywhere, no bones were broken. Stiffly he got to his feet and stumbled up the hill away from the tracks.

Through the night he walked steadily. The pain from his rough tumble down the embankment began to ease off as he kept hiking. As daylight began to move into the countryside, he knew he was near the German-Swiss border. Soon he spied the barbed wires and pulled himself through. Walking along a little road near the wires, he suddenly heard voices.

"Now I'm in Switzerland and free," John thought. "These fellows can take me to the authorities, where I can identify myself and get on back to Lyons."

The voices came from two men, to whom John explained, "I've just escaped from a slave labor train headed for Germany. I am a Dutchman and want to see the police so that I can get help to get back to Geneva and then back into France."

"We'll be happy to take you to the police," the two men offered, and Weidner followed them as they moved off down the road. As they went, he felt lighthearted despite the night of constant hiking and a badly bruised body.

When at last he looked up to see the swastika flying from the flag atop the police headquarters, John's light heart suddenly became heavy. "I'm still on the wrong side of the border," he moaned as he stood there before the building. "There must have been two, or maybe three, barricades along the border, and I went through only the first one, which leaves me still in Germany. How stupid can I be?"

The door of the police headquarters opened, and a gray-coated German policeman came out to investigate the stranger standing fallen-faced in the village street. When the two men with John explained the story he had told them, the policeman shouted at Weidner, "So you are a lazy fellow and don't like to go to Germany to work, eh? Well, we'll fix that. Tomorrow morning you will be on the next labor train east, and you won't get off that one!"

Early in the morning the train, with Weidner aboard, sped eastward, deeper into Germany. Just before noon they came to a stop in a small German village. Confident that the prisoners, who fully realized that they were well inside Germany, would not try to escape, the guards left the train to get refreshments at a café inside the train station. When John found himself unguarded, he simply walked off the train, too. He calmly stepped out onto the station platform and walked carefully along to the end of the train. There he followed the narrow space between the fence and the railroad tracks to the first street that crossed the railway. He left the tracks and moved through the streets of the town until he came to a shop that sold food. There, speaking passable German, he purchased some bread and other supplies. Stopping at another store, he purchased a map of the countryside. Then he set off toward Switzerland, where the Rhine River forms the boundary between that country and Germany.

Through the night John hiked toward freedom. When daylight came, he found a wooded shelter and slept. That night he was hiking again. He rested much of the following day. For three hours that night he walked rapidly until he came upon the swift-moving Rhine at about ten o'clock.

"They say this river is very swift," John reminded himself as he peered down into its inky waters from the high bank where he stood. "And the Germans have a number of machine-gun posts along the bank here somewhere. I could be carried under by that current, for it looks very swift. Or they could get me with the machine guns while I'm swimming. But I've got to try. I've *got* to try!"

He rested for a short while to gain as much strength as possible for the rugged swim he knew was ahead. Then he plunged out into the waters.

The current, John found, was just as swift as he had been told, maybe even stronger. He swam powerfully, pulling with all his might against the swift flow, but he was still being carried downstream. After ten minutes of desperate work he was near midstream. A rush of current caught him and pushed his head beneath the water. When he came up, he thought a star had burst on his head. Then he realized it was a powerful German searchlight slanting across

196

the water at him. In a moment another beam hit the water nearby. Then a deadly chatter rose over the rush of the water. The water all about him began to splut and hiss in a weird symphony of sound.

"They're firing at me with the machine guns," he choked. "I've got to get moving!"

Tired now, bone tired from the fierce struggle against the rushing current, John stuck his head under the water again to avoid being seen and kicked with desperation toward the opposite shore. Now he was in a frantic fight to live. The water, the bullets, the lights, all combined to confuse and frighten. Weidner flailed the torrent with his arms; he kicked with legs now grown feeble. He rolled on his back and let the current take him, then swam again for that cherished shore. When he felt he could not stroke another time, his foot hit some mud. He saw that he was safely out of machine-gun range. The ghostly glare of the searchlights suddenly dissolved into inky blackness.

"I'm safe! I'm safe! I'm safe!" he mumbled through his exhaustion.

Friendly hands found John that night and helped him out of the near full shock that gripped him as a result of the river-crossing ordeal. Then, when he was fully rested and restored, these newfound friends sent him on his way to Bern, to Geneva, and then to the familiar border crossing and on to Annecy.

XIV

GOING UNDERGROUND

IN 1943, as the cold grip of winter clutched the land, the full power of the invader's iron rule was brought to bear on France. All of the country was now covered with the SA, or Storm Troopers, and the black-shirted SS Elite Guard. Through this complex network of suppressive organizations there also moved the SD, or Security Service, and the Gestapo, or secret police, who often scorned uniforms in their work. Adding to the terror brought by these units was the collaborating activity of several French police and semimilitary groups who were looked upon by the French people as traitors to their country. The effect of this giant network of spy, counterspy, and collaborator could be graphically observed on the fear-drawn faces of the people in those cold, gray days when the war reached its high-water mark.

Despite the rapidly increasing terror brought to the country by the Nazis, Weidner's efforts to solidify an effective unit which could spirit threatened refugees to freedom in other lands sharply increased. When winter came, he had a three-hundred-member organization operating through the help and cooperation of seven major agencies. The escape of Jews, other civilians in danger, and Allied airmen shot down over occupied Europe was being planned and executed over routes running from Holland and Belgium through Paris and then to Toulouse or Lyons. From these two staging points in southern France the escapees were led via several routes into Switzerland or across the Pyrenees into Spain.

Regularly now Weidner's agents were carrying out of the Netherlands nonmilitary information gathered from other occupied countries for use by Dr. Visser 't Hooft. Information for World Council member church groups was also flowing via Dutch-Paris back from WCC headquarters in Geneva into the occupied countries. World Council headquarters, through the continuing efforts of Dr. Visser 't Hooft and his secretary, Joop Bartels, was also assisting in the refugee work through both messages of encouragement and financial aid.

For the Netherlands Ministry in Bern, Dutch-Paris was bringing information relating to the plight of Dutch refugees in France and Belgium on a regular basis. Bosch Van Rosenthal, Netherlands minister in Bern under orders of the Dutch government in exile, provided financial aid to John's organization. He also assisted diplomatically, whenever possible, to speed the flow of Jews to Switzerland.

The military-related aspects of the work of Dutch-Paris was given aid through the office of Gen. A. G. Van Tricht, Netherlands military attaché in Bern. General Van Tricht provided important financial help to escaping Dutch military personnel and maintained liaison with Allied offices. Dutch-Paris also carried out missions for the International Red Cross in Geneva.

Charles Guillon, of de Gaulle's French Red Cross, asked Dutch-Paris to help get supplies and messages to prisoners of war throughout France. The Jewish organization in Switzerland, The Joint, directed by Sally Mayer, sought the aid of John's underground group in its refugee work. His activities also included gathering information about churches and members for the Southern European Division headquarters of the Seventh-day Adventist Church at Bern. As a devout member of this faith, John assisted Pastors A. V. Olson and Walter R. Beach, Southern European Division leaders, by carrying information into France and other occupied countries. He also brought messages about Adventist church operations in the occupied countries to Bern and carried money and messages from Bern to the churches.

In addition to work for these groups, Weidner's group operated closely with Alliance, the underground unit in which his friends Gilbert Beaujolin and Annie Langlade played such an important role. Through Pastor Marc Boegner, he maintained liaison with the Federation Protestante de France, which helped all Protestants in France in special need during the war, and with Cimade, a Protestant organization which also aided needy persons. This unit was directed by Madeleine Bardot, a devoted Christian. Pastor Boegner, president of the French Federation of Protestants, had encouraged the Cimade and Protestant ministers of France to give special help to the Dutch refugees.

This friendly relationship which Pastor Boegner recommended dated from the time Calvinism was accepted in Holland and the Dutch Reformed Church was established. From that date friendliness had characterized the lives of Dutch Calvinists and Calvinist Protestants in France. When the French Protestants were persecuted in the seventeenth and eighteenth centuries, they found refuge among the Calvinists of Holland. Now, in the great war setting Europe aflame, it was the Dutch who were finding refuge with the French. And, of course, the queen of Holland was a descendant of the Frenchman Gaspard de Coligny, prime minister of France, who was the first man killed in the St. Bartholomew's Day Massacre. Thus, the ties between France and Holland, especially in times of strife, were strong.

Into the inmost circle of confidence in operating Dutch-Paris John now drew two men whom he had come to trust implicitly through scores of life-or-death episodes in which they had all been mutually involved. There was Jacques Rens, a young Hollander who spoke fluent French, and Salomon Chait, a rabbi's son who was a lumber merchant from Rotterdam and who also spoke flawless French. All three were extremely clever and possessed that special daring so necessary to underground work.

In Holland, as the organization of the underground group continued, the escape route which John's members used was known as Switzersche Weg, or the Swiss Road.

In Paris his organization was officially directed by Herman Laatsman; in Belgium, by Benno Nykerk; in Toulouse, by Mr. Aarts, assistant to the Dutch consul; and in

Lyons by Consul Maurice Jacquet. Every other member of Dutch-Paris took direction from this small, close-knit group of men.

Moving from one area of operation to another, Weidner endeavored to make each member of the group more efficient. He constantly reminded them to shun close contact with friends or those they led to safety.

"The day will come," he warned, "when you will be seen in the same place once too often, or your friend will forget himself at the wrong time, and the work you are doing will be revealed. It is difficult to work alone, but that is the safest way." That was the way John worked more often as the war went on. He moved constantly, making sure he did not return to the homes of friends too often.

Weidner's headquarters were at his business office at 13 Rue du Griffon in Lyons, although he did not sit at the desk there often. He was active in his church, in his business, and in the far-reaching underground unit which he directed.

He traveled extensively throughout France and into Belgium and to the Dutch border in the late summer and fall of 1943. He also journeyed regularly from Lyons to Annecy. Each time he went, a group of refugees bound for Switzerland accompanied him.

One day at the height of the war while he was in his store in Annecy, Weidner took a telephone call from an underground associate in Lyons. The message was in the code language which Dutch-Paris leaders used.

"The Gestapo has been to your store in Lyons to ask many questions about you," the voice on the other end of the line said. "Maurice Jacquet has been arrested again. So has Paul Duvivier, the French consul general. You must leave the office in Annecy immediately, because they are probably coming for you right now!"

Five minutes after the telephone conversation ended, John was out of the store, heading for the home of a friend in another part of the city. An hour later the Gestapo arrived at the store. From his new location John telephoned his friend in Lyons.

"I am going to Morzine in the mountains," he explained. "Tell Raymonde that she should come there to meet me and to let me know what has happened. She should be extremely careful not to be followed."

During the afternoon Weidner, with the aid of the man he was staying with, obtained complete new travel and identification papers made by de Gaulle underground agents working in the prefecture office in Annecy. The new documents were officially registered by the agents so, should John be questioned, he could refer his questioner to the Annecy Prefecture Office. His new name, one of fourteen he used during the years of terror, was Jean Cartier. That night he slipped out of Annecy and went to a ski resort at Morzine, high in the French Alps.

Raymonde arrived safely the next day with a report for her underground chief. "The Gestapo burst into the office without warning," she explained. "They made everyone put their hands against the walls while they searched us and the office. Then they began to question all of us as to where you were, but no one gave any information. They looked in the files, though, and found the address of the store in Annecy. The officer in charge called the Gestapo there to arrest you. That's why we were afraid you might have been caught.

"I'm not sure just why they arrested Mr. Jacquet," continued Raymonde, "but we think you are being sought because of connections with him."

John told the girl she should return to Lyons to obtain more news about Jacquet.

"I will stay here in Morzine until you bring further word about him," John said. "Until I find out what they are doing with Jacquet, I can't determine how much they know about me or what I should do. When you get more information, come back. Then with more news I can begin to make plans for the future."

Within twenty-four hours she returned to the ski resort with further word about the consul.

"Jacquet was released yesterday," she told Weidner happily. "He was arrested because one of the refugees gave his name when he was taken into custody by the Nazis. Some underground people were arrested too—people with whom Jacquet had been in contact. In searching the papers at the consulate they found letters addressed to Jean Meunier— one of your underground names. Jacquet cleverly avoided implicating you, but then they asked him if he knew John Weidner. He told them that he did, that you had helped some Dutch refugees, and had been of service to the consulate at different times. Then they brought out the big file they have on you and showed it to Jacquet. 'Here is one of Weidner's many aliases—Jean Meunier,' they sneered at him. Jacquet got off lightly enough, but the Gestapo is sure now that you are 'big underground,' and they are determined to get you, John.

"Because of your first arrest," Raymonde continued, "the Gestapo has pictures and fingerprints of you. I think it better that I don't go to the consulate anymore. But Renée, Jacquet's secretary, will keep in touch with me."

"So they are after me for sure now!" John sighed as the two walked through the snow near the resort buildings. "I'll just have to move faster and more often in the future. You go back to the office in Lyons, Raymonde. Close up the business there. Ask Mrs. Langlade and Beaujolin to get rid of everything in Lyons. Then go to Annecy, and keep the store there open as long as you can. I can never go back to the business in Lyons now. The Germans will be watching every day."

"All right, John; if that is what you want, I'll do it," Raymonde said. "But it will mean loss of a lot of money."

"Yes," agreed John, "but money sometimes has very little value. I will get along without the business as best I can."

Later that evening Raymonde returned to Lyons. John went for a walk outside the hotel again after she had left. He wanted to take an evening stroll before starting for Switzerland the next day. As he looked at the snow-capped peaks glowing rose-colored in the fading sun, the danger of his present situation seemed to slip away. His mind wandered back to the other times he had come to Morzine. Once, earlier in the war, he had been here studying a new escape route into Switzerland when a young Dutch refugee, as good a skier as John himself, had asked to be shown how to get across the mountains to Switzerland and freedom. Having skied out of the resort many times, John was happy to help him on his way.

The two men had left the resort before the German mountain patrols or other skiers at the resort were up. For four hours they inched up the mountain on skis covered with skins to stop slippage on the snow. Finally they stood in the Col de Joux, where they could look many miles into Switzerland. An awesome quiet blanketed the pass that morning. The only sound was the faint whisper of wind. Far below they could see the Rhone River snaking through the white countryside. Beside its banks lay the little towns of St. Maurice, Bex, and Aigle.

The sight of Aigle sent John's mind back through the years to 1924. That had been a year he would never forget. It held too many memories. Each week his father, a Seventh-day Adventist minister, had gone to the prison in the Castle of Aigle, where he was greeted by the jailer, then taken to one of the cells and locked in. As he stood in the frosted pass, John could remember going with his mother to the castle, where they would sometimes see a handkerchief flutter from one of the prison windows telling them their father was there and that he saw them even though they might not see him.

John's father was paying the price a prejudiced community demanded so that his son would not have to attend public school on Saturday, which the Weidners observed as holy time in accord with their reading of the Scriptures. The sad little weekly ritual left John with the deep impression that his religion was something he would never take lightly —his father had paid too high a price for the privilege of observing it.

After gazing for a long while at the far-off village, he had turned to the young Dutchman standing beside him.

"That's Champery down there," he pointed out. "It is all downhill from here. If you travel fast, you can be there in two hours. We are standing on the border right here in the pass, so you are now a free man."

When they had taken the skins from their skis, John gave the refugee a slap on the shoulder that sent him flying through the pass toward Champery. John turned back to Morzine. Descending toward the resort, he passed several parties of skiers on the slopes out for an early morning workout. German patrols were also skiing across the snow, but John had been able to avoid contact with them.

Now as he strode through the gathering darkness back to the resort hotel, he knew that another chapter of his life was finished. He could not go back to Lyons openly anymore, not as long as the war lasted. Each future visit would have to be made in disguise or complete secrecy. If the Gestapo in Lyons had a file of information on him, he could expect every other Gestapo unit across France to have a similar file.

"My travels will now have to be even more carefully planned than before," he decided. "I wonder how long I can evade the Gestapo?"

207

Early the following morning he slipped from the resort and set off for Switzerland. In Geneva he met with Dr. Visser 't Hooft once again, this time to explain his latest problem.

"It may not be such a bad blow after all, John," Dr. Visser 't Hooft said. "You see, I have just received a request from the Dutch government to implement completely the organization we have discussed before. Now we can organize regular trips from Switzerland to Holland and back to get the information we need. Now that you are completely cut off from your businesses, you can work closely with us in this new function and still carry on your escape work. We have received funds to do this new work. You have no funds. So working together we can benefit each other.

"I have sent my secretaries, Jan Borsum Buisman and Joop Bartels, to organize the collection of social and religious news in Holland and to set up a committee for transmission and reception of news. All that has to be done now is to develop a regular liaison with Holland, and that is your task."

The plan of the kindly clergyman was one which John recognized as ideal for his present situation. He would make his headquarters in Geneva but would still be able to travel to the various Dutch-Paris units, and at the same time cooperate with Dr. Visser 't Hooft.

"Yes, you have come at just the right time," Dr. Visser 't Hooft told Weidner. "As a matter of fact, I sent a message to you in Lyons two days ago, asking you to discuss this work with me."

208

Having decided that the new arrangement would provide mutual help for his underground organization and the other groups with which he was working, John turned his thoughts toward France and the other occupied countries and the work still to be done there.

Recently the Italian government had signed a surrender agreement with the Allies, and Mussolini had been overthrown. Now the Germans had completely replaced the Italians in the border area between France and Switzerland. Before, the Nazis had only directed the border security complex; now it would become much more difficult to cross the border than when the easy-going Italians guarded it. The area from Annecy to the border itself, a thirty-mile stretch, was now teeming with German security agents. John's trips toward Lyons would have to be made in strict secrecy.

Laying plans for future operations in a context of increased secrecy, John recalled an incident that had occurred before he went completely underground which had shown the need for security. To his store in Annecy one day came a man in the uniform of the French police.

"I am Jean Massendes, inspector of police for the government of Vichy. Are you John Henry Weidner?" he asked.

"Yes, I am John Weidner."

"Mr. Weidner, the French Gendarmerie in Annecy has just arrested a man by the name of Kanegiter, an Alsatian. Do you know him?"

Kanegiter! Of course John knew him. But what were the police doing with him? Why did this inspector want to know if he knew Kanegiter? That name brought instant recollection to Weidner. He had been recommended as a reliable man through Dutch refugees Weidner had helped. On their recommendation John had asked him to send any refugees he found in real need. In order to recognize the refugees as having come from Kanegiter, John gave the man a supply of coded bonus coupons which he used in his store. These identified refugees as having been sent by Kanegiter.

The police inspector asked his question again.

"Do you know Kanegiter, Mr. Weidner?"

"It is very possible that I might know him," answered John after a moment's hesitation. "I have many buyers of cloth in my store. It is just possible he might be one of my customers whose name does not immediately come to mind."

"We believe you know him well, Mr. Weidner. Kanegiter, as I said before, has been arrested because of his underground activities. We have searched his apartment, and do you know what we found there? We found a booklet in which Kanegiter keeps notes. In the booklet is a complete story about you, about the people you are helping, and about the system of using coupons so that you will recognize those coming from Kanegiter. The gendarmes passed this information along to our headquarters, and my chief has assigned me to investigate. I must make a report. What would you suggest that I put in it, Mr. Weidner?"

Dumbfounded that Kanegiter would be so careless as to put on paper a plan which should have existed only in the mind, John had no answer.

"We have no other evidence to go with what we have found in Kanegiter's apartment," continued Inspector Massendes. "But we will probably find what we need. We always do. I shall have to place you under arrest. You will, of course, be sentenced to prison. But since you have lived in France for such a long time, I don't think you will be turned over to the Germans. And, as you know, that is lucky for you."

"If all is as you say it is, then I probably will go to prison," John agreed with the inspector. "But I will go in the knowledge that I have done right, never anything wrong. I have only tried to help people and to do what I believe God wants me to do."

The two men talked for a long time. John spoke of the divine direction he felt he was receiving in his work for refugees. In their conversation Inspector Massendes said he had been reared as a Protestant, that he knew the Protestant minister in Annecy, Pastor Chapal, who was also a friend of John's. During their talk Weidner admitted that he was helping those whose lives were threatened, that he had given coupons to Kanegiter, and that he felt the man had proved himself very unreliable in keeping a record of the arrangements about the refugees.

Weidner had the feeling in their discussion that Massendes wanted to say something, but he could not discover what his reason for holding back might be. Then, little by little, he realized that the inspector wanted to be sure about him before he would declare himself a sympathizer with the underground. Weidner himself, before saying too much, also wanted to be sure about Massendes. But when the name of Pastor Chapal was mentioned, he felt he could speak more

211

freely. And when Massendes realized that John was a friend of Pastor Chapal's also, he quickly gained confidence in Weidner. Once the bond was established between them, Massendes told of his desire to meet Count de Menthon to give him information about a secret police order which had been handed down from the Pétain government for the count's arrest.

Days later John managed through Gilbert Beaujolin for Massendes to meet the count in Beaujolin's office. The inspector told de Menthon about the Vichy government's secret order for his arrest in Annecy. This important piece of information made the count decide to go completely underground at once. In the following months Massendes gave useful help to John, which made the implementation of numerous Dutch-Paris plans easier.

XV

tRAIN WRECK

ON SATURDAY NIGHT, October 30, 1943, Weidner was at the train station in Lyons en route to Paris. According to the schedule—and no one could believe a wartime train schedule—the train should arrive in Paris at eight o'clock on Sunday morning. Trains ran infrequently from Marseilles through Lyons to Paris during late 1943, and they were invariably crowded. The army had commandeered most of them, and the underground organizations, through sabotage, were beginning to disrupt the schedules of the others.

Several kinds of special papers were required before the ordinary, workaday citizen could get aboard one of the trains. And when one finally arrived in a station, there was little assurance a seat would be available, even though all the extra papers were in order and a ticket had been purchased. Getting off an incoming train had become a nightmarish battle, with hundreds, sometimes thousands, of people pushing and shoving to get on even before passengers had gotten off. Bodies flew through opened windows or were

213

jammed against the detraining mob at the compartment doors. Even the restrooms were full of passengers seeking a place to ride.

Such a battle took place in the Lyons station when the train from Marseilles pulled in at nine o'clock that Saturday night. Because he knew by experience the intensity of the crush of humanity that would take place, John had given money to a railway worker to tell him where the first two coaches usually stopped. These often carried fewer people because it was known that if the train was blown up by the underground, those in the front coaches would most likely be killed.

John therefore waited at the spot the railway worker had indicated. And when the hissing engine came to a halt, he stood opposite the doors of the two forward coaches. Most of the crowd was fighting a terrific battle to board and detrain a few yards to the rear. Strangely, though, no one opened the doors of the two front coaches, no one jumped out through the windows. John tugged the door of the forward coach open. People were jammed inside, and there was absolutely no room. He ran to the second coach and finally got the door open, but it, too, was filled with people.

"This is impossible," he mumbled above the hiss of escaping steam from the nearby engine. "I've never seen a train so crowded!"

He ran quickly back to the first coach to see if the mass of humanity inside had shifted so that he could squeeze in. But when he got the door open again, it was even more jammed than before. He turned back toward the crowd fighting along the platform for space on the coaches farther back. As he did so, he spotted a space on the connecting mechanism between the first and second coaches. Several persons were on the coupling already, but there was a small place where he could stand. He leaped aboard, thinking as he did that it certainly wasn't much of a bargain for the price of the ticket and for the trouble he had gone to in getting the special papers for the trip.

The train was not due to leave Lyons until ten o'clock, and he had about fifty minutes to wait—if some delay did not hold things up longer. He tried to relax on the coupling, but when he moved, the heavy metal on which he stood felt colder and harder.

"This is a foolish way to ride to Paris," he told himself as he tried once again to get comfortable. "If anything happens, even a little jolt, all of us could be thrown off between the cars and killed. It really isn't worth the risk. I must try to find some other place."

He jumped back onto the platform and began searching for another place to ride, and behind him a shout went up from the others who had been huddled on the coupling. Now that he was gone, they would have a bit more space for their torturous journey.

Back along the train John went, searching for any niche in the human jam that clogged every available space. He walked the entire length of the train, looking anxiously, searching carefully. There was nothing.

But just as he was about to turn away, he noticed something that made his heart leap. Railway workers were pushing a new coach from a siding up the tracks toward the rear of the train. In joyous fascination John watched as the coach came closer and closer to the end of the train. The crowd, still shoving up ahead, didn't see the new coach approaching. As the men jolted the car onto the end of the train, the door was only inches from John's nose. He got aboard and chose a good corner in the compartment at the middle of the coach. Five minutes later the entire coach was jammed.

Seven other passengers joined him in the small compartment and settled down to enjoy the comfort of a seat. Fifteen minutes later, when the train started to move, he took off his jacket, turned out the small compartment light, and said good-night to his fellow passengers. He wanted to get some sleep, but more than that, he needed to think over plans for the talks he would have when he arrived in Paris the next day.

He was to meet Herman Laatsman, head of his Paris underground group, who was to give him information about the work being done to move refugees through the city. He was also to receive secret information which he would take to Switzerland. In the middle of thinking over his plans, John went to sleep—but for less than two hours.

A shuddering crash abruptly catapulted him out of his seat and across the tiny compartment against the passengers on the other side. Dazed, they stared at one another numbly as they disentangled themselves.

"What happened? What happened? What happened?" a small man kept repeating.

Weidner reached up and flipped on the tiny compartment light. At the front of the train something was sending
forth a faint hissing sound. It was exactly midnight. John
pushed the window of the compartment up and leaned far
out to peer into the darkness ahead. "I can't see a thing up
there," he told the others. "There must be some kind of accident, though, because the engine is whistling in a very
strange way—as though lots of steam is escaping."

In a few minutes several German soldiers came along
the aisle from the front of the train. John asked them what
had happened.

"We've had a very bad accident," one of them said. "The
train was traveling about seventy miles an hour when we
hit a bridge that was blown up by the underground. The first
eight coaches are scattered all about the tracks, and many
people are hurt. We're near Tournus, about one hundred
miles out of Lyons."

If there were people hurt, maybe dying, John knew he
should try to help. At least he could give some comfort to
those in pain, even if his elementary knowledge of first aid
might not be enough. He climbed out of the compartment
and made his way along the tracks in the darkness to the
accident area, which was a confusion of horror. Coaches lay
scattered about the tracks and embankment. Everywhere
cries and screams cut through the night. The eerie whistling
of the locomotive played a ghastly background music to
the scene.

He wanted to do something for the injured, but hardly
knew where to start. A young girl crawled out of the wreck-

age, blood gushing from a deep wound in her head. He went through a broken window and began to help lesser-injured people out of the overturned coach. Others joined him, and soon they were able to lift out some of the seriously injured. As he worked his way slowly from one car to the next, helping wherever he could, he saw many mangled bodies, and blood soon covered him. Twisted metal, broken glass, and mangled bodies lay in a horribly fused heap all around.

Finally there was little more he could do in the coach which had been second from the engine. As he crossed to the first coach, he glanced at the spot where he had stood for some time while the train was in the Lyons station. The two coaches had been jammed together by the impact of the crash, and the people who had stood with him there the night before were now compressed in a metal coffin, all dead. John turned from the awful sight, convinced that the hand of God had made him leave that spot between those coaches, saving his life.

Hour after hour Weidner worked at the grisly task of lifting mangled, lifeless bodies from the coaches. Many passengers were trapped in the broken metal or lay under pieces of the coaches too heavy to be moved by hand. At least 250 persons were removed from the wreck during the night. Five hours afterward official railway help finally arrived. Heavy equipment was brought in, and slowly the trapped people were set free.

With better equipment and adequate railway employees on hand to do the remaining work, John went to the rear and reported to the railway rescue chief that he was going to leave the accident scene.

"Well, that's all right with me," the man said, "but you won't find any coaches back there where yours was anymore. They've taken all that were still on the rails back to Lyons. They will be rerouted to Paris."

The rescue chief's words alarmed Weidner. In the shock of the wreck and the spontaneous impulse to help the injured he had left his jacket on his seat in the coach. In the jacket were his papers and messages. He knew that if the messages were lost, all the work they represented would have to be done over again. And the underground in Holland was waiting for those messages—their schedules would be disrupted too! What of the precious identification papers and the considerable sum of money in the jacket?

In a surge of silent desperation Weidner started back through the maze of wreckage. Those cars just couldn't be gone! Suddenly he felt sick—sick with apprehension, sick at the flickers of reflection he allowed himself of the grisly task he had just been about. As the early morning light began to break over the wreckage, he saw more clearly the bloody, twisted destruction he had been working in through the dark hours. He jumped down the embankment away from the carnage and ran. As he came nearer the end of the cars which were wrecked, he strained to see if some coaches were still on the track. There was a coach still on its wheels! And another. And still another.

"They're still there," he shouted as he ran along beside the embankment. He raced up the embankment and pulled himself up the steps of the coach and ran down the aisle. As he neared his compartment he was almost thrown off balance as the train gave a jerk. He pulled open the door of his compartment and looked frantically. In an innocent heap on the seat lay the precious jacket!

John sank down in relief and exhaustion as he picked up the document-laden jacket. And at that moment, with another series of jerks, the coach started moving back toward Lyons!

"We were worried that you would not get back in time," one of the passengers in his compartment said. It almost seems as though they were waiting for you to return before they left."

The train picked up speed through the brightening morning, and John felt strongly that divine agencies had kept the coach from rolling until he returned.

One of the women in the compartment handed him a bottle of detergent with which he was able to clean some of the blood from his skin and shirt. Having recovered his jacket, and with a better outlook now that most of the blood of the accident was washed from his body, Weidner joined in the conversation of those around him as the train sped back toward Lyons. Back in Lyons, John caught another train for Paris. Traveling over a different route, this train ride was uneventful, and he arrived in Paris safely.

One day after the war while visiting Dr. Visser 't Hooft's home in Geneva, John again met the woman who had befriended him on the train. She was a relative of Dr. Visser 't Hooft and at the time of the train wreck had been a member of another Resistance group working against the Germans.

It had been at the train station in Lyons, John recalled, that he had recently been confronted with the reality of the war in a most shocking and maddening way. Waiting for a train that day with many others on the station platform, he saw a group of Jewish women who had been arrested and were being deported. One of them carried a fretful baby in her arms, and despite everything she could do, the child continued to cry. Nearby stood a Nazi officer who personified the worst the war could offer. He ordered the mother to keep the child quiet. But there was no way of stopping the cries of the baby. In furious anger the Nazi snatched the child out of the mother's arms and slammed it to the concrete platform of the station. Then he brought his great boot down on the baby's head, and the child was dead.

When the officer had grabbed the child, the woman broke into a high, almost inhuman scream. Her stabbing cry echoed through the station, piercing every corner of the place. As she witnessed the heartless murder of her baby, the woman apparently lost all her reason and appeared to become completely deranged.

From just a few feet away Weidner had watched the shocking drama, and everything he had learned in the past about human decency revolted.

"How can there be cruelty like that?" he raged inside as he saw the anguished mother huddle on the platform over the small, lifeless form. "How can any man face his family or friends after doing a thing like that?" Every part of his body cried out for John to leap at the fellow, to beat him even as he had crushed life from the child. But caution prevailed. Deep inside, where the issues of life are hidden, another voice spoke to John.

"That officer's own dark reward will come to him. But for you, John Weidner, you know that life is not yours to take." Yet as he stood there, trembling in rage, he was not sure what he would have done if he had held a gun in his hands at that moment.

As the war progressed, on many other such occasions he saw the cruelty of the invaders. He was forced to see inhuman and unnatural things. And somehow they always brought to mind a saying of the Apostle Paul: "This know also, that in the last days perilous times shall come. For men shall be . . . without natural affection, truce-breakers, false accusers, incontinent, fierce, despisers of those that are good." 2 Timothy 3:1-3.

In 1943, during a trip to Switzerland, Weidner stopped at the office of Gen. A. G. Van Tricht, the Dutch military attaché in Bern. There he was surprised to find something special waiting for him. The general had previously mentioned to Weidner that the Dutch government also wanted his family to realize at least some financial benefit if their son should die while serving his country.

"It has arrived, John; your commission is here," the general told him. "The government in London is very proud to send this commission and their greetings with it."

He handed John an official paper with the names of top Dutch officials scrawled on it. "Congratulations! You are now a captain in the Dutch Army!"

The commission brought a quiet joy to John's heart. He thought back to the days just before the war when he had applied for a place in his country's service and was refused only because he had been living in a foreign land for several years. Now he was a captain, accepted fully because of his record of faithful service in helping his countrymen and others to gain freedom.

Before he left the general's office, Weidner learned that some of his companions were to receive commissions also. Jacques Rens, Armand Lap, and Salomon Chait were to become lieutenants.

Leaving the general's office, John Henry Weidner walked a little straighter. After all, he was a captain now. Even if he couldn't wear the uniform of the soldier, he could walk like one!

XVI

terror's months

NOW OCCUPYING all of France, German soldiers and secret agents spread like a great cloak everywhere, and John Weidner's movements became ever more hazardous. To avoid capture he began to travel under many false names, to use different routes, and to avoid familiar haunts and friends. Already arrested on four occasions, he knew that his file in the Gestapo office in Lyons was fat with facts. The only way to stay free was to outwit every new trap set by the Nazis. He had also changed his physical appearance. He had previously parted his hair, but now he combed it straight back; and he also began wearing glasses and grew a moustache.

Travel through France and the other occupied countries was becoming both physically and diplomatically more difficult as the war progressed. Special documents were needed for even the simplest of travel plans, and the priority given military personnel made it next to impossible for civilians to obtain passage from town to town. The increased activity of the numerous French underground units gave rail travel a particularly dangerous quality. Railway bridges were being blown up by the underground almost every day, and buses, trucks, and cars were often ambushed or demolished.

With the tension of his struggle to stay free increasing daily, John continued to rely on divine help in his efforts to save others. Even in worship, however, he was careful not to attend one church regularly, knowing too well that the Gestapo would not respect the sanctuary in their efforts to capture him. He turned more often to private worship and spent as much time as possible reading from the Bible he carried with him at all times. He also found solace and guidance through frequent times of prayer.

As he continued making contacts in Geneva and Bern with Dr. Visser 't Hooft, of the World Council of Churches, and Gen. A. G. Van Tricht, Dutch military attaché, Weidner was asked to add to his duties transmitting special information. Nonmilitary messages needed to be carried out of the occupied countries, then transmitted to England via Switzerland. An increasing amount of information was also needed by the World Council relating to its member churches in the occupied countries. It was this type of message that John was asked to carry during his trips along the escape lines of Dutch-Paris.

A young Dutch engineer living in Switzerland had discovered a process which permitted the upper layer of microfilm to be detached from the body of the film, thus making it possible to carry hundreds of microfilm messages in a tiny space where only a few could be carried previously. This process was explained to Weidner, and he was instructed in the best methods of carrying this delicate, but highly valuable, film. A representative of General Van Tricht, and his wife, Mr. and Mrs. J. G. Van Niftrik, skilled in handicraft, developed various objects, such as a set of keys, a pencil, or a brush, into which tiny rolls of microfilm could be inserted. To the unskilled eye these objects seemed ordinary enough, but they were packed with filmed messages. In all written or spoken communication these keys, pencils, and other items were referred to as "the objects."

Since the information contained in the objects was of such a secret nature, John told only a select few of his group about them, including Jacques Rens, Salomon Chait, and Paul Veerman. As the war progressed, they were asked to help carry them. Since crossing each additional border brought greater chance of being caught, two agents in Holland were assigned the task of bringing the objects across the border into Belgium. Then Weidner or one of his three lieutenants would carry them over the border into Switzerland.

Once the information reached Switzerland, it was carefully studied, and the most important items were reduced to code for transmission to London by radio. Then the documents themselves were sent to England by two different methods: Young Dutchmen, having reached Switzerland, were given copies to carry with them when they went to England to join the Netherlands forces in that country. Other copies were concealed in the binding of books which were sent by mail through Germany to Sweden. From Sweden the books were flown to England.

In the days before Weidner was forced to go completely underground, a young Belgian refugee, Fanny Van Hof, received a special paper from Colonel Lisbonne, chief of the refugee internment camp at Chateauneuf-les-Bains, where she was confined. The paper was an authorization for her to go to Lyons, under police escort, where, she said, she had to care for important business matters. In the city she contacted Weidner. Her fiancé, Armand Lap, who had been helped across the border by Weidner, had notified her that the underground chief could give her help.

"Yes, I believe we can make arrangements for you to get to Switzerland," John told the girl, using the Dutch language so that the French gendarme would not understand what he was saying. "First, I will need to get in touch with my friend at the immigration office in Geneva so that your name will be placed on the records there as eligible to enter the country. If your name is not in their records, the guards at the border will send you back to France, even if you get into the country successfully.

"Now, in just a moment, I am going to get this guard interested in something in the window over there," John said as he nodded toward the display in the front of his office. "When he looks that way, I want you to take a paper I am going to give you. It is a forged document authorizing you to come out of Chateauneuf-les-Bains to Lyons once again. It was prepared for cases such as yours."

John spoke to the gendarme in French, calling his attention to the attractive display window. When the guard looked at the display, Weidner slipped the paper to the girl.

227

"Use the paper in about a week," Weidner told Miss Van Hof in Dutch. "By that time I will have everything arranged in Switzerland."

About eight days later Fanny showed up at John's store again. "I made it!" she exclaimed. "The paper must have been a good one, because no one asked me any questions about it. What do I do now?"

"Tomorrow we will go to Annecy," John explained. "There we will have to work out the rest of the details."

The following evening they arrived in Annecy and the next morning left for Cruseilles. They got off the bus at the familiar spot shortly before coming to the town itself.

"We must go around the control point at Cruseilles because the guards are checking everyone very closely these days," Weidner said. "I know a farmer near here who will take us to the other side of the town in his hayrack. We'll be hidden under the hay. The guards probably won't think anyone would try to get by them that way."

John's plan worked perfectly. Within a few hours they were on another bus which ran through St. Julien toward Collonges. Shortly before reaching Le Chable, Fanny, as she had been told before boarding the bus, left the vehicle.

"A guide will meet you and take you around the control point of Le Chable on to Collonges," John had told her while they were still in the hayrack. "There your fiancé will meet you. Then the two of you can make your way into Switzerland easily since he will know the way."

Later John learned that Fanny's escape had been successful and that she was now Mrs. Armand Lap.

228

On another occasion a small, feeble Jewish woman, too old and sick to walk a long distance to cross the border or to travel through the mountains, had been listed for execution by the Nazis during the months of terror. Weidner was able to bring her by train to Annecy, then by bus to the now-familiar stop just outside Cruseilles. There he dug deeply into his source of ideas for a way to get her from that point to the border.

"I cannot try to cross the Saleve with her," he reasoned. "She is so sick I couldn't get her more than a mile at the most. Even if I do get her to the border, most of the crossings are several miles in length. She couldn't make it that way either."

Then he had an idea. Dr. Pierre Toureille, a physician in Collonges, could help. If he would sign a paper stating that she had to be hospitalized, then she could be taken to the nearest hospital. And that hospital was in St. Julien, only a few hundred feet from the border.

The doctor was happy to sign the paper; and with the paper in hand, John called an ambulance, and she was rushed to the hospital in St. Julien.

In the morning Weidner again contacted Dr. Toureille. "When you see the woman today, tell her to be at the rear door of the hospital at six o'clock in the evening day after tomorrow," he told the physician.

A friend of the Resistance movement, the doctor readily agreed to give the instructions.

Two nights later John found the old woman at the hospital door as arranged. They rapidly covered the two hundred yards of wooded area which separated the hospital from Switzerland. When over the border, they went to the Swiss authorities, who cleared the woman's entry into the country. John put her in a taxi, which took her to Geneva.

Henri Gazan, brother of Nico Gazan, whom John had earlier led to Switzerland, had one of the special qualifications needed by Weidner's organization—he spoke perfect French. When asked to join the group as a guide, Henri agreed at once.

John crossed the Swiss border into France with Gazan in the middle of the day near St. Julien. Under ordinary circumstances this was not especially difficult or dangerous. Normally the border in that area was not heavily guarded, particularly at midday.

Now as the two men approached the border, John cautioned Henri to move slowly as they came through the barbed wire onto the road that ran beside the wire barricade. In his excitement, however, Gazan jumped from a low-lying wall onto the road, and a gendarme nearby noted the sudden movement. Moments later both men were being questioned. Their answers obviously did not satisfy the gendarmes, and they were arrested.

Marching along the road toward police headquarters at Etrembiere, Weidner realized that this arrest could put him out of action for days at least and might lead to his being turned over to the Gestapo. If that happened, not only his rescue work but his life as well might come to an abrupt end. He had to do something—and quickly.

Determined to try anything to avoid being put in prison, he suddenly knelt on the road as though tying his shoelaces. Only three yards away were the barbed-wire strands. The gendarme yelled at him to keep going, but John waited until the guard got so close that he had no room to unlimber his rifle, then Weidner leaped for the barricade. In an instant Weidner grabbed the top of the heavy barbed wire and jumped. As he sailed into the air, he could feel the barbs cutting deeply into his hands. At the top of the barricade his body came down onto the wire, and he rolled, got another grip with his hands, and pulled again. Then he lay on the ground—clothes torn; hands, arms, and body bleeding badly; but in Switzerland! The gendarme screamed at him through the wire as John picked himself up and set off to get aid for his lacerated body. The action had happened so fast that the gendarme hadn't had time to get off a single shot; and with Weidner now moving rapidly away in Switzerland, he could do nothing!

After receiving medical attention, Weidner made his way to another point along the border and crossed once again into France. In St. Julien, where he knew Gazan would be tried, Weidner sought out friends who might know what could be done for the unfortunate Henri.

"Well, the judge and his assistant are both sympathetic to the underground, John," Weidner's friends revealed. "Why don't you appeal directly to them?"

Heartened by this information, John went to the judge's assistant, asking that he contact the judge and tell him that Gazan was a member of the Resistance.

At the trial the judge, acting on his assistant's information, said he needed more information about the incident at the border. He said he was allowing Gazan freedom in St. Julien for three days while he collected the additional information. When Henri left the courtroom, he met a gendarme, who took him back along the border road.

"You are going across the border here," the policeman explained. "I am a member of the Resistance. The judge has told me to make sure you get safely back to Switzerland. Now come on—I'll boost you over the wire."

For the Jewish people in conquered territory the passing months of war brought increased terror. Almost every day they faced another restriction, another method devised by the Germans to eliminate them. In Holland, on October 3, 1940, for example, all officials of the Dutch government had to sign declarations stating they were Aryan. On November 23, 1940, all Jewish administration employees were dismissed. The tide of death for the Jews was irreversible, their restrictions becoming progressively more stringent, as the following examples show.

January 9, 1941—Movie houses and theaters out-of-bounds for Jews.

June 4, 1941—Jews forbidden on public beaches.

August 8, 1941—All Jewish moneys must be deposited in a special bank.

August 11, 1941—Jews must register all household possessions.

August 29, 1941—Jewish children can no longer attend public schools.

October 22, 1941—All Jews need special permission to work anywhere.

November 1, 1941—All Jewish textile merchants ordered to close shop.

April 1, 1942—Jewish patients forbidden care in public hospitals.

April 29, 1942—All Jews must wear the Star of David on their clothing.

June 30, 1942—Jews must be in their homes between 8 P.M. and 6 A.M.

July 14, 1942—Systematic arrest of large numbers of Jews begins.

October 2, 1942—Jewish work camps in Holland emptied—Jews deported to concentration camps in Germany.

April 13, 1943—All Jews must turn themselves in to the concentration camp at Vught, Holland.

For most of the Jews the months rolled irrevocably toward only one destiny—death. Multiplied thousands were caught in the Nazis' planned program of annihilation. For some, though—those with large sums of money—there was a chance for freedom if the Nazi officials could be bribed. Jews who successfully bribed the Nazis set off through the escape lines running southward, led by members of the underground such as Weidner and his agents. Others tried to travel without help. Most of these were caught and thrown back into the concentration camps. For Jews whose talents in science and other fields were of use to the Nazis there was a special hostage-holding camp in Germany at Theresienstadt.

233

In Holland a special camp at Westerbork housed hundreds of Jews who claimed citizenship in neutral countries. Since Germany was not eager to incite other nations to join the Allies, the nationality of these Jews was studied with some care before action was taken regarding them. Often the difference between release or deportation to a concentration camp in Germany was whether the Jew in question had a document which showed his nationality.

In Switzerland relatives and friends of Jews without proof of citizenship in this special camp made great effort to help their loved ones. If a document of citizenship could be gotten into the captives' hands, they were told, then the Nazis would keep the relative or friend at Westerbork or send him to Theresienstadt or, in some rare cases, set him free. Treatment in both camps was not nearly as bad as in the other concentration camps, and the danger of death was not so immediate as elsewhere.

In Switzerland relatives of the special-case Jews often found help at the consul offices of neutral countries. For a "consideration"—usually between $100 and $500—the consuls of such neutral countries as San Salvador or Paraguay would prepare a document which appeared to be a valid citizenship paper. The fact that the top officials of these governments at home did not know of this illegal trade by their consuls, or that the documents would most certainly not be honored in these neutral countries, made little difference to those who sought them. They might, they just might, convince the Nazis that their loved ones should not face the execution squads.

It was one thing to obtain the document, quite another to get it to the person it was supposed to help. Since they were already traveling regularly from Switzerland through France and Belgium to the border of Holland, Weidner and his agents were often asked to carry these citizenship documents to the camps. Of course, if Weidner or members of his group had been caught with the documents, they would have been shot. But, on the other hand, if they got the papers into the camps, lives would be saved.

Usually the citizenship paper was placed in a new book whose pages were not yet cut apart. If the books were examined by guards, it would seem there was nothing inside the uncut pages. When he had to leave the train or bus to be checked at a control point while carrying the documents, Weidner left the book lying innocently on the seat he occupied. Not once was he or any of his agents caught while carrying forged citizenship documents into Holland. The only time the papers were ineffective was when they arrived at the camp after the Jew they were supposed to help had been deported to Germany.

"I will get the message through; you can count on it," John told Jonkheer Loudon, retired minister of foreign affairs for the Netherlands, as he left the old gentleman's home in Cannes on the Riviera during the months of terror.

"It is more difficult to travel now with the bridges and railroads being blown up so often," Weidner explained, "but I should get to Geneva in two days anyway. The message will go immediately from there to London."

The message, John knew, was of top priority importance to the Dutch government in London. With his knowledge of the war situation gleaned from visits with friends from all over France, and with his long government service, whatever Loudon had to say was important to his government.

Despite his eagerness to take Loudon's message as quickly as possible, John realized that in going to Geneva, choosing a less-traveled route would be wise. Heavily traveled rail lines were being bombed by the Allies or blown up by the underground almost every day. He decided to take a little train from Cannes to Nice and then to Digne in the mountains. From there he wanted to join the main train line from Marseilles to Grenoble, which ran on to Annecy.

Although his decision to take the back routes had been a wise one, the train on which John traveled still had to stop several times so that broken rails could be repaired. Shortly before they reached Digne, the train stopped once again.

"There is a big battle going on between the Germans and the maquis up ahead," a train crewman announced. "The Germans want us to take the train back to Nice. They say we can't go through."

The news disturbed John. If he went back to Nice, he still had no assurance that he could get through on the Marseilles-Lyons-Annecy line, because that route was under almost constant attack by Allied bombers, the marauding maquis, and other underground units. If he got off the train here and tried to continue by foot, it was possible he would be killed or wounded in the battle in the mountains that lay ahead.

As he sat in the coach thinking the matter over, a young Frenchman nearby seemed to be reading John's mind. "If we go back, we might not make it through—or we might get mixed up in the battle."

Weidner smiled at him. "But I have decided," he said, "I am going on from here by foot. I can't waste time going back."

"Good," replied the Frenchman. "I'll go with you."

Together the two men set off into the mountains. John knew they had to reach Grenoble, which was beyond where the fighting was taking place, before he could get transportation to Annecy. There, if lucky, they could catch a bus.

After three hours of climbing through the wild, rugged mountains, they had covered only three or four miles. Again John was thankful for his mountaineering experience. He was happy too that his French companion was able to keep up with him as they worked their way through the dense undergrowth and up the steep ravines. Hiking along, Weidner thought of the maquis who were engaging the Nazis in combat up ahead. A closely knit, tough organization, they were a law unto themselves. Their best fighting was done in the mountains, but they had been making things hot for the Germans in the lowlands also.

Several times as they struggled up the slopes, the two men saw German soldiers, fortunately spotting them first. Suddenly, as they topped a new rocky ridge, John and his friend stood exposed to heavy firing between the Germans and the maquis. Just as they came over the ridge, the noise of machine guns and rifles split the air.

"Quick, get down! Follow me!" John shouted.

Crouched low, they ran, not knowing which way to go. But John soon determined the direction from which the maquis were firing, and he and his friend raced in that direction. Seeing the two men, the maquis threw up a tremendous hail of bullets at the Germans. John and the Frenchman dived into a small shelter among protecting rocks and shortly found themselves in the midst of the maquis.

Following a soldier through the rocks and trees, John suddenly realized that he would have to prove his identity to the maquis. "I could be an agent of the Nazis for all they know," he thought. "Well, I'll tell them about my work and the contacts I've had with the maquis in the Savoy area. That will persuade them to help us reach Grenoble."

The commander, however, was not impressed by John's explanation.

"Maybe your story's true, maybe not," he replied. "But that's not my worry. You will go to our headquarters. If they believe you there, fine; if not——" Turning to one of his men, he ordered the two blindfolded.

In a few moments they were hustled into a car and taken farther into the mountains to maquis headquarters, and only then were their blindfolds removed. All about they could see men wearing the Cross of Lorraine, the insignia of de Gaulle's Free French Fighting Forces. They were taken to the commander, and John told his story once again.

"We have no contact with maquis units fighting in the Savoy," the chief replied when John mentioned his contacts to the north. "We need some other way to check on you before we can let you go."

"I see you have a radio transmitter here," Weidner said to the commander. "If you will contact London, I'm sure they will give you a recommendation for me."

The suggestion impressed the maquis chief. "All right," he said, "but it takes several hours for our messages to be answered from London. In the meantime you and your friend will spend the night with us. By tomorrow morning we will have the answer."

That night John slept well, confident that London's answer would satisfy the maquis chief. His French companion had no identification problem since he was from the immediate area.

The next morning, after John had shaved and eaten, the maquis commander showed up with word from London.

"They say you are all right," he said. "We have detained you, but we must make sure of everybody these days. One of our cars will take you to the edge of our area of operations. From there some of our contacts will take you on to Grenoble."

When John left the car about an hour later, he was picked up by other agents who had German authorization to travel. They passed through several German checkpoints but were not detained.

Grenoble was swarming with people who had come for the weekly market day. John made his way easily through the crowds and caught a bus full of people returning home from market. That evening he arrived in Annecy without incident. The next day he crossed the border into Switzerland with Jonkheer Loudon's message.

One day as he met with Jacques Rens, one of his "right arms," John heard some amazing news that made him wonder if the usually good cooperation between the various allies in the war was breaking down.

"We have just picked up two men coming from Holland with an almost unbelievable story," Jacques told him. "They escaped from prison at Haarlem and are members of the Dutch secret service in London who were dropped into Holland by parachute to transmit secret radio messages to England."

According to their report, the British originally set up the mission with a secret code in which certain letters were left out of sentences in radio messages to warn London if the operation was discovered by the Germans.

Shortly after the first of the Dutch operatives was dropped, he was caught by the Germans. The Nazis had already broken the regular code by listening for some days to the transmissions these operatives had been sending to London, but they still did not know the secret code which was to signal that something was wrong. They had forced Lauwers, one of the captured operatives, to send messages to England asking for secret information, supplies, and more operatives.

At first Lauwers cooperated, but left out parts of the transmission to thus warn London that something had gone wrong. To his great surprise London ignored his warning code and sent back the requested information and materials. They even began to drop more operatives. At first Lauwers thought London might have missed his security check messages hidden in the code; but as day after day passed, and London kept sending back what was requested, he realized that whoever was at the receiving end in London was asleep at the switch.

From the time the first operative was dropped into Holland near the beginning of 1942 until November, 1943, nearly fifty were sent by London in answer to the messages Lauwers was forced to transmit. Each of the agents had been picked up immediately when he hit the ground in Holland. At one time Lauwers even sent in regular code, "We are in the hands of the Gestapo," but London evidently thought he was joking and continued sending operatives as requested by the Gestapo.

"We have to get these men to Switzerland to General Van Tricht right away, John," Jacques said. "They must get word through him to England so that whoever is sending the operatives and supplies will be relieved of his post at once. The Germans are extremely concerned about the escape of these two men because if they get word to London, the Gestapo's little game will be ended."

A short time later the two men—last names of Dourlein and Ubbink—were moved safely to Switzerland and General Van Tricht's office.

When the messages had been received in London, word came back that the two should be taken back across France to Spain and then brought to London at once. General Van

Tricht asked Weidner to escort the two men to Spain.

After careful planning Weidner arranged their passage across the increasingly difficult Swiss-French border to Annecy. Together they traveled by train to Lyons, where he turned them over to one of his agents for the trip to Toulouse. In Toulouse, Jacques and Moen (Salomon Chait) kept the two operatives hidden until Weidner joined them a few days later. The three underground leaders planned a careful trip for Dourlein and Ubbink into the Pyrenees. By the end of November they were in Spain, on their way to tell their strange story in London.

Near the end of 1943, while he was in Paris, Weidner was asked to contact Victor Swane, who said he was working with a small underground group.

"We are directed in our work by Christian Lindemans, whom some call King Kong," Swane said. "We have been bringing refugees from Holland and Belgium, trying to get them to Spain. We've gotten some out of the country, but now we have no more money. Lately we've been having trouble on the Pyrenees because without money we can't get guides to help us. What we'd like to do is join your organization," Swane said. "I think you might want to talk with King Kong about the idea. He would like very much to see you."

Weidner told Swane he would be happy to talk with Lindemans to see if something could be worked out.

Within a few days he met the underground leader in a Paris café. King Kong was a handsome man, tall and powerfully built, but he was also loudmouthed and extremely touchy. As they talked, John noted that King Kong kept fingering a large revolver.

When their conversation ended, King Kong said he had to catch a train for Brussels and invited Weidner to walk with him to the station. During the walk and after they had arrived at the station, King Kong played with the gun he was carrying. As they waited in the station, he accidentally dropped the weapon on the station floor. Quickly he scooped the gun up as people standing nearby scattered to the other side of the room. John stood frozen, hoping that no Nazi or gendarme had seen King Kong's clumsy action with the gun.

The next day Weidner met Swane again to talk more about the idea of King Kong's group joining Weidner's. Swane admitted that this bizarre man was more adventurer than idealist, and that, although he had courage, he was not morally stable. The fellow maintained improper relations with a number of women, Swane acknowledged, and he was fond of using his gun. Weidner saw contrasts which he knew would not make it easy for the two groups to merge. Weidner's own underground members were practically all of a very high moral level. And no one in his organization carried a gun or used one. That was one of the rules by which they operated: they did not take life; they only saved it.

In reply to Swane's continued plea for funds, John turned over fifty thousand francs to King Kong's group. He told Swane he thought giving the Lindemans group financial help, but keeping the two organizations separate, would be best.

On two later occasions he saw Swane again and gave him additional funds. Then in July, 1944, Weidner lost contact with the go-between.

After the war ended, Weidner heard that Swane was arrested by the Germans and later died in a German concentration camp. Lindemans—King Kong—continued his work and his adventures. But in March, 1944, his brother and one of his girl friends were arrested by the Gestapo. Lindemans, greatly disturbed, went to the Gestapo and offered to work for them secretly if they would free the pair. The Gestapo accepted the offer, and from that time on King Kong turned traitor to his own underground group. His agents began to be captured with strange regularity. One of those who disappeared into the hands of the Germans as a result of Lindemans' traitorous activity was Victor Swane!

Near the end of the war King Kong infiltrated the Netherlands secret service and gave news of their operations to the Germans. But on his return across Allied lines to Holland he was arrested by the Dutch. As information about his dark activities came to light, he denied everything; and later in a prison hospital he committed suicide with an overdose of sleeping pills obtained from a nurse who had fallen in love with him.

When Weidner heard the end of King Kong's story, he realized what could have happened if he had maintained contact with the unprincipled man.

XVII

suzy kraay

AMONG the scores of persons who worked for Dutch-Paris, few moved along its escape and message routes more often than did tall, gangling, plain-faced Suzy Kraay. Recommended to Weidner by Herman Laatsman, whom she met when she first arrived as a refugee in Paris, she fell easily into the underground group's activities.

In mid-1943, however, Suzy's luck began to run out. Against Weidner's advice she tried to cross the Pyrenees to Spain, but was arrested in the foothills and imprisoned at Gurs, where she remained until November, 1943. After many appeals, she was released. During long months behind barbed wire she received numerous messages, packages of food, and other supplies from Weidner, which let her know that Dutch-Paris had not forgotten her.

After her release from Gurs, Suzy went to Lyons, home base for all Dutch-Paris operations. John sent her on an assignment to Toulouse, which she handled successfully. Next she was sent to Holland to help guide a family of refugees, the Simons, back through Belgium and France to freedom in Switzerland. She successfully located the Simons and started back with them. At the Franco-Belgian border the group was arrested by customs officials but released after questioning. Suzy proceeded with the family to Paris, then to Lyons, and finally to Annecy, arriving after John's store had closed for the night. The little group spent the night at Miss Meunier's store in Annecy. Early the next morning a Dutch-Paris border passer took charge of them.

She returned to Lyons and received instructions to go to Paris, where she contacted Herman Laatsman for further assignment.

"There are a number of American pilots in Toulouse who need help," Laatsman said. "Tomorrow you should leave for Toulouse to guide them. I'll give you money at breakfast time in the morning so that you'll be able to move as you feel best. Tonight you are to stay at the Hotel Ibis. We've made good contacts there; they will keep your name out of the hotel register."

Although she was somewhat apprehensive, Suzy met the Paris underground chief at breakfast the next morning and received the funds. Against her wishes, she also agreed to take some black-market food packages to the pilots.

At three o'clock that afternoon Suzy entered the Paris Metro station to catch the four o'clock train to Toulouse. Since it was still an hour before the train was to depart, she decided to get something to eat. She eased the three sacks of food Laatsman had given her onto the seat, and as she studied the menu, she suddenly became aware of someone standing by her side.

"Where are you traveling, Miss?" one of two French police inspectors asked.

"I am catching the four o'clock train to Toulouse," she answered.

"And these packages, what is in them?"

"Food I am taking to prisoners in the camp south of Toulouse. It is not forbidden to aid friends in the camps, is it?"

"No," replied the policeman. "But you appear Jewish. Let me see your papers."

"I am not a Jew," Suzy replied hastily. "Here are my papers. They show clearly that I am not Jewish."

"Yes, yes, I can see that," the inspector agreed roughly. "Papers have a way of being false these days, though. One doesn't know what papers are telling the truth anymore. But we shall soon know if you are Jewish. Pick up your packages. We're going to headquarters, where we can find out more about you."

Her protests that she had to catch the four o'clock train did not impress the French police who led her out of the station. Moving along the street, Suzy slipped a small book of addresses and other data from her purse and dropped it to the sidewalk. She did this in a movement of sheer terror, for in carrying the book she had gone against the constantly repeated rule of all the Resistance groups, especially of Dutch-Paris, that members were never to carry names of other members or important contacts in any written form. Suzy had committed an unforgivable act, and now she realized how important the instruction had been.

247

"Mademoiselle has dropped this little booklet on the sidewalk," a gray-haired little Frenchman murmured beside Suzy a few moments later.

One of the inspectors grabbed the book. "Yes, indeed, we do want the book." He smiled at the little man. "Thank you for retrieving it for the lady."

"It is nothing," Suzy stuttered through teeth clenched with fear. "It is only something I didn't want."

"Ah, yes, something you didn't want. A list of addresses and other information, it looks like to me," said the inspector as he leafed through the pages. "I'm sure you don't want this, Miss—especially not while you are with us."

At police headquarters Suzy was ordered into the office of Bissoir, head of the Brigade d'Interpellation, a special section of the French police which took orders directly from the Germans. Suzy waited in the police chief's office until 6:30 that evening, when he arrived from an appointment.

"Good evening, Miss. How are you?" asked Bissoir. "They tell me you are an interesting young lady. Something about a 'little black book' you had with you, eh?"

Suzy said nothing.

"You also seem to have false papers," Bissoir said. "And you are traveling with a large amount of food supplies, much of it illegal, which you have not explained to my men. You say you are not a Jew, but your papers show you have been in Holland. Are you living in France now?"

"Yes," Suzy replied. "I now live in France. The food I am taking to prisoners in the camps south of Toulouse. I am not a Jew, but it is true that I have fled from the Germans in Holland. Many people have come to southern France from there, and not all of them are Jews. Now, isn't there some way I can be released?" she asked. "I am telling the truth, and I should be on my way to Toulouse."

"Of course," soothed Bissoir. "Of course you can be released—just as soon as you tell us *all* the truth. You might tell us all these things openly and still be an agent of the Gestapo checking up on us, you know. If your story is not true and we release you, we will be in bad with the Gestapo. A friend of mine recently released someone like you because she was supposedly truthful. A few days later the Gestapo mysteriously heard about it. Do you know where my friend is now? He is in a German prison camp. So I must be sure your story is true before you can be released. And I am not yet convinced that you are telling me the truth—at least not all of it. For example, Miss, is this your real name here on your papers? It doesn't seem to be the same as the one in your little book!"

"I have told you the truth," Suzy said. "I will admit that I have taken a false name because it is easier to get around with one. My real name is Suzy Kraay. But that is not such an unusual thing in this crazy war. Everyone is doing two things in life—one is known everywhere; the other is not known."

"So, now we are making progress," Bissoir said as he leaned back in his chair. "You have taken a false name. Now that leads to a few other things we must know. There are many things we must know, young lady, before you can be released!"

"But I am telling the truth," she said, now caught in a feeling of panic at the commissioner's suggestion of worse questioning to come. As the conversation continued, however, Bissoir's questions appeared mild enough, and Suzy relaxed a bit. She began to feel that he thought she was working for the Germans to test his organization's abilities. To counter this idea, she thought that, without revealing too much about her work for Dutch-Paris, she could convince him she was part of the Resistance, even as she thought him to be. After all, she reasoned, he was a Frenchman, part of the French police. Why should he not be in sympathy with the Resistance?

"I'll prove to you I am telling the truth," she said. "I'll help you in your work. Tomorrow afternoon there is a group of men—escapees—going through the train station bound for Toulouse. These will be airmen, and they will be led by underground people. You can go there and check on them. Then you will know I am truthful with you."

This information had been passed along to Suzy by Herman Laatsman just before she left him earlier that day.

"You are a help, Miss Kraay; you are a help indeed," conceded Bissoir. "We shall see about your suggestion. If you are right, this may help us decide to let you go."

After lunch the next day Suzy was brought from her cell to a large hall. In the room were thirty-five French policemen. One of them turned to the girl as she entered. "We are going to meet the group you told the commissioner about yesterday," he declared. "Those airmen will never get to Toulouse!"

SUZY KRAAY

Suzy was horrified that her suggestion, given with the thought that the man to whom she gave it was sympathetic to the Resistance, might mean the arrest of airmen scheduled to pass through the train station at about five o'clock that afternoon. She had told Bissoir about them thinking that, as a loyal Frenchman, he would merely go personally to check on the movement of the airmen, then realize she was to be trusted. "How could he be so disloyal to France as to turn those men over to the Germans?" she asked herself, trembling with fright as she was taken past the waiting crowd of police to the commissioner's office.

"We have decided you should accompany us to the railway station to point out the group you mentioned yesterday, Miss Kraay," Bissoir said. "You can put your complete confidence in me that all will be well if you are cooperative. It will result in your release, I can assure you."

"No, I will not go with you. You have betrayed my confidence in you. I thought you would only want to check on the truth of my story. Now you have a gang of inspectors waiting at the station. I will not go with you," cried Suzy.

The commissioner's face reddened. Then he scowled at the girl as he pushed his chair back from the desk. "So you will not go. Very well, we shall go alone." He left the room quickly.

A few minutes after eight that night the commissioner had another meeting with Suzy. "You have sent us to the railway station for nothing, Miss Kraay," he rasped at her. "There were no airmen there. We saw nothing. Now I cannot trust you at all."

Had not plans for this group of escaping airmen been changed at the last moment, they would have been trapped at the train station. Leading part of the airmen, Weidner, as he often did to avoid detection, changed the departure plans, and the group took an earlier train to Toulouse. The information Suzy Kraay had given to the commissioner had been truthful, but she did not know about the last-minute change of plans.

Covering her surprise that Bissoir had not found the airmen, Suzy said, "There was nothing to my story about the group at the train station. I only told it to be set free. But everything else has been true. You must believe me."

"We would like to believe you, Miss Kraay, but you are making it increasingly difficult with these lies and fabrications. We must get at the truth, or you will never be released."

"All I want is to be free, to go on my way," moaned Suzy to the commissioner. "I have done nothing. I am telling the truth. Why don't you believe me?"

"Believe you? How can I believe you when you are not telling me what we need to know? Here is an interesting document," he said, picking up the book of addresses she had attempted to throw away on the street. "It says here you were to meet Caubo. Now who is Caubo? And here is the name of Moulonguet. Who is he? And Milleret—who is he? And the Hotel Ibis is on your list here, too. What were you going to do at the Hotel Ibis? Until you can tell us what all these names and places mean, we cannot possibly release you."

252

"I don't know about those things," mumbled the girl. "All I can say is that I have been trying to be truthful with you, and you do not believe me. What else can I say?"

"Your truthfulness takes strange turns," responded Commissioner Bissoir. "We shall start to find out something more concrete tomorrow."

The next morning, Saturday, February 11, a group of Bissoir's inspectors appeared at Suzy's cell. "You are going to the Hotel Ibis with us, Miss Kraay. We want to see if anyone there can recognize you," one of the officials said.

The visit proved fruitless to the police. No one at the hotel admitted knowing the girl. When she was returned to her cell, a man handed her a note from Bissoir's secretary.

"Mr. Caubo, the railway official, has been arrested by the police," the note said. "He is being held in this prison."

For long moments Suzy thought about the words. "Could it be a trick?" she asked herself. "Or is his secretary sympathetic to the Resistance?"

Shortly after lunch Suzy was taken again to Bissoir's office.

"Now, Miss Kraay, you must put your confidence in me," the commissioner said. "It is possible that if you will speak truthfully, putting your confidence completely in my good judgment, then we can have you released very soon, perhaps even by tomorrow. But that means you must tell me everything you know. You can trust me to use discretion with the information you give."

"You did not use discretion with the information I gave you about the airmen at the railway station, even though it was false," the girl replied. "Besides, you are still assuming that I have more information than I really have."

Signaling to the guard just inside his door to take the girl back to her cell, Bissoir growled, "You have the information all right. The only question is when we will get it from you. Tomorrow perhaps, maybe the next day. Perhaps not till next week. But we'll get it, Miss Kraay; we'll get it!"

On Sunday morning Suzy was returned to Bissoir's office.

"Now here is a letter which seems to concern you," he said, holding out several pages. "It is signed by you, and it is addressed to Mr. Caubo, your friend from the railway. Now I want you to read this letter to me, since it is written in Dutch. Perhaps from it we shall be able to learn a bit more of your true character."

The letter made Suzy catch her breath. It meant beyond any doubt that Caubo, a fellow member of Dutch-Paris, had been arrested. They had probably gone to his home after seeing his name in her address book. The letter was one Suzy had given Caubo to hand to her mother the next time he was in Holland on railroad business. There were no addresses or other important information in the letter except a part which referred to Suzy's father's being transferred from Vught Prison to Utrecht. As she translated the letter, she left this part out.

"Very good; that's very good," Bissoir said when she had finished translating to him. "That kind of cooperation is what we need, Miss Kraay. If you continue to be cooperative with us, I'm sure you will be released soon."

254

She was taken to her cell, but late that afternoon the guards appeared again, and back she went to Bissoir's office.

"I just wanted to tell you again how much I hope you will cooperate with us," he stated. "I have already promised you that I will keep your information in confidence, but I just wanted to tell you once again. You know, of course, that it will be to your advantage to stay here in the prefecture headquarters rather than being transferred to the prison where the Gestapo is in charge. Our German friends are not as easy to deal with as I am. So I'm sure you want to be cooperative and avoid being transferred there, don't you?

"Now," he said, handing Suzy's purse to her, "here are your funds and other items. We have kept your little book and some other small things, but we wanted you to have your purse back. All women need their purses, don't they?"

That night in her cell Suzy tried to review everything that had happened so far, and to plan what she would do next. But she did not have enough information about what Bissoir knew to be able to settle on a definite course of action. "I'll just have to find answers as I go along," she reasoned. "If they don't turn me over to the Gestapo, I can probably be released in a day or two."

On Monday morning Suzy went back to Bissoir's office. This time he returned the packages of food she had when she was arrested, but required her to sign a paper declaring that the food in the packages was considered black-market items. Just after noon she was taken from her cell to the office of Bissoir's secretary. After he had made sure the door was closed and locked so that the guards outside wouldn't intrude, the young secretary turned to Suzy.

"You must be careful in your talks with Commissioner Bissoir," he began. "He is working with the Germans. Everything you tell him will find its way to them. You will probably be transferred to the Gestapo in a few hours; but when you go, be sure you tell them exactly what you have told Bissoir. Otherwise they will know you have changed stories, for the commissioner tells them everything. I have already told Caubo this same information so that he will know. He is being held in another part of the headquarters here."

"You are one of us, aren't you?" Suzy said with relief when the secretary had finished telling her about his chief. "It is good to know there are still honest people willing to help others. Thank you for the information."

Late that night the guards returned to Suzy's cell. With them were six German soldiers and Caubo. Suzy was taken from her cell, and she and Caubo were handcuffed together, then marched into the cold night air. Within half an hour they arrived at Gestapo headquarters in Rue des Saussaies. For the next hour Suzy was questioned by a Gestapo officer, and she repeated the story she had told Bissoir during the previous two days. After the questioning Suzy was taken to prison at nearby Fresnes for the night.

The next day Suzy was returned to Gestapo headquarters, where she was questioned again. While this was going on, an officer entered the room.

"I am happy to have found you, Miss Kraay," he said. "You can help us very much. Here is something I want you

to see. I believe you can establish the identity of this man."
The officer took a large picture from a book. The photograph was of John Weidner.

"Do you know this man, Miss Kraay?" he asked.

"I can't say right now," replied the girl, steeling herself not to show the surprise she felt. "There are many men who look like that."

"That's true, but this man is someone special to us. And he is special to you, too. I think you ought to come with me to the office upstairs. We'll see if you can't remember a little more about this picture."

The officer motioned to the guards who stood nearby, and they led her upstairs.

"Now we can get down to business," he said when they were seated. "The picture is of John Henry Weidner. We know he is leading a large underground group. We know you have had dealings with him. We know you have not been telling the truth either at the prefecture headquarters or here. We want some much better answers from you, Miss Kraay."

"How could they connect me with John Weidner's name so quickly?" thought Suzy as she looked at the officer sitting across the desk from her. "I didn't mention his name at any time I can remember. I haven't told anyone of my connection with Dutch-Paris. How could they know?"

"I want to warn you we are not very patient with people who tell lies," the Gestapo officer said. "We know too many things about you and about Dutch-Paris as well. We will use every means available here to bring your memory back for you. And," he paused, letting each word fall heavily, "I assure you we have many different ways of doing that."

"I cannot deny that I know John Weidner," responded Suzy. "In November, 1943, I was released from the prison at Gurs. When I left there, I went to Lyons, where I saw Mr. Weidner. But I have not seen him since that time."

"And how did you get out of Gurs?" the officer wanted to know.

"I was released. I appealed many times, and finally they said I could go."

"And after seeing Weidner, where did you go?"

"To Holland, via Paris and Brussels."

"So you went to Holland. And in Holland I guess you just stayed there twiddling your thumbs? Quite a story you tell! Quite a story! Next you will be telling me you have never been to Toulouse in your life. Your story is a lie. You are nothing but a liar! I've already told you we have many ways here to help you get back your memory. It seems we shall have to use some of those ways. You think about that in your cell tonight!"

Back in the prison at Fresnes, Suzy did think about the Nazi officer's words. She shuddered at the thought of what might happen the next morning. But no soldiers came to her cell the next day, and the following day also passed without incident.

On Thursday morning, however, the keys rattled in the cell door, and Suzy was ordered back to Gestapo headquarters, where she was summoned before the same officer who had threatened her three days earlier. With him were two other officers. They again warned her of their torture methods, then asked for her life story.

"If you can't remember better than before, things will not go well with your father," one of the officers declared. "You see, we know him; and I am sure you wouldn't want further harm to come to him, would you?"

Deeply troubled by the officer's words, Suzy began to recount the events of her life. "I went to Paris from Holland in October, 1942," she said. "Then I tried to cross the Pyrenees into Spain, but I was caught and imprisoned at Gurs. After getting out of Gurs I went to Lyons, then back to Holland."

The questioning continued for hours. About six o'clock in the evening two more Gestapo agents came in and began to ask questions.

Suddenly one of the officers blurted, "You know, don't you, Miss Kraay, that your father has been condemned to death at Utrecht for his underground activity? Nobody can change that except you. If you begin telling us the truth, you can save your father's life—think of that!"

The frightened girl did not answer. In a few moments she was on her way back to her cell in Fresnes.

At seven the next morning she was returned to Gestapo headquarters. The officers began by showing her pictures of many different people, but she could recognize only one as an acquaintance. Soon a high German military official arrived. Then two more officers came into the room. The four men began to fire questions without pause. Every few minutes two questions were interspersed between the others: "Where is John Weidner? Where is Herman Laatsman?" After two hours of brutal questioning they began to slap and kick her. After thirty minutes of this treatment they suddenly left the room, and Suzy was alone.

But they soon came back. The military official leaned over the exhausted girl. "If you think we are going to continue wasting our time on your lies, you are mistaken! I warn you that this will be the last time we question you. If you can't do better this time, something worse is going to happen! Give us the names and addresses of all Dutch-Paris leaders, then your father will be set free. We know about your mother in Holland. If you don't tell us what we want, we won't guarantee what might happen to her. We'll give you five minutes to think about this, then we will begin again."

"I don't need the time," Suzy responded. "I have nothing else to say. I've told you everything I know. I don't know why you won't believe me."

"Very well, if that is your answer," the officer said coldly. He ordered the guards to take her downstairs.

She was led down the stairs along a hall to one of several heavy wooden doors. The guards opened the door and shoved her inside.

At first Suzy saw only a bare room. Then she turned to the wall opposite the door. What she saw there chilled her to the bone. Three handcuffed men were hanging on the wall, great steel hooks through the handcuffs, their feet suspended about two feet above the floor. They did not appear to be alive; they did not move. One of the men had been stripped

260

of his shirt, and his back was a mass of blood and torn flesh. Suzy's stomach turned at the awful sight.

In a few minutes an SS guard stepped into the room and led her back along the hall and up the stairs to another room where the four officers were waiting.

"You have seen how it goes with others, Miss Kraay," one of the men said. "Have you changed your mind yet?"

"No, I have nothing else to say."

"All right. Guards, get her ready!" he said.

Four soldiers stripped the clothing from her body, hand-cuffed her hands behind her back, and clamped shackles on her feet. As she twisted, trying to get away from the men, she saw the dreaded bathtub which was a standard part of Gestapo torture. She was thrown into the tub of cold water, and strong hands seized her hair and shoved her head under the water.

Long moments went by; then she began to thrash about violently. Suddenly one of the officers tapped the guard on the shoulder, and he jerked her head out of the water.

"Now tell us, who are the leaders? What are their addresses?" shouted the officer.

Suzy shook her head.

Again her head was forced under the water.

The water treatment continued for five minutes, ten, twenty, then thirty minutes. At the end of an hour, Suzy was dragged from the bathtub and thrown to the floor. The officers left the room in a rage.

In twenty minutes they came back. This time they began to kick her. When she tried to get up to avoid the blows,

261

they slapped her onto the floor again. During every minute of torture the questioning went on: "Where is John Weidner? What are the names of Dutch-Paris leaders? Who are the members in Paris? How often do agents move from Paris to Brussels? What are the lines of escape used by Dutch-Paris?"

Abruptly they stopped. One of them turned to an SS officer standing nearby watching the girl.

"Take her to the Table Room," he directed.

They jerked Suzy to her feet and pushed her from the room. Downstairs again, they entered a room in which torture was in progress. A man lay strapped to a table, and four soldiers stood around him flailing the poor fellow with their heavy leather belts. The belts cut deeply into his naked flesh. His body was a mass of blood. He was screaming pitifully.

As Suzy tried to turn away from the scene, the SS officer held her head and forced her to look. In a few minutes she fainted. When she awakened, she was again forced to watch the bloody scene. Then she was taken upstairs.

"Your turn will be next, Miss Kraay. If you tell us what we want to know, your father will go free, your mother will not be harmed, and you will not have to go to the table. But it won't disturb us in the least if you have to go there. Eventually we will get the information we want. Are you ready to go downstairs again, or do you have something you want to tell us?"

Faced by the threats on the lives of her parents and the horrible torture on the table, Suzy's reservoir of strength and determination suddenly ran dry. She dissolved into great, broken sobs. Fear, such as she had never known before, took possession of her mind. She suddenly became so frightened that she could no longer hear the officers' voices as they shouted at her. Her world seemed to be collapsing, and she lost all control of herself.

"I will tell! I will tell! I will tell!" she screamed. "Just don't hurt my parents! Don't hurt me anymore. I can't stand it!" Her body heaved with the sobs of sorrow, pain, and fear which she had endured.

They led her to a desk and an officer took her statement. She gave the names of the underground leaders, told where they lived, what their habits were, where they were most likely to be found. She gave the Gestapo the addresses of Herman Laatsman; Gabrielle Weidner, John's sister; Miss Meunier in Annecy; and Pastor Paul Meyer, of the Seventh-day Adventist church in Lyons. Other names tumbled from her trembling lips. She recounted Weidner's habits, named his friends and the places he sometimes went. But she could give no address for him because he now lived somewhere in Geneva and his time in France and the other occupied countries was a constant series of movements from one place to another.

That night Suzy huddled on her cot in Fresnes prison, quivering and broken by the Nazi torture.

On Sunday she was questioned again at the prison, but it was obvious she had given all the information she knew. Then on the twenty-eighth of March she was taken from Fresnes to the prison at Romainville, then transferred from Romainville to Ravensbruck in Germany on April 16.

The Gestapo kept their word about her father, who was released from prison. But they jailed him again the next day. He died in a concentration camp.

In the hour of torment when her spirit broke before the Gestapo's threats and torture, Suzy Kraay was probably slow of realizing what would result from her confession. But the results were inevitable. Nearly 150 members of Dutch-Paris were arrested. At least forty of this number were destined to die in the concentration camps to which they were sent.

XVIII

the net closes

WEIDNER ARRIVED in Paris from Vichy on February 14, 1944, and received the distressing news of Suzy Kraay's arrest.

"She was picked up by the Brigade d'Interpellation," an agent informed him.

The Brigade, although unknown to John at the time, was a special section of the French police which worked with the Germans. Their task was to check the papers of persons in the Paris streets and buildings, and if their suspicions were aroused, to take any suspects to headquarters.

But Weidner was not greatly concerned when he first heard about Suzy's arrest. It was not the first time a Dutch-Paris member had been taken into custody by French police, but every time they had been released—sometimes worse for their encounter with the law, but released nonetheless. John knew that the regular Paris police were not working with the Germans directly, and in any case they would not turn Suzy over to the Germans or give the Germans information she had given them. But what John didn't know was

265

that Suzy was in the hands of a new police section, headed by the pro-German officer Bissoir.

A short time later Weidner learned that Caubo, with his wife and children, had also been arrested. Another Dutch-Paris agent filled in these details:

"The police found Caubo's address on a paper Suzy had with her. At Caubo's home they discovered considerable food and some gold watches. Herman Laatsman says there is a suit in Caubo's house with a new set of identification papers in it for you and Jacques Rens. It is quite possible that the police have this suit, too."

The following day Pierre, a Dutch-Paris underground agent, was dispatched to Caubo's home to see if he could learn whether the suit had been taken by the police. As he moved toward the door of the house, a French policeman sprinted across the street.

"What are you going to do in that house?" the policeman shouted.

"I am a friend of the man who lives here," responded Pierre. "I have come to see him."

"He is gone. We have arrested him for illegally operating in the black market," the policeman said. "I also suspect that he is a member of the underground. If you know him, you might be part of the underground, too. You are lucky I stopped you instead of my partner, who is eating his lunch down the street. He is a 'bad' Frenchman. We are stationed across the street to arrest anyone who comes here. I don't believe your friend has told anything about his underground activities—if he is a member, as I suspect."

"And a girl—her name is Suzy Kraay—do you know what happened to her?" asked Pierre, quickly sensing that the policeman was a friend of the underground.

"I know nothing about her," the policeman said. "We are on the Caubo case. Now you get away from here fast—before my partner returns. He would arrest you without any questions asked if he were here."

Pierre hurried away to take the information to Weidner. That night John called Laatsman, Rens, and others of the Paris unit of Dutch-Paris to discuss the arrest of the two underground members.

"Caubo has had only limited contact among our group lately, mostly with you, Herman," Weidner stated when the group had gathered. "I feel sure he will not give information which would cause us to change our operations."

The others agreed that Caubo was trustworthy, that he would not give the police any vital information about the work or leaders of Dutch-Paris.

"And Suzy is reliable," John continued. "We can trust her. She has moved about frequently, and she has never dropped a name in the wrong place. She is certainly clever enough to come out of this situation. Neither she nor Caubo would say anything to help the police in questioning the other. We can trust both of them to keep the Nazis thrown off the trail of the organization. With the food Suzy was carrying it will certainly look as though she has been operating in the black market, but she can explain that, too.

"We will continue to try to get more information about them and go ahead as we have in the past," John said.

The next morning he left for Belgium to carry out assignments for Dutch-Paris in Brussels. He reported the two arrests to members of the Brussels group and reassured them of the trustworthiness of both Suzy and Caubo.

When Weidner returned to Paris on February 16, Suzy was still in the hands of the French police. He told the Paris group to continue trying to get information about her and Caubo and to continue moving refugees and airmen from Paris to the southern part of France.

On February 23 Weidner visited his sister Gabrielle in Paris and left her some of the objects used for concealing secret messages—the pencil and the keys. Gabrielle agreed to hide the objects in her apartment.

That evening Weidner learned that Mrs. Caubo and her daughter and sons had been released by the French police. When he sent agents to talk with the family, they got little information they did not already know. Worried about his own plight, Caubo had failed to give his sons a message for the organization about his and Suzy's situation. They did learn, however, that the police had not found the suit in which the papers for Jacques and John were hidden. Caubo had given the suit to a neighbor, who had burned all the papers when Caubo was arrested.

On Friday, February 25, several meetings were held between Laatsman, Nykerk, Rens, Chait, and Weidner. They discussed the Caubo-Suzy situation thoroughly and finally came to a solution they felt was reasonable:

"Suzy has been in jail for so long now that if she has given any information, something would have happened by this time," they agreed. "She has probably been put into prison. We will have to find out where she is and see if something can be done to help her escape."

During the day John's youngest sister, Annette, arrived from Holland with several messages for him. When she had delivered them, she went to Gabrielle's apartment. Earlier John had told Gabrielle that he would be sleeping that night at the home of Pastor Oscar Meyer, president of the Franco-Belgian Union Conference of Seventh-day Adventists. She was the only one who knew where he would be. He had also told her that he would leave Saturday night for Brussels, but had not told her where he would be staying in the Belgian city.

The next morning Weidner decided to go to a nearby park to read his Bible rather than attend worship services at the Seventh-day Adventist church as he usually did. He could not take a chance on being seen at any church—his presence would almost surely implicate members of the congregation if the Gestapo were to capture him during the services. So he dressed and walked slowly to the little park, where he read from his worn Bible until about 11 A.M. At noon he was to meet Gabrielle and Annette there, and they would have lunch together.

Suddenly Annette came running across the leaf-strewn lawn, her eyes filled with tears.

"They came to the church," she sobbed. "They came to the church and took Gabrielle away!"

The words slashed into John as he held his sister close to comfort her. "They," he realized, were the Gestapo. And they were probably questioning Gabrielle at that very moment.

"Now," he said to Annette when she had calmed down a bit, "let's hear all about it. How did it happen? Tell me all you know."

"It was just after ten o'clock," began Annette. "We were in church when someone told Gabrielle two men wanted to see her in the foyer. She left and didn't come back. So I went to the foyer to find her. She wasn't there. Then I ran to the apartment; and when I opened the door, I found her there with the two men—they were both in civilian clothes.

"Just as I opened the door, Gabrielle began to yell at me that she was busy talking with the men. 'Why do you keep sticking your nose in my business?' she yelled at me. And she said, 'Don't disturb me; can't you see that I'm busy? I don't want to be disturbed! Get out of here!'

"I knew then that they were the Gestapo, because she never yells at me. She was only trying to save me. So I got out quickly and came here. I'm sure they are gone by now."

Annette's story tore at John's heart. He wanted to run to the apartment, to try to save his sister from the Gestapo, perhaps by asking them to take him in her place; but he realized that they had almost surely gone already. As Annette gave more details of the terrible experience, John thought about how he had always kept Gabrielle out of the Dutch-Paris organization because of her close connection with his church. As secretary to Pastor Meyer, the Adventist administrative leader for France and Belgium, John had felt that she should not take an active part in Dutch-Paris. He

270

had been careful not to even mention her name to any but his closest associates—Chait, Rens, Laatsman.

"We've got to keep our heads and think clearly about this, Annette," he told his sister. "They have probably taken Gabrielle by this time, but that does not mean they have searched the apartment. But they are sure to do that. If they find the objects there, it will implicate Gabrielle, so we've got to get them out of the apartment, and also the false papers I brought for you to get into Switzerland with. You call one of your friends who lives in the apartment building and ask if anyone is in Gabrielle's place right now. Ask her if she can tell whether the building is being watched."

Annette went to make the telephone call while John stayed in the park. He knew now that wherever he traveled in the city he was in real danger. Something had happened, he could not tell exactly what, but he knew that danger was everywhere in Paris for him that Sabbath day. The best place, for the present, was in the park.

Annette returned soon with the news that there was no one in Gabrielle's apartment and, as far as her friend could tell, the building wasn't being watched.

"Then you go there at once," Weidner said. "Be very careful as you approach the building. If you see anyone who looks even a little like the Gestapo, just walk on past and don't go in. If there is no one around, then go to Gabrielle's apartment and look for your identification papers, which I'm sure she has hidden. And look for the objects I left there Thursday night. Get one of your friends to act as lookout while you are inside. You shouldn't spend more than ten minutes at the most in the apartment, because the Gestapo could return at any time. Come back here as quickly as you can."

An hour later Annette was back in the park. Triumphantly she whispered that she had the objects and had located her identification papers.

"I found them quickly," she explained, as she pointed to her purse where she carried them. "I knew Gabrielle might have put the papers in one of her books, but I didn't know which one. In the first book I opened, there were the papers. The pencil and the keys were in the record player."

They went quickly to Pastor Meyer's home, and John gathered his things, including a briefcase with more than one million francs in it. The briefcase was Dutch-Paris's "treasure chest," from which Weidner paid the expenses of the far-flung underground organization.

He also telephoned news of Gabrielle's arrest to Moen (Salomon Chait), asking him to come to the park immediately. After returning to the park, Weidner arranged for Annette to stay at the home of a trusted friend.

"Oh, here is something else I found in Gabrielle's apartment," Annette said, handing John a small picture of himself. "It was on the bed, face down. She must have put it there to let you know the Gestapo is after you, too."

After meeting Moen and another man in the park, Weidner went to the apartment of his friend Gilbert Beaujolin, who had given him the use of the apartment any time he needed it. He let himself in quietly and settled down to an uneasy night's rest.

272

Early in the morning John met Annette, and together they returned to the park, where Moen and Mrs. Laatsman were waiting for them.

"Herman was arrested yesterday morning!" Mrs. Laatsman said. "They came at seven o'clock, before we were even up, and dragged him away. Anne-Marie, Okkie, and Pierre have also been arrested. There has been a mass arrest throughout the city, but just how many of our group is gone I don't know."

How, John wondered, could all these arrests be occurring at the same time? Yesterday he had felt that Gabrielle's arrest might have resulted from a review of his file by the Gestapo, although he did not believe they had her name in that file.

But now, with all the arrests coming at once, there had to be something more important than just a review of files. He searched through his memory over the names of those in the organization for clues to an answer. Who could be responsible for these mass arrests? Who had made contact with most of the organization's leaders? Who knew where they all lived? Finally, the answer became clear.

"I believe it is Suzy," he said to Moen and Mrs. Laatsman.

They stared unbelieving at him.

"Only Suzy knew the addresses of all those who have been arrested," John continued. "She didn't know the addresses of those who have not been arrested. She must have kept names in a book or recorded them somehow. I can't believe it either, but it has to be Suzy. Even Gabrielle's

10   273

name was known to her. I gave Gabrielle's name to Suzy, and she gave Suzy some clothes smuggled in from Switzerland."

Even after detailing his belief about Suzy in full, not everyone thought as John did, and even he did not want to believe what his mind told him must be true. But they had to agree that someone had talked to the Gestapo to cause the mass arrests. Every member of Dutch-Paris was now in grave danger; anyone could be arrested at any moment—and worst of all, no one knew how much information the Gestapo really had!

Shocked still further by this latest blow, John struggled to form a plan of action. He sent word to Brussels by Jacques Rens to warn the group there to disband and scatter immediately.

He sent Moen to Lyons and Annecy and returned Annette to the home where she had been staying to await further word.

Weidner went back to Beaujolin's apartment to wait out the hours until his leaders could give him information from Brussels and Lyons. He knew it was probably the safest place he could be—right in the heart of Paris—with the Gestapo searching all of France for him.

A few days later his lieutenants arrived in Paris with news far worse than John expected.

"In Brussels nearly the whole group had been arrested before I got there," Jacques reported. "Paul, David, Hans, and many American fliers whom they were leading toward Paris have been captured. Fortunately, Pastor Ten Kate, one of the Brussels leaders, is still free. Nearly thirty of our people are gone, and there have been arrests of our agents in Holland as well. The Gestapo must have been given many names of people, whose houses they watched, because they arrested anyone who visited suspected homes."

David Verloop, a brilliant young Dutchman in Belgium, tried desperately to save his friends in the Brussels group by telling the Gestapo he was the Dutch-Paris leader in the city. Others in the organization tried to stop him, but he would not listen to them. When the Gestapo took him to the sixth floor of the jail, he suddenly broke away from his guards and hurled himself down the long stairway. He was dead when he landed at the bottom. The Gestapo, seeing his heroic act, really believed he was the leader and that all the plans and responsibility of the Brussels group died with him. A devout young Christian, Verloop was at that time the youngest person to hold the doctor of philosophy degree in all of Holland.

Things in Lyons were no better than in Brussels. Weidner's secretary, Raymonde; Pastor Paul Meyer, of the Lyons Adventist Church; and Jacquet were all arrested. About twenty others had disappeared. In Annecy several people, including Miss Meunier, had also been taken into custody.

In Vichy, Mario Janse, who had succeeded Arie Sevenster as the last unofficial Dutch representative in France, was arrested as part of the mass roundup of Dutch-Paris members. When he was in Vichy a few days after this, Weidner heard of Janse's arrest. Leaving Vichy that same evening, John went by train to Paris. As he stepped from the train in Paris, he saw Janse. Around him were six guards, and he was heavily shackled. The two men looked at each other only a split second, but soundless conversation passed between them. "Go ahead with the war," Janse's fleeting glance told John. "Don't let this blow stop the work of saving lives." And Weidner's look told the faithful Janse, "Take courage, Mario. We will care for your family."

The mass arrest was a catastrophe for Dutch-Paris. In one day the core of the organization had been swept away by the Gestapo. Now, as Rens and Chait reported further on what they had found, John realized that nearly 150 members of Dutch-Paris had been arrested in the carefully executed plan which had certainly been aimed at trapping him, too.

"We have made a big mistake in having Suzy travel so much," he told the two men. "The responsibility, of course, is mine. But I had full confidence in the girl. She was recommended very highly by Herman, and she did good work, too. She has probably been tortured, but I didn't think she would talk even under torture. And why would she give the name of someone like Pastor Paul Meyer, who wasn't even a part of the organization? He has done nothing but give some food and shelter to the Jews."

Although the Gestapo had all but ruined the operation of Dutch-Paris, the four biggest names in the group were still not in their hands—Nykerk, who had been selected to replace Laatsman in Paris; Rens, Chait, and Weidner.

"Although we have suffered a great disaster, we can still rebuild," John told Jacques and Moen. "We must leave

276

Paris and start recruiting and reorganizing from Switzerland. The loss of Herman is a heavy one, but the four of us can still operate the main escape lines. We still have about 150 members left, and we can add new agents. The organization must go on, for the work is far from finished."

A few hours later Benno Nykerk got in touch with the trio, and Weidner began to give basic directions for Dutch-Paris's work in the future.

Nykerk was sent back to Brussels to contact Pastor Ten Kate and anyone else left who could be trusted. Chait went to Toulouse, and Jacques took Annette to Switzerland and reported to Dr. Visser 't Hooft and General Van Tricht. Weidner remained in Paris for a day to organize another nucleus there. He arranged to go to Lyons, then Annecy, and back to a rendezvous with his leaders one week later at the Restaurant la Provencale in Paris.

Annette arrived in Geneva exhausted. For several months she lay critically ill as a result of the emotional strain of the Dutch-Paris disaster and the arrest of her sister.

The Gestapo posted a five-million-franc reward for Weidner's arrest, and he was considered one of the most-wanted underground leaders in France. So desperate were the Gestapo that through German diplomatic channels they protested to the Swiss government because of the refuge John had taken in that country.

In Switzerland shortly after he began reorganizing Dutch-Paris, he learned that Gabrielle was imprisoned just outside Paris, as bait to tempt him to make a rescue try which the Gestapo hoped would result in his capture.

She sent word that she had not been tortured and that her treatment was reasonable. But she warned John that under no circumstances was he to try to help her.

During her stay in Fresnes a German Seventh-day Adventist soldier, with whom John had studied at Collonges, heard that Weidner's sister was in the prison and went to her carrying words of comfort and a Bible which she might read. When he came out from his visit, however, he was seen by suspicious officials, arrested, and sentenced to one month in jail for this humanitarian act.

In Switzerland Weidner spent long hours weighing the possibilities of rescuing Gabrielle. If he tried to help her and his plans did not succeed, it could only make things worse. If she was to be kept in France merely to tempt him, and was not mistreated, he felt sure of seeing her when the war ended. And, much as his heart ached to go to Gabrielle, he knew he should not jeopardize the existence of the entire organization for his own interests. He thought of arranging the exchange of Gabrielle for himself, but nothing in the Gestapo's past actions suggested they would honor such an arrangement. Even as he weighed the possibilities in his mind, he knew he could not help her.

XIX

toulouse journey

DURING April, 1944, Dr. Visser 't Hooft advised John about his future action. "You must be extremely careful in your movements here in Switzerland from now on," he said. "The Germans have made unofficial protests to the Swiss government, stating that you are organizing underground activities from Swiss territory. They say this is a violation of Swiss neutrality."

As he listened, John realized that he would have to devise even more secret methods. Nazi undercover agents followed him even when he was in Switzerland.

"More information has just come from London, too," Dr. Visser 't Hooft continued. "The Allied command wants an underground leader in England who will represent all the various units that are now active in Holland. The Dutch underground troops have chosen Gerrit van Heuven Goedhart, who took over as a leader of *Het Parool,* one of the Resistance newspapers, after the arrest of Frans Goedhart.

"As you know, John, Gerrit Goedhart has been one of those who have helped us send information to London. And

279

we want you to see that he gets safely from the Dutch border to Spain. You will have to plan the operation carefully, because Gerrit is a very important man—especially if he should fall into German hands. You will use the code name ZBM (Dutch for VIP) in all references to him. He is one of the most-wanted men in Holland, and the Dutch government in exile is putting high hopes on the success of this operation. If we can get Gerrit out of occupied Europe, it will be a real blow to the Nazis. He can provide valuable information to officials in London. You should be on the Belgian border on Monday, the 24th, and Lejeune, our agent from Holland, will bring ZBM to you there. Your job is to get him safely from that point into Spain. Spend whatever money is necessary to make the mission successful."

Leaving Geneva, John slipped once again through the border to Annecy, then to Lyons, and finally to Paris, where he spent hours planning the operation with Moen and Rens. Weidner assigned Moen to bring ZBM from Belgium to Toulouse. Jacques Rens was directed to take the underground leader over the Pyrenees into Spain.

On Monday, April 24, Weidner was in Belgium at the assigned rendezvous point with Moen to meet ZBM. The contact was made very smoothly without difficulty, and John turned the underground chief over to Moen for the trip to Toulouse.

A short time later John returned to Geneva and reported to Dr. Visser 't Hooft that the first phase of the Goedhart operation was successful. The information was radioed to London.

While Weidner was with the church leader making his report, Dr. Visser 't Hooft relayed further orders to him from London.

"They want you to come over there now and talk with them about Dutch-Paris and explain the general situation relating to the morale of the Dutch people you have been contacting. And there is some important, highly secret information you must take when you go."

John agreed to carry the information to London. First, however, he would need to visit all the operations centers of the newly reorganized Dutch-Paris. He would leave direction of the different units in the hands of Jacques, Moen, and the others while he went to England.

On May 4, Joop Bartels, Dr. Visser 't Hooft's secretary, gave Weidner instructions for his trip to London. Bartels also gave him two objects—a large clothes brush and a flashlight—in which he would carry the secret information. Into the brush were stuffed two thousand microfilms. The flashlight contained microfilm showing various underground newspapers published in Holland—information which the Nazis already possessed. If apprehended, John would surrender the flashlight decoy as though it contained all the information he was carrying. When he reached Toulouse, Bartels said, John could expect to receive more information to be carried to London. He would also stop at Vichy to make financial arrangements for continuing the refugee work.

Weidner crossed the Swiss-French border safely and arrived in Annecy without incident. There he talked with his underground members about future work, then took the train for Paris. On Friday, when the train arrived in Paris, there was good news from Jacques.

"We have heard from Gabrielle," he told John. "She is still in Fresnes and has not been tortured. But she says again you should not try to help her in any way because the Gestapo is still using her as bait in a trap set for you."

The news cheered John considerably. At least his sister had not been mistreated, and perhaps the Gestapo might realize, after all, that she was not part of the underground.

Other messages had been picked up from Dutch-Paris members who were in prison at Fresnes and Compiégne. Paul Veerman arrived from Brussels about the same time John reached Paris, carrying several important messages from members captured in the Belgian city. The three leaders talked through the day about their plans for action while John was in England.

On Tuesday, May 9, John met Rens and Veerman in Toulouse and made final arrangements for Gerrit van Heuven Goedhart's departure to Spain the next day. He was being kept in the city after the trip with Moen from the Belgian border.

Moen would stay in Toulouse to handle operations there. Jacques, instead of going with Goedhart, was to return that evening to Switzerland to pick up any last-minute information for delivery to London. Veerman was to take charge of Goedhart on the first leg of his escape through the Pyrenees. With Moen, John visited a group of Quakers who had been giving important help to Dutch-Paris in Toulouse.

On Wednesday night they were aboard the late train leaving Toulouse. They went to Vichy, where Weidner introduced Chait to officials as the contact who would be taking his place while he was in London. While there they also visited Mrs. Mario Janse, wife of the imprisoned Dutch official. She expressed confidence that she would be seeing her husband again soon. On Thursday night the two men left Vichy for Lyons, where John gave some money to the families of Dutch-Paris members who had been arrested by the Gestapo as a result of Suzy Kraay's confession.

Two young Dutchmen from a refugee group in Toulouse were selected to carry the same information as Weidner to help assure that the messages got through. They were to enter Spain via the *wagon plombes,* sealed railway boxcars, which Dutch-Paris used infrequently.

Trains which carried merchandise between southern France and Spain were always inspected by the Germans, then each car was sealed with a lead seal before the train left its last stop in southern France, often Toulouse. The enterprising railway employees who worked for the Resistance had succeeded in stealing lead and a copy of the official seal. After the seals had been affixed by the Germans and before the train pulled out of the yards, these underground workers would break the seals, spirit refugees or couriers aboard the cars, then reaffix the seals with their stolen materials. Sometimes refugees who were not strong enough physically to stand the rugged climb over the Pyrenees were put aboard these boxcars. The underground seldom used this plan, though, because the Germans had learned about it.

The *wagon plombes* method of transport had been discussed for Goedhart by the Dutch-Paris leaders, but it was later dismissed because of the hazard of detection by the Germans. Several bad experiences convinced Weidner the safest route for Goedhart lay in the hard climb over the mountains. Following a hazardous trek over the Pyrenees into Spain, the underground leader proceeded to Portugal, from where he flew to England.

After his arrival in London, Gerrit van Heuven Goedhart became Minister of Justice of Her Majesty the Queen's government of Holland in exile. After the war he became executive editor of the daily newspaper *Het Parool,* the same paper published underground during the war. In 1947 he was named to the United Nations subcommission on press freedom. On December 14, 1950, he was appointed United Nations high commissioner for refugees. In 1955 he accepted the Nobel Prize for work done by members of his commission.

On Saturday night, May 20, Weidner, Rens, and Veerman were joined at Le Club Restaurant by Gabriel Nahas, who knew the Pyrenees route very well by now. They avoided speaking of John's trip across the mountains as they ate to minimize the risk of being overheard by someone sitting nearby. There were many other important matters to be discussed, however, and the pleasant meal passed quickly.

Out into the fresh, evening air of Toulouse they came, four happy men, confident about the future. But that future suddenly disappeared with explosive swiftness.

284

"Get your hands up!" roared a man with an outthrust gun as they turned away from the restaurant. "Get your hands up, or we'll shoot you like dogs!"

The four men quickly raised their arms. Looking around, John counted five men in civilian clothes, each armed with a pistol. The underground leaders were shoved against the wall, arms still up, and searched for weapons; then one of the captors began taking their papers. As he reached into Nahas's coat pocket, the papers he had collected from the others dropped to the sidewalk. When he stooped to collect the documents, Nahas pushed himself from the wall and ran as fast as he could down the street.

"Shoot him, shoot him; he's getting away!" shouted the leader of the armed men. Although the man collecting the papers brought his pistol up to shoot, no sound came from his gun, and he was blocking the line of fire of the others.

"My gun's jammed—it misfired or something," he stammered as he lowered the weapon. At that moment Nahas, running for his life, turned a corner and disappeared.

"Fine time to have a jammed gun!" fumed the leader. "Well, come on, let's get these others to headquarters."

They handcuffed their prisoners and marched them down the street.

Walking ahead of the menacing guns, John tried to think who these men could be—what part of whose government they were. When he saw the symbol on the building to which they were being taken, he instantly recognized it as the headquarters of the Milice, that special police group which operated under the direct orders of Joseph Darnand, arch Nazi collaborator in Vichy. Neither of the French leaders, Marshal Pétain or Pierre Laval, trusted Darnand fully. But in January, 1944, his cooperation with the Nazis brought him a cabinet position, chief of all French police, and, of course, director of the Milice, which he had now been directing for some time.

The Milice operated completely independent of the regular French police forces; they took orders only from Darnand. They were, in fact, at odds with the regular French police more often than not. They were not an actual part of the German Gestapo, but were often called the French Gestapo because they had the same aim and used the same techniques. They worked closely with the Nazis to destroy the Resistance.

Inside the building each of the three men was taken into a different room for questioning.

"It is good to see you, Mr. Dupont," said the interrogator as John sat down in the room to which he had been taken. "We have been looking for you everywhere, and here you are right in the heart of Toulouse."

John was confused by the greeting. To his knowledge he had never used the name Dupont in his work. His papers, which the Milice had taken at the restaurant, were made out in a false name, that was true. But John could be sure of them; they had been prepared by de Gaulle agents working in the French documents office, and they were registered throughout France. Jacques and Paul had similar papers.

"Dupont—I know no Dupont," John replied to his interrogator. "I am not Mr. Dupont, believe me."

"You aren't, eh?" responded the Milice officer. "You have a moustache—Mr. Dupont has a moustache. Your features are those of Mr. Dupont. Everything about you says you are Dupont, but you deny it. Here, take a look at this picture. Is this not you, Mr. Dupont?"

John looked at the photo which the officer held out. Yes, he had to admit, he looked like the man in the picture. In recent weeks to cloak his true identity, John had grown a moustache, and he had started wearing glasses. In assuming this disguise, he had unknowingly begun to look remarkably like the man in the photograph.

As the questioning continued, the Milice officer insisted that John was Dupont, and Weidner continued to deny it. From the questions he was able to learn that Dupont was a young leader in the French underground who had killed several members of the French Gestapo. He had been arrested and tortured, but had escaped in another part of France. When he escaped, his description was sent throughout France, and orders were issued for his immediate arrest. Finally another officer came in.

"Your friend Jacques has confirmed to us that you are Dupont," he stated. "Now what do you have to say?"

"There is nothing to say except that it is impossible since I am not Dupont," John countered.

"All right, I have had enough!" the interrogator shouted. "We'll give you a little taste of our electricity here and see if that will help you think more clearly!"

In the corner of the room Weidner could see the wires of the infamous Milice torture device, which they coupled with the bathtub torture adopted from the German Gestapo. The officers shoved him across the room and stripped away his clothes. Then the electrical wires were attached to sensitive parts of his body. When the switch was thrown, a hot, burning current jolted his body with terrible pain.

"Wait a minute," said one of the men. "The report we got says Dupont should have fresh wounds on his shoulders. This fellow hasn't got a scratch. Maybe he isn't Dupont after all. Let's phone Vichy. The original report is there."

In a few minutes they came back. "Well, Vichy says if you don't have fresh wounds on your right shoulder, then you are not Dupont," one of the Frenchmen said. "So you are not Dupont, and we'll have to let you go."

The handcuffs were removed from Weidner, and he put on his clothes again and started for the door.

"But just a minute." An officer stopped him as he was about to leave. "We still don't know your real name."

John now tried to avoid giving an answer as to what his name was. He was not willing to give his real name, of course, knowing that to give it would put him in a worse position than if he were actually Dupont. This reluctance on his part made the Milice deeply suspicious, and they began to fire a barrage of questions at him once again. His answers were evasive.

"We have plenty of ways of finding out what your name is if you don't cooperate, you know," an officer asserted.

"Yes, I know," agreed John. "But I do not care to tell you my name. I have done nothing wrong. You know that I am not Dupont, so why don't you just let me go?"

"No, not until you tell us your name; we want that name," insisted the officer. "Guards, take him to the bathtub!"

The guards started stripping his clothes from his body once again.

"Here it comes," John thought. "Here comes that tub again!"

Another officer rushed into the room just as they were about to throw the underground chief into the tub of cold water.

"Of course he isn't Dupont!" the man shouted. "He is John Weidner. Here is the file on him from the Germans. Here is his picture without moustache, but you can see that he is Weidner all right! This is John Weidner, chief of Dutch-Paris. We have really caught a big fish this time!"

"Very good! Very good!" said the officer in charge, a note of triumph in his voice. "Well, Mr. Weidner, you please us very much. We wanted Dupont, but we are ten times happier to have John Weidner. Now you will tell us where you live here in Toulouse!"

John, knowing that important documents were in the room where they were staying, would not give the address.

"I will not tell," he told the Milice.

"Well, you can rest a bit." The officer questioning him smiled. "We'll see what your friends in the other rooms have to say."

The officers then went to the room where Jacques Rens was being questioned. They told him Weidner had confessed everything. Using John's real name, which they had discovered from their files, they were able to make Jacques believe that a confession had actually taken place, since Rens knew Weidner was operating under a false name. As the Milice dropped further facts about Weidner, taken not from John but from his files, Jacques became further convinced that his companion had actually confessed. When they put the question of where the underground leaders were staying, Rens gave a correct answer, thinking that he was only confirming facts Weidner had already confessed.

Immediately the three prisoners were assembled in one room, then marched off to the apartment. John realized one of his companions must have given the address.

"Take whatever you will need overnight, because you will be staying in the prison," the men were advised when they reached the room.

John picked up his shaving kit and a small bag of clothes. He was about to take the clothes brush in which microfilm was hidden, but then he stopped. "If I take it with me, they will probably go over everything thoroughly at the jail to see if we have anything hidden," he thought to himself. "The microfilm might never get to England if I leave it here, but at least it won't fall into the hands of the Milice and the Gestapo."

He turned away from the table without a flicker of recognition crossing his face. "We've got everything of importance," he said. "We're ready to go now."

At Milice headquarters the men were placed in separate cells. The next morning John was brought before the French Gestapo for more questioning.

"Captain Weidner, we know what you have been doing. We know everything about you and your organization. Your organization has many Frenchmen working for it. Some were caught in the mass arrest in February, but many are still at work. We want you to tell us the names of these people. We are not interested in the names of Dutch or Belgians, only the French."

"I know what you want," responded Weidner. "If I give you the names of these French people, then you will have them arrested. Some will be tortured; many will be deported to Germany or Poland. Some will be killed. The French people working with us have confidence in me. They know I will never give their names, because my conscience would not let me do so. You can cut my tongue out, put out my eyes—anything—but I will not give their names. I will not betray those people."

As he spoke, Weidner suddenly felt supremely sure that God would give him strength to withstand any torture which might come. He also felt sure that this hour might be the worst he had ever experienced, and he prayed that his mind would stay clear, his mouth closed. He knew that if he gave the names of Frenchmen working for him, that would not be the end. Next the Milice would demand other information, and the process could go on for days or weeks. If he talked once, there would be no stopping until everything had been told.

Again he was stripped and led to the bathtub, this time to face water torture combined with the electrical shocks. The added torment would make the ordeal almost unbearable. In a desperate effort to avoid the tub, John turned to the officer.

"I would like to speak with your chief," he said. "I have something to tell him that I cannot tell you—it is for his ears only."

"You want to speak to l'Intendant Marty?" asked the officer with a smug expression on his face. "He is too important a man for you to deal with."

"Yes, but I have something that I will say only to him," replied Weidner. "He will want to hear what I have to say. Ask him; he will listen to me."

The officer finally agreed. "Put his clothes back on him, and we shall see," he said to the guards.

John was taken back to his cell.

Two hours later they returned. He was handcuffed, then led through the corridors to the huge office occupied by Milice Chief Marty.

This man, Weidner realized, was one of the worst collaborators in all of France. He had worked his way up through one collaborationist post to another, always keeping a false front to the French people while actively accepting assignments for the Nazis. Underneath it all, though, he was a Frenchman who should have some sense of honor as a citizen of his country. It was to this honor that Weidner had decided to appeal.

"You have asked to see me?" the Milice chief said, a sour look on his face. "What do you want?"

"You know that your men have arrested me," began Weidner. "And you know that I am the chief of an escape organization. But it is also true that none of the people in my organization, or I myself, have ever used violence or killed anyone among the French or Germans. We love our country and want only to be free. But the Germans have occupied my country and your country against our will. They are arresting people whose only crime is that they do not think like the Germans. But what is worse, they are arresting many people just because they are Jewish. I feel it is my duty, as a human being, to save lives. That has been the reason for my organization.

"We don't want to harm France," continued the Dutch-Paris leader. "But we have to go through your country in order to find freedom in Switzerland or Spain. Our consuls have been arrested. We cannot get transit visas through France, so we have to work secretly. Your men have arrested us and are asking questions about the names and addresses of people helping us. If I give these addresses, your men will arrest these people. These French people have confidence in me. It would be horrible for me to deceive them, to betray their confidence.

"You know by the reports you have received on me that I have never spoken even under torture. I will not speak now, even if your men kill me. I am, as you know, an officer in the Dutch army, and you are an officer in the French army. If I had arrested you and asked you to give the names of your agents, would you do it?"

John was trying desperately to make the Milice director feel exactly as he felt, hoping to awaken a spark of honor between two military officers. Even though the chief was working with the Germans, John felt he still had a sense of personal honor.

Marty sat deep in thought for several minutes.

"I see what you mean," he said at last. Turning in his chair toward the door, he shouted, "Guards, take the handcuffs from this officer." To John he said, "I will not ask you any further questions, and I will give orders to my men not to ask you anything further, either."

"I hope you will see fit to release me," Weidner pressed, now hoping that his words might cause the Milice chief to set him free. "And I hope, too, that you will not give information to the Germans about my arrest. They have condemned me to death and are looking everywhere for me."

"I would personally be happy to release you," conceded Marty. "But I cannot do so. I can arrest people, but to release them I need authorization from my chief, Darnand, in Vichy. I am going to send a confidential report to him about you, though. I will tell him I think you should be released. I'm sure he will accept my recommendation, and in a few days you can be set free."

Then the Milice leader called in his officers to tell them of his decision to stop questioning Weidner. He also warned them not to take Weidner back to the torture room again without specific authorization.

Later in the day one of the officers who had arrested John outside the restaurant came to his cell. "Are you a Protestant?" he asked Weidner.

"I am a Seventh-day Adventist," the Dutch-Paris chief answered. "But why do you ask me a question like that?"

"Well, I found this Bible in the pocket of your jacket," the officer said.

"Oh, others besides Protestants carry Bibles. I have many Catholic friends who carry Bibles, as do many of my Jewish acquaintances," John explained.

"Maybe so," said the officer, "but I thought yours was a Protestant Bible. I am a Catholic myself, and I know Protestants read the Bible more than we do. I have much respect for those who read the Bible. I studied for some time in the University of Montpellier. There I met several Protestants who read their Bibles regularly, and I learned to respect them for their moral values."

Now, as he heard the officer's words, John was happy that he carried the Scriptures with him at all times. The little Bible the officer had found, however, was not the regular, larger one he usually carried. The small volume had been given to him as a present in the restaurant by Gabriel Nahas as they sat eating the night they were arrested.

The officer standing outside the bars continued to talk with John. His name, he said, was Rene Brunner.

The two men talked for a long time, with Brunner bringing up many of his personal problems. Often their conversation returned to religious questions, and Brunner seemed to gain strength from the advice John gave him.

Shortly after he had been returned to his cell from Marty's office, John learned some exciting news when the guards brought Jacques to his cell.

"Where is Paul Veerman?" John asked the guards, afraid something had happened to him.

The guards summoned one of the officers, who, red-faced, said, "Ah, that is quite a problem. You see, we were so interested in you two that momentarily we forgot about Mr. Veerman. Somehow he was able to escape. We are most interested in him, because if the Gestapo finds him in the city, they will learn that the two of you are here, and we cannot keep them from taking you."

John did not think too much of the officer's reasoning, but he was concerned that Marty might change his plans to contact Vichy if he found out about Veerman's escape. Still, Weidner could not help but rejoice silently at his friend's good fortune.

Brunner returned to the cell a short time later to ask John if he had any idea where Veerman might have gone.

"We must get him back, or it will go badly for you," he said. "If you will come with me to look for him, I will agree not to follow you as you go into buildings—if you agree not to try to escape."

John decided to go along with Brunner's suggestion. Brunner was putting his confidence in Weidner, and John would not betray this confidence.

He did not hope to persuade Veerman to return to the Milice headquarters, even if he found him. But he saw the unusual arrangement as an opportunity to tell other members of the underground in Toulouse what was happening to their leaders.

John felt a surge of happiness as he stepped into the sunlight again. When they were about a block from the first address John wanted to visit, he stopped Brunner.

"This is the first place," he explained. "You stay here, and when I get up the block a short distance, turn around. I'll be watching; and if you turn toward me, I won't go inside at all. You keep your word, and I'll keep mine."

As he walked up the street, John could see that the Milice officer had turned away from him. He went quickly to the apartment of Abbe de Stegge, a Catholic priest who was a member of Dutch-Paris. The young clergyman had information about Veerman.

"He went to the apartment and got the objects," the priest said. "Then he gave them to one of the young Dutchmen, who should be over the mountains by this time. Right now Paul is on the train traveling toward Switzerland to tell Dr. Visser 't Hooft what has happened to you."

John left the building and found Brunner, still standing with his back turned, far down the street. Apparently he was keeping his word.

John next went to the homes of several other Dutch-Paris members, telling each what had happened. Finally he reported to Brunner.

"There is nothing I can do. Veerman has left Toulouse," he said.

The long hours in a fifth-floor prison cell were punctuated almost daily by the screams from the Milice torture room. Often a prisoner, more dead than alive, was dragged past their cell. Brunner stopped at the cell frequently, and he and Weidner continued their discussions.

One morning an officer came to the cell. "I am sorry," he said, "but Darnand has refused to release you, Mr. Weidner. Vichy has also informed the German Gestapo of your presence here. Tomorrow they are coming to take you. Preparations for your execution are already made at their headquarters. If you have any letters to write to your family or other papers you care to make out, you should do that today. Here is some paper and a pencil. I'm sorry not to have better news for you."

Both John and Jacques were shocked by the news. They had believed Marty's appeal in their behalf would be favorably received in Vichy and that they would be released. But now the opposite had happened. They had only one more day of life left.

Some time later Brunner came to their cell.

"I've just heard the bad news," he began. "I'm really sorry for you. I wish I could do something."

Hearing the officer speak, John had a sudden inspiration. "I'll try to get him to help us escape," he thought. "We have to escape; it is our only hope."

"You know that the war is coming to an end soon, Brunner," John said to the officer. "Soon the Allies will be landing in France and in the rest of Europe. After the war you and all the members of your group will be arrested. You will have no chance to escape; there will be no place to go. You will doubtless be shot because you have killed so many underground people.

"Now let's make a proposition," John ventured. "Help us escape from here; go with us to Switzerland. It is a neutral country; nobody can touch you there or bring you to trial. I will speak for you in Switzerland and will give you help to start a new life. You will be saved, and we will also be saved."

The two men waited for an answer from Brunner with agonized impatience.

"I'm sorry, but I can't do it," he replied. "I have been with this outfit since the beginning, and I will stay with it till the end. Whatever happens to me will happen."

John took another desperate tack. "We don't want to be shot by the Gestapo. We must try to escape by ourselves then, but we really need your help."

"Well, what do you want from me?" quietly asked the officer.

"First, we need to be placed on the third floor of the prison. From there we can reach the office where the windows look out onto the street. We can try to escape the same way Paul Veerman did. Then we need the keys to the cell so that we can open it tonight."

"Probably I can help you to get down to the third floor," said Brunner. "But I can't give you the keys, because the jailer is the only one who has them."

"All right, but you can get us some tools to force the door on the cell," John pleaded.

The Milice officer thought that over and finally agreed to help.

"The door will not be too hard to force, because cells down there are not made for dangerous prisoners. But don't escape before ten o'clock. The guards will be looking in on you every half hour before that time. You can't see them, but they can see you. And don't try to escape outside between 10 P.M. and six in the morning. That is the curfew time, and you will be picked up on the street if you do get out. Try to escape just after six in the morning. Good luck," he said as he left the cell, "and God help you."

A little later Weidner and Rens were transferred to a cell on the third floor. The jailer didn't like the idea, and he tried to get the two prisoners to give their word of honor that they wouldn't escape from the cell in which they were placed. They avoided answering him directly. Brunner, standing nearby as the jailer pressed them for a guarantee, smiled as Weidner engaged the key-keeper in a two-hour conversation to avoid committing himself.

When they were alone again, John confided to Rens, "I'm not absolutely sure about Brunner. After all, the Gestapo is known to encourage people to escape just so they can shoot them down."

For the next several hours John turned again to God for help in the attempt to escape. He recalled the miraculous Biblical story of Peter's escape from a jail cell. Yet he also remembered the fate of John the Baptist, who lost his life in somewhat similar circumstances.

About an hour after a nearby church clock tolled ten that night, Weidner and Rens began working at the door of their cell with the tools Brunner provided. They had the door open in about an hour. Weidner stepped out quietly to check the corridor. Near the door on the right side of the cell was a guard—asleep on the floor. Cradled between his legs was a machine gun. John returned to the cell, and he and Rens removed their shoes. Then, closing the door carefully behind them, they tiptoed past the sleeping guard. They turned a corner and saw another guard—also sleeping. Moving silently past him, they entered another corridor and made their way quickly to the office, whose door was open. Quietly they closed the door, then went to the window and pushed it open. On the street below a sentry was on duty, his gun slung over his shoulder.

There was nothing to do but wait until the soldier pacing his beat moved out of sight. Weidner and Rens both knew they would stand no chance in the streets during curfew. The five hours that crept by were, John remembers, probably the longest of his life. They lived the moments in fear that one of the guards near their cell would wake up and sound the escape alarm.

Finally the church clock struck six. Everything had worked smoothly, largely, he felt, because they had followed Brunner's instructions.

He had been honest with them thus far.

Waiting a few moments after the curfew ended, John opened the window again, and Jacques crawled through it when the sentry was at the farthest point from the building. Rens let himself stretch full length from the third-floor window sill, then dropped to the street below. Not able to see in the semidarkness, Weidner dropped to the sidewalk a few moments later. He landed on the ground with a sickening, stinging feeling in his legs, but no bones snapped.

Instantly they were on their feet, running madly down the sidewalk. After two blocks they turned a corner and then slowed to a normal pace, fighting to control themselves as they walked slowly along the streets. Half an hour after their escape, they reached the apartment of the Abbe de Stegge, where they were joined by Moen and three men, also on the run from the Germans.

"These men," Moen said, "are eager to get to Spain. I need your help in planning for them. This is Bob Van Der Stok, who escaped some weeks ago from Sagan camp, up near the Polish border.

"The other two are Rudy Schreidemakers, a Dutch secret service agent on his way to London; and Father Lodewyck, a Catholic priest who has been called to England to care for the needs of the Dutch Catholics in the army there."

After the brief meeting Weidner and Rens hurried off to the Maurice Lejeune home, where they entered a hidden bunker. During the week, while police combed Toulouse for them, they helped Moen plan the escape of the three men he had brought from Belgium.

In March, 1944, seventy-six airmen in one of the most thrilling of all World War II escapes, slipped through a tunnel under a specialized prisoner camp for Allied airmen at Sagan in Germany. Unfortunately, nearly all were recaptured, and fifty were shot on their way back to the camp. Only three of the seventy-six reached England. Among them was Bob Van Der Stok, a Dutchman in the RAF. Van Der Stok had reached Holland on his own. Underground friends got him to Belgium. There he came in contact with Dutch-Paris. John instructed Chait to help Van Der Stok to Toulouse, then over the Pyrenees to Spain. This assignment was successfully accomplished.

TOULOUSE JOURNEY

By June 1 new identification papers had been prepared for Weidner and Rens. Lacanal, one of the Toulouse underground agents, took them by car to Carcassonne, where they stayed in the home of a pharmacist named Billot until they caught a train to Annecy. They finally reached Geneva on Friday, June 2, nearly one month from the date of their arrest in Toulouse.

About the Illustrations

The editors were privileged to examine many documents and photographs relating to the John Weidner story. These substantially added to the documentation and provided a wider selectivity, from which were chosen the following thirty-two pages of illustrations.

and Basil Zarov, Montreal

Council of Churches, Geneva

Above, left: Arie Sevenster, Netherlands consul general in Paris and a close friend of Weidner's. He aided Dutch-Paris until imprisoned. Below, left: Dr. W. A. Visser 't Hooft, general secretary of the World Council of Churches from 1938 to 1966. Right: Skiing was often Weidner's safest method of travel between remote mountain villages along the French-Swiss border.

11   All illustrations were supplied by John Weidner.

S. A. Wehrli,

In the turreted towers of this castle at Aigle, Switzerland, Weidner's father served a prison sentence for his religious convictions.

Left: The village of Collonges. The road which runs from left to right in the lower part of the picture is the highway between St. Julien and Annemasse. Right: A determined climber scales the rough face of the Saleve.

Above: Seminaire Adventiste du Saleve, where Weidner attended school before the war. Right: Weidner and officials of the Franco-Belgian Union headquarters of Seventh-day Adventists in Paris prepare to leave the city ahead of the advancing German army.

Above: St. Julien customshouse, on the French-Swiss border. Below, left: The highway between St. Julien and Annemasse. Right: Salomon Chait, one of Weidner's underground assistants, who was entrusted with the "object."

Photo Helios, Geneva

Above, left: Jacques Rens, another leader in Dutch-Paris. He and Weidner were arrested and escaped together from the Milice prison at Toulouse. Right: A farmhouse just inside Switzerland which became a haven for escaping refugees. Below, left: Typical barbed-wire border blockade between St. Julien and Annemasse. Dozens of times Weidner crawled on hands and knees through similarly guarded borders. Right: Swiss customshouse at Collonges.

Photo Helios, Geneva

Above: Three typical members of the maquis, underground fighters who operated in the Savoy area of southern France. Below: The maquis check identification papers of people traveling through their district.

Photo Helios, Genev[a]

Above: British, French, and American flags fly above the customshouse at St. Julien. Some Dutch-Paris members worked in this building throughout the war. Left: Herman Laatsman, a member of the Dutch consulate in Paris, was ordered to Holland by the Germans when the war started. Instead, he joined Dutch-Paris and became head of the Paris group. Below: Gendarmerie at Cruseilles, where Weidner was severely beaten.

Above, left: Catholic priests pose for photographs in Lyons before being evacuated by Dutch-Paris. Right: A priest and two other refugees prepare to leave Lyons. Below: The city of Geneva, with the Saleve and Mont Blanc in the background.

aeger, Geneva

Above, left: Street scene along the lake in Geneva. Right: The rugged Saleve. Left: Marie-Louise Meunier, a close friend of Weidner's, operated a store in Annecy which sheltered many Jewish refugees. Below: Lake Annecy and part of the town of Annecy.

Photo-Eclair, Annecy

Weidner's shop was to the left of the double doors. Through his store window he could watch the swans swimming peacefully in the lake.

Compagnie des Arts Photomécaniques

A typical street in Annecy where Weidner's shop was located.

Compagnie des Arts Photomécaniques

Castle of Count de Menthon near Annecy. Weidner helped the count and members of his family escape to Switzerland.

Above: Interior of the Paris Seventh-day Adventist church. Gabrielle Weidner was captured here by the Gestapo during a Sabbath morning service. Below: When the Gestapo was closing in on Weidner's store in Annecy, he fled to this hotel at Morzine.

Above: Railroad station at Toulouse where Dutch-Paris members frequently brought escapees from Paris. Below: City of Toulouse, the jumping-off point for the Pyrenees escape route.

Gabrielle Weidner, shortly before her fatal arrest.

Left: David Verloop, brilliant young co-leader of Dutch-Paris in Brussels. Verloop took his own life rather than disclose Dutch-Paris activities to the Gestapo. Below: The Milice prison in Toulouse from which Weidner and Jacques Rens escaped. They jumped from the small window in the third story to the courtyard below.

Picturesque road and village of the Pyrenees.

Pau-Billere

A group of refugees with their Dutch-Paris guide ready to cross the Pyrenees.

Dutch-Paris refugees plow through knee-deep snowdrifts in a rugged Pyrenees pass.

Gabriel Nahas, who organized Dutch-Paris escape routes and directed the Pyrenees operation.

Pastor Paul Meyer, who died in a concentration camp.

Control station at Andorra on the border between France and Spain.

Photo Helios, Geneva

Above: The first American liberation forces, who drove to the Swiss border from landings on the Mediterranean coast, arrive in St. Julien. Below: Captured Nazis bury their officers who were killed in the invasion.

Foto Verheu

Above, inset: Informal meeting after the war brought together (left to right) Benno Nykerk's brother, Mrs. Paul Veerman, Salomon Chait, and Paul Veerman. Above: Full-scale reunion of Dutch-Paris members after the Armistice. Left: Col. Frank M. S. Johnson, U.S. military attaché, pins Medal of Freedom with Gold Palm on Weidner in ceremonies at Het Binnenhof, The Hague, Netherlands.

Godfried de Groot, Amsterdam

Above, left: Queen Wilhelmina, of the Netherlands, with whom Weidner had an important conference in London just before the end of the war. Right: Queen Juliana and Prince Bernhard, of the Netherlands, congratulate Weidner at a reception in Paris. Below: John and officials march to the "Mont Valerien" overlooking Paris, where the first Dutch resistant in France, Yan Doornick, was executed by German firing squad.

Above, left: Ambassador Boetzelaer looks on as Weidner and the Dutch military attaché lay wreaths on the spot where the first underground members were killed. Right: A monument at Senlis, near Paris, honors members of the Dutch underground who aided France. Among those named are Gabrielle Weidner, Benno Nykerk, and Paul Meyer. Below, right: Weidner honors the maquis in a ceremony at Plateau des Glieres.

Photo Dubost

EN HOMMAGE
A
MAURICE JACQUET
CONSUL GÉNÉRAL DES PAYS-BAS
MEMBRE DU RÉSEAU DUTCH-PARIS
QUI FUT ARRETÉ DANS CET IMMEUBLE
PAR LA GESTAPO LE 28-2-1944
DÉPORTÉ-RÉSISTANT A
MAUTHAUSEN
DÉCÉDÉ DES SUITES DE SA DÉPORTATION
A LYON LE 18-10-61

n honor of Maurice Jacquet, consul general of
e Netherlands, a member of the reseau Dutch-
ris, who was arrested in this building by the
estapo the 28th of February, 1944. Deported
esistant at Mauthausen [concentration camp].
ied as a result of his deportation at Lyon 18
ctober, 1961."

Weidner participates in ceremonies in Paris, October, 1945, at the Arc de Triomphe, for the underground of several European nations.

reception in Paris before Weidner leaves for the United States. Between Weidner and Gilbert Beaujolin (leaning forward at left) sits former Netherlands ambassador to France, Baron Van Boetzelaer Van Oosterhout. Below: Weidner receives a special award from the American Jewish Congress (AJC) in Los Angeles for his service during the war. Left to right: I. M. Prinzmetal, national vice-president of AJC; Hon. W. P. Hasselman, consul general of the Netherlands; Weidner; Hon. Mordecai Shalev, consul general of Israel; and Cree Sandefur, president of the Southern California Conference of Seventh-day Adventists.

Les Reportages de France

V. M. Hanks, San Francisco

Above: Weidner chats with Admiral Chester W. Nimitz at a reception in San Francisco's Palace of the Legion of Honor. Below: In a letter dated September 6, 1944, Xavier de Gaulle asks Weidner to take a message to his brother, Gen. Charles de Gaulle.

FROM THE GOLDEN BOOK OF
THE JEWISH NATIONAL FUND

למזכרת נצחי; מכתב תעודה
מספר הזהב שלקרן קיטת לישראל

JEAN WEIDNER

בין ויידנר

A group of Jewish businessmen in Holland whom Weidner helped during the war gave generously to enter his name in the Golden Book of Jerusalem.

This certificate states that trees have been planted in Israel to honor Weidner for his aid to Jews during the war.

Left: False identity card used by Weidner for wartime travel. Opposite: Another identity card with the name "Jacques Vernet." Weidner used fourteen different names in his underground work. Left: Identity card in the name of "Paul Lins." Opposite, right, Weidner's real travel permit issued in 1942. Within a few months after this permit was issued, he was forced underground. After that all permits were made in false names. Opposite, left, Weidner's permit in the name of "Paul Rey."

8110 SÉRIE: H

PRÉFECTURE DE la Haute-Savoie

Carte d'identité

Empreinte digitale

Nom: VERNET
Prénoms: Jacques
20 Novembre 1910
à Alger
Département Alger
à Alger sous-Alézy

Taille: 1 m. 74   Nez: droit
Cheveux: bruns   Forme générale
Moustache: du visage: ovale
Yeux: gris-vert
Signes particuliers: néant   Teint: mat

le 10 Avril 1943
Le Préfet.
Pour le Préfet et par délégation
Le Chef de Division

CARTE D'IDENTITÉ

Jutel Paris n° 5   D P 5
Empreintes Digitales

Nom REY
Prénoms Paul
Profession représentant
Nationalité fr.
Né le 8 février 1908
à Clermont-Ferrand (P. de Dôme)
Domicile Lectore

SIGNALEMENT

Taille 1,76   Cheveux châtain
Bouche moyen   Yeux verts
Visage ovale   Teint clair
Signes particuliers: —

Signature du Titulaire,

Établi à Lectore
Le 7 Octobre 1946
P. Le Maire ou le Commissaire

3 FRANCS
DA 10 FRANCS

Enregistré sous le N° 268

CHANGEMENTS SUCCESSIFS DE DOMICILE

PRÉFECTURE de la CARTE D'IDENTITÉ FRANÇAISE
Vu pour validation
2 9 MARS 1947
Cachet Officiel

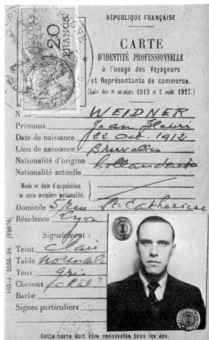

RÉPUBLIQUE FRANÇAISE

CARTE
D'IDENTITÉ PROFESSIONNELLE
à l'usage des Voyageurs
et Représentants de commerce.
(Lois des 8 octobre 1919 et 2 août 1927.)

Nom WEIDNER
Prénoms Jean Henri
Date de naissance 22 Oct. 1912
Lieu de naissance Bruxelles
Nationalité d'origine hollandaise
Nationalité actuelle

Mode et date d'acquisition
de cette dernière nationalité

Domicile 5 rue St. Catherine
Résidence Lyon

Signalement:

Teint clair
Taille normale
Yeux gris
Cheveux noirs
Barbe
Signes particuliers:

20 FRANCS

Cette carte doit être renouvelée tous les ans.

REISEBESCHEINIGUNG NR.
ATTESTATION DE VOYAGE NO. 2 322
REISEBEWIJS NR.

Nur gültig in Verbindung mit der Identitätskarte NO.
Valable seulement en corr... ation avec la carte d'identité NO. 239
Slechts geldig vergezeld ...

ausgestellt von der Bürge...
délivrée par l'administre...
uitgereikt door den burge...

am
le .....7-10-1932.../.2...
den

Der/Die Staatsangehörig...
Le/La .....REY....Carl...
De Staatsonderdaan   (...

von der Firma
au service de la firme
van de firma

reist in der Zeit vom ..
voyagera du ..23...
reist van den

mit der Bahn/PKW-Nr
en chemin de fer ...
per spoor, per auto,

von   Toulouse
de ....
van

nach Annemasse-...
à ....
naar

Er/Sie hat Auftrag...
Il/Elle a reçu de s...
Hij/Zij heeft opdr...

Grund der Reise
Motif de voyage ..
Reden der reis

Die Bescheinigung
nachstehende Dien...
La présente attes...
ment au service o...
Dit bewijs moet n...
den hiernavermelden ove...

Abgefunden mit Verpflegung bis
Pourvu(e) en aliments jusqu'au ....
Verpleging ontvangen tot

Ausgefertigt am
Etablie le ..18..Mai..... 1944
Opgemaakt den

Dienststelle Feldpostnummer 21535B

.... Reg. Baurat a.K. ....
(Unterschrift, Dienstgrad, Dienststellung
Signature, grade, fonction
Handteekening, dienstgraad, betrekking)

Dutch Paris p 11   D P 11

PRÉFECTURE DU RHONE   ETAT FRANÇAIS

Nº 132

SAUF-CONDUIT
pour le département de la Haute-Savoie

VALABLE du XXXX 28 mars   au   28 avril 1944

(Application de l'Arrêté du 28 Janvier 1944, de M. l'Intendant de Police.
Directeur des Opérations de maintien de l'ordre en Haute-Savoie.)

NON et Prénoms   LINS, Paul
né le 28 octobre 1912 à Dunkerque   Départ. P. de C.
Profession   courtier   Nationalité   Fr.
domicilié à   LYON, 111 Quai Pierre Seize

est autorisé à se rendre à

en Haut-Savoie

MOTIF DU DÉPLACEMENT
affaires professionnelles
Pièce d'identité: Nature: carte
Nº   8072
délivrée le   7 mai 1942
police Lyon   par

Mode de transport autorisé:

Autorisé à conduire l'automobile, marque   chemin de f.
Nº
à M   Carte grise délivrée le

Permis de conduire Nº   par
par   délivré le

Autorisation de circuler Nº
par   délivrée le

délivré à Lyon, le
P. le Préfet du Rhône délégué,
Pour le Intendant de Police

Le Conseiller de Préfecture

Voir au verso les prescriptions pour visa.

Safe-conduct certificate issued to "Paul Lins" (one of Weidner's substitute names) and Nazi travel permit issued to "Paul Rey." Both were used by Weidner in his underground activities.

Blank travel permits, properly signed and stamped, were frequently provided by Dutch-Paris to help move people along escape routes. Use of these forms was dangerous, however, because refugees were not registered by name at the point of issue.

False identity papers for Jacques Rens, one of Weidner's chief lieutenants in the Dutch-Paris operation.

CONSULADO GENERAL
DE LA REPUBLICA DE EL SALVADOR. C.A.
GINEBRA
SUIZA

Dos. I.594/943.

Certificat de Nationalité.
===========================

Le Consulat Général de la République de El Salvador
/Amerique Centrale/a Geneve,confirme par ces présentes que...
ISRAEL Raphael,né le 10.I.1904 et sa femme
Johanna ISRAEL-SCHRAVEZANDE,née le 2 IV.1915 et ses enfants
sont reconnus comme citoyens de la République de El Salvador
avec tous les droits et devoirs inhérents a cette nationalité.

Si les intéressés voulaient envisager une émigration,
il leur appartiendrait d,aviser ce Consulat Général en temps
opportun de leur intention a ce sujet,en meme temps une photog-
raphie de date récente pour passeport de chaque membre de la
famille.Ces photos devraient porter chacun au verso une certi-
fication légalisée par une autorité ou un officier ministériel.

Ginebra,le 20.III.1943.

PREMIER SECRETAIRE DU CONSULAT GÉNÉRAL

A typical certificate of nationality given to Jews by neutral countries. Such documents, which could be purchased for about $500 in Geneva, often saved Jews from certain death in Nazi prison camps.

AU NOM DE LA RÉPUBLIQUE DE PARAGUAY

LE CONSUL
DE LA RÉPUBLIQUE DE PARAGUAY
À BERNE

SIGNALEMENT	
Âgé de 10 II 1882	
Profession /	
Taille MOYENNE	
Nez NORMAL	
Cheveux FONCÉS	
Yeux FONCÉS	
Bouche NORMAL	
Dentier NORMAL	
Visage OVALE	

Invite par les présentes toutes les autorités et les employés chargés du maintien de l'ordre public et de la sûreté générale de laisser passer librement et sans obstacles le porteur de la présente: MADAME Vve ESTHER FLESSEMAN - DA SILVA

originaire de PARAGUAY

allant EN EUROPE ET EN OUTRE-MER

Le porteur est recommandé à la protection et aux bons offices des autorités.

Le présent passeport délivré est valable pour ━ 2 / DEUX / ANS.

Donné à Berne sous notre sceau le 30 / TRENTE / du mois DÉCEMBRE 1942 / DEUX /

Signes particuliers: /

Signature du porteur:

Le Consul:

A passport from the Republic of Paraguay which was prepared to help Esther Flesseman Da Silva escape the gas chamber.

XX

flight to london

WHEN Weidner and Rens reached Geneva after their prison escape in Toulouse, they found the Swiss city almost electric with excitement about the impending arrival of Allied troops in France. To Weidner and his group those last days of waiting were full of strain, of not knowing what the situation would be from day to day, but always knowing "It is coming! For many months the undergrounders had suffered. Many of them were now in concentration camps, and some were already known to be dead. Now every moment brought closer the day when Allied armies would sweep onto the continent and a brighter era would dawn.

The Allied landing, however, did not mean that killing, terror, and hardship would end overnight. From the landing date until Paris and Brussels were liberated about three months later, the situation in France and the other occupied countries became even more confused. Some areas were liberated by the Allies; others, as around Annecy for example, were liberated through the combined efforts of the maquis and other underground forces. The continual bomb-

13 337

ing, underground destruction, bitter German last-ditch hatred, and other factors made the occupied countries contradictions of confusion, joy, and death.

John and Jacques, when they returned to Switzerland, once again took over direction of Dutch-Paris, along with Moen and Armand Lap. They sent agents ranging across the utterly confused patchwork of liberated and captive areas. Travel was confined almost entirely now to bicycles and other slow off-the-road methods. Contact, though sketchy, was maintained by Dutch-Paris between Brussels, Paris, Toulouse, Lyons, and Switzerland.

Paul Veerman, off on an assignment, had been arrested by the Nazis in Belgium and deported to Germany, then had escaped from the German camp only to be recaptured just before reaching the Swiss border. Other agents of Weidner's organization had also been arrested. Mr. Mohr, chief of the Dutch Red Cross in Paris, and Baron Brantsen and Benno Nykerk had been arrested in Paris. Again Dutch-Paris began to crumble; but Allied victory seemed in sight, and the work of the organization seemed to be nearly over.

Early in August Weidner made another attempt to go to London. Dutch officials in England wanted to see him to get information about the status of their consulate and embassy offices, as well as to discuss arrangements for helping members who had served so faithfully in Dutch-Paris during the war.

Just outside Paris he asked help of members of the French underground, who were working with English agents parachuted into France.

"We may be able to help," one of the British agents ventured. "We'll talk with London on the radio this evening. They can probably work something out."

Early the next morning the answer to the radioed request came back from England: A plane would pick up Weidner and several others within a few days.

A few nights later John crawled into a vehicle which arrived at the little underground camp where he was staying. About two o'clock in the morning they drew up to a seemingly deserted farmhouse.

"The plane will be here soon. There are many planes in the sky tonight, but there is a special one for us," John was told.

Glancing upward, Weidner could see the truth of the statement. Swarms of aircraft filled the night sky, and the high-altitude drone of bombers beating their way toward Germany sounded almost constantly. At the edge of the little field lights flicked on and then off in a signal, and a lone plane flashed an answering signal back to earth, as it began to drop lower toward the small clearing.

"Move out into the field with the others," one of the men said to John. "When the plane lands, it will drop off a couple of boxes of guns and ammunition; then you jump aboard fast. There'll be three others with you, so you will have to act quickly. The plane must not be on the ground more than five minutes."

The tiny craft skimmed the treetops as it dropped into the clearing, and John started running toward it. As it rolled to a stop, a door was kicked open and several boxes hit the ground. When he saw there were no more boxes, Weidner pushed through the door into the small aircraft. Three other men squeezed in behind him. The door slammed shut, and the pilot began to move the plane toward the end of the field. In a few minutes they were climbing into the night sky heading toward England.

Security control for all persons coming into England from France during those closing months of the war was extremely rigid, and clearance to leave the point of entry usually took several days. But word had gone ahead about Weidner's mission, and he cleared the airfield security inspectors in a few minutes.

He was taken to the Mayfair Hotel in downtown London, where he slept through the remainder of the night. In the morning at Dutch headquarters he met the Netherlands Minister, President Gerbrandy.

"You have done a great service for your country," said the Dutch official as Weidner was introduced to him and handed over the documents he had brought from France. "We have been in regular communication with Dr. Visser 't Hooft, who has often told us of the heroic and selfless job you have done in saving the lives of our people and in carrying vital information. The Netherlands is very proud of your example, Mr. Weidner!"

In the next few days Weidner met many people whom he had helped to escape through France. He saw them in several of the government offices he visited.

As soon as Gerrit van Heuven Goedhart, who was now Minister of Justice for the Netherlands government in exile, heard that John was in London, he called the underground leader, and the two recounted the experiences they had had during the war. Goedhart told Weidner about his escape over the Pyrenees and how he had gotten to England.

The Dutch Minister of Foreign Affairs, E. N. Van Kleffens, wanted a full report of Weidner's work during the war. The Netherlands Secret Service also asked for a similar report; and through the week John met with first one group, then another, to give information.

During his stay in London, Weidner also took parachute training at a nearby Royal Air Force base. Dutch officials felt he might have to parachute in when he returned to France, and they wanted him to be fully prepared if he had to jump. Despite bruises and strained muscles he got through the concentrated course, which included several jumps into the English countryside, without mishap.

But the war on the continent was moving faster than many persons realized, and Dutch authorities decided that John should return to one of the liberated areas in his uniform as captain in the Dutch Army. He was given a diplomatic passport and assigned to work with the security sections of the American and British forces in control of movements of people through the newly liberated areas.

A few days before he left London a thrilling surprise came to John. General Van 't Sant, private secretary to Queen Wilhelmina of the Netherlands, called Weidner on the telephone.

"Captain," he began, "Queen Wilhelmina has heard of the work you have been doing throughout the war. She has asked that you come to tell her the things you have done. A private audience has been arranged for you at her home."

That afternoon John drove to the queen's modest home in the London suburbs for a two-hour audience. When he was presented, the queen dismissed her private secretary, then turned to John.

"Now, Captain," she said, "you tell me exactly what you know, what you have been doing, just as it is. I want all the direct information I can have about our people."

As he spoke of the cruelties he had seen, tears came to the eyes of the queen several times. John could clearly see the love the gracious monarch had for her people and for all who were suffering because of the war.

Not long after his visit with the queen a British bomber landed at Brussels with John aboard. The city had been liberated only a few days earlier.

Now a new challenge, the challenge of helping those who had helped others in the war—the members of Dutch-Paris themselves—faced John. Soon he met Jacques again, and Moen, and others of the Dutch-Paris organization. Word came, too, that Arie Sevenster, for whom John had an especially warm spot in his heart, had been liberated.

But while many were liberated, others remained in prison, or worse. There was Miss Meunier, Paul Meyer, Nykerk, and John's sister Gabrielle, along with many others. What of them? What was to be their fate?

XXI

at war's end

WATCHING the military trucks roll through Brussels toward Holland, John felt a desperate urge to be reunited with his family, whom he had not seen for years. They were living in The Hague, not more than 150 airline miles from Brussels. It would not be long now, though, he was certain. Paris had been liberated on August 25, Brussels on September 3. If the Allies kept to that swift-moving schedule, he would be able to visit his parents before October. The British Second Army, under the command of Gen. Bernard Montgomery, even now stood at Nijmegen in Holland, ready to assault the city of Arnhem on the Lower Rhine. Once Arnhem and its strategic bridges across the river fell, all of Holland could be liberated.

But the schedule did not work out. On Sunday, September 17, the 1st Airborne Army under the command of the American General Brereton, using 1,544 planes and 478 gliders, swept down out of the sky onto the Arnhem side of the Rhine to blaze an advance trail for Montgomery's forces. British, Polish, and American paratroopers made up the huge force which literally blackened the skies over the Dutch city. The parachute and glider landings occupied a forty-five-mile strip of land. Some bridges along the river were taken, but in the immediate area of Arnhem the situation became confused as rain and fog settled over the land.

Seeing the huge airdrop developing, the German commander of forces occupying Arnhem fired a message to Western Headquarters of the German General Staff. A message came back over the radio that two armored divisions—the 9th and 10th of the 2nd SS Armored Corps— were already moving toward Arnhem to give help. As dawn came on September 18, these battle-hardened troops and their huge Tiger tanks clanked into positions in and around the city and began to whittle away at the liberated island of territory the 1st Airborne had won the day before. By September 25 the Allied high command saw that the operation across the Rhine was a loss and decided to withdraw all troops still fighting at Arnhem. Eventually 2,200 Allied airborne troopers got back across the Rhine to the British Second Army. But they left 7,000 across the river either killed, wounded, or missing.

In withering, but ineffective combat, the two armies lay locked for one cold and sickening day after another. September, October, November, and December passed, and still the Allies could not move ahead in Holland. Through the long winter the British were unable to move across the river because the Germans were so well dug in they could withstand repeated Allied bombings and artillery barrages. Even when spring came, the great deadlock held. The Allies, finding easier going straight into the heart of Germany, relegated Arnhem to a holding action and moved swiftly to the east.

In Holland the eager members of the Dutch underground heard rumors of the fast-moving Allied schedule of liberation. September 17, later known as "crazy Tuesday," found Dutch streets teeming with thousands of excited people. "They'll be here soon!" they called to each other. "They aren't far away; it can't be long now!"

With unwavering confidence in the invincibility of the Allied military machine, the underground poured from bunkers, basements, and other hiding places into the bright winter sunlight. They unlimbered their light guns and with great courage began to make war on the Nazis. But the Allies remained entrenched across the Rhine before Arnhem. The great guns spoke, but the army of the Allies didn't move.

In those long, bitter days of disappointment while the Allied army was immobile on the Rhine, the Dutch people, especially those who had shown their hatred of the enemy in scattered small-arms actions, began to suffer almost unspeakable torment. Bitterly angry in the defeat they knew was coming, the Nazis began a reign of unprecedented terror against the hapless members of the underground who had exposed themselves.

To no one did this unforeseen delay of the Allies bring greater sorrow or more anxiety than to John Weidner. It had been months since he had heard from his parents. He knew they were suffering both torment and starvation. The static situation of the Allied army made his heart ache.

But while this massive program of brutality was building up in his homeland, he was getting down to the big task of helping his organization and his nation meet the chaotic days ahead. He was in Brussels only two days before he left for Paris, where his headquarters office was to be. He had heard earlier that Paris had been liberated and hoped Gabrielle had been set free and was now at the home of some friend. But his hope turned to disappointment when he arrived in the city.

The day before the arrival of the American troops in Paris, the Germans had taken all prisoners eastward on the last trains leaving the city. Searching for some word about his sister, Weidner finally turned up someone who had seen Gabrielle as she was being put aboard the prison train.

"She seemed full of courage and faith," John was told. "She was a real comfort to those around her. As she was about to get aboard the train, she slipped this note to me."

John opened the tiny piece of paper and gazed at the handwriting of his sister. Tears sprang to his eyes as he read the words of love the girl had penned to her family. Four words were penciled heavily at the end of the message: "Courage! *Vive les Allies!*"

So Gabrielle was gone! Where had they taken her? What was happening to her right now? The agony of waiting for more news couldn't be drowned, even by the challenge of John's new job. Constantly his mind was preoccupied with concern about Gabrielle. "At least she was well when she left Paris," he thought. "The war should be over soon.

Surely, if her health continues to be good, she can make it even under bad conditions. The big question is, How long will the war continue?"

Despite his anxiety about his sister, Weidner had an important assignment which was vital to thousands of persons. One of his tasks was to help the families of those who had died or who were imprisoned because of their work with Dutch-Paris. To aid French members of his group he worked closely with Agnes Bidault, president of COSOR, the organization which rehabilitated French underground members. Agnes was the sister of Georges Bidault, leader of all French underground groups. Aid for Dutch underground members was sought, after Holland's liberation, through Stichting 40-45, an agency representing the Netherlands government. Information which brought help to Belgian, English, and American underground workers was given to agencies of these countries.

In his new role Weidner had numerous complex battles to win, some of them more mentally taxing than the cloak-and-dagger episodes in which he had been engaged during the height of the war. As he now sought to help those who had helped the Jewish people and Allied airmen, a tangle of newly created red tape blocked practically every major move he tried to make. It was sensitive, frustrating work, which required utmost tact and diplomatic maneuvering.

The Dutch government also asked John, as he worked at his other duties, to prepare a report on the activities of Dutch people living in France during the war, along with a record of Dutch underground achievements in France. In addition, he was directed to screen all Dutch citizens living in France who requested a passport from Dutch authorities in France.

In these new duties he used all the available members of Dutch-Paris, scattering trusted agents across France to make security checks on those requesting passports. Thousands of Dutch people were screened, and many of them were arrested because they were found to be in dangerous collaboration with the Germans. Others had engaged in war crimes of a most serious nature. This vast screening program was not an easy task, but John felt it was his duty to do it. He knew of persons who, seeing the war coming to an end, made false accusations against others for personal gain.

A number of cases uncovered showed one person falsely accusing another of being a Nazi collaborator so that the accuser could take over the business or property of the accused when he was jailed. In this work Weidner operated an organization as elaborate as the German Gestapo, but his group's manner was a complete opposite of the Nazi security group. Brains, not fists or torture, were employed to obtain the truth in the checks made by Weidner and his agents. Truth for truth's sake was the goal in all the work that he directed.

At the request of the British and American governments he submitted a report on those who had worked with Dutch-Paris to help Allies, and as a result of this report many were honored by the Allies. He fought hard to have jobs reinstated to those deported during the war. Others who had escaped German punishment had taken their places in the shops and factories, and John reasoned that the jobs should rightly be returned to all who had been snatched away by the enemy.

"It was astonishing, too," he recalls, "how many people who were afraid to do anything for their country during the war suddenly turned very patriotic and began soliciting high positions in the embassies and other offices when, with the war ending, there were no more risks, only honors to be gained!"

To carry out his new duties effectively Weidner received diplomatic status from the Dutch government. Now he was traveling throughout liberated Europe with diplomatic passport and in the uniform of a captain in the Dutch army. How strange to cross the Swiss border now—to pull through the border checkpoints in a diplomatic car, flash a diplomatic passport, and receive the honors reserved only for diplomats! Now there was no sneaking through clumps of trees, no risking electrocution on the strands of barbed wire, no chatter of machine guns. Only weeks before he had crossed this same border, but the night was moonless then, and death lurked close by.

One day, free from heavy duties, Weidner picked up Pastor Marc Boegner, president of the French Protestant Federation, and took him to Geneva for a visit with Dr. Visser 't Hooft and the Marquis de Maillardoz, a diplomatic courier for the Vatican, whom John knew well. After visiting in the Swiss city for a short time, John and Pastor Boegner returned to Paris, bringing Dr. Visser 't Hooft and the Marquis de Maillardoz with them.

349

In the complex new duties he now directed, the days sped by for John, but with each new dawn came the continued chilling nag of worry about Gabrielle and members of Dutch-Paris. Finally he assigned two men to follow the Allied armies eastward. They were to report on Dutch-Paris members as they came out of concentration camps, and to find out, if possible, what had happened to Gabrielle.

On May 5, 1945, the Germans surrendered. The next day John was in The Hague, where his parents lived at 13 Columbusstraat.

When the door opened, his mother stood there.

"John! John! John!" she cried as her son stepped into her outstretched arms.

Tears streaming down their faces, the two clung together. When at last he spoke, it was in fear, for John could not see his father anywhere about.

"Where's father? What has happened to him?"

"He's all right. He's only out for a few minutes. He'll be back very soon," answered his mother. Then she asked anxiously, "Where is Annette? And what of Gabrielle?" Her voice trembled as the questions came.

"Annette is doing well in Switzerland. She will be able to come home soon."

As he was talking, the front door opened, and his father came in. Again the tears came as John embraced his beloved father. Both his father and his mother, John could see, were terribly thin. During the last few weeks before the liberation, they had existed on only a quarter-pound piece of bread. Starvation had caused the death of hundreds all around them. John realized that they, too, had suffered much in the war.

As soon as he had turned from his father, his mother pressed him for more information about the girls.

"Gabrielle, where is she?" his mother insisted with growing anxiety in her voice.

"As you know from underground messages, she has been taken from Paris, Mother," John said with a heavy heart. "But when she left, she was in good spirits and in good health. She has been gone only a few months, and I'm certain she will be all right," he said. "We'll just have to be patient for word about her. I am checking constantly for information. When it comes, I'll let you know at once."

"We haven't seen her since Christmas, 1943," his mother recalled with great sadness in her voice.

Soon after he returned to Paris, news began trickling in about members of Dutch-Paris who had been sent to concentration camps. Some of his underground companions also began returning to Paris. The Hotel Lutetia in Paris became a reception center for the former prisoners, who were a pitiful-looking lot, some of them little more than skeletons.

One day Mario Janse, the last Dutch diplomatic representative in Vichy, walked into John's office at 45 Rue Taitbout. With him was Herman Laatsman, former head of the Paris unit of Dutch-Paris.

"Hello, John!" the two men exclaimed as Weidner reached for their outstretched hands. They said his name quietly, almost serenely; and he knew they were as glad to

351

be back as he was to see them again. But there were no shouts of joy, no loudness. They had all seen too many bad sights, had spent too long in suffering and torment to feel like shouting. So they were quiet, and the emotion was deep inside. They were joyful, yes; but it was a silent joy that said, "We are back; we are safe!" Nothing else needed to be said. The two men were thin, half-dead products of Nazi inhumanity.

The quiet conversation held some deep sorrow. "Kolkman, Testers, Mohr, Baron Brantsen, are all dead," the two men explained sadly. "The devils at Mauthausen killed them."

At the reception center John also found Maurice Jacquet, who had been arrested in Lyons following Suzy Kraay's confession and sent to Mauthausen. Jacquet had suffered greatly in the concentration camp, and he looked far from well. Paul Veerman, Weidner's trusted lieutenant, also came back one memorable day. Other joyous meetings took place at the center when Anita, Miss Roume, and Raymonde Pillot, his faithful secretary, came through the door.

Then one day news about his sister finally came. Madeleine Billot, a friend and member of another underground group, found John at the hotel. She lived at Carcassonne, and it was her parents who had helped Weidner and Rens in their escape from Toulouse.

"I was with Gabrielle at Ravensbruck," she said. "Then we were transferred to Konigsberg. All the time Gabrielle gave a wonderful testimony of her faith in God. She was in the infirmary at Konigsberg, and even there she was always encouraging the others. She had been very much affected by the death of one of her friends, a young Christian girl, but she still tried to be of help to the others. She was never a really strong girl, as you know, even though her health was good when she left Paris; and the lack of food and the intense cold in the freezing buildings began to kill her little by little.

"But while still at Ravensbruck, Gabrielle was placed under the direction of another prisoner, Eva Amstela. Eva had become a *kapo,* a trustee placed in charge of other prisoners. The girl had become a *kapo* to save her own life. She put Gabrielle to work handling strong acids which diffused vapors very dangerous to Gabrielle's already feeble lungs despite Gabrielle's pleas that such work would be very hazardous to her health. That is where Gabrielle really began to lose her health.

"In February when the Russians advanced near the camp, the German guards decided to leave. As they left, they set fire to the barracks and the infirmary, with the prisoners inside.

"Gabrielle was farthest from the door in the infirmary; but even while the fire was raging through the building, she astonished everyone by her calmness and her lack of concern for herself. They got her out just before the flames touched her, but she was overheated by the fire, and bringing her out into the intense cold made things worse.

"The Russians arrived the next day. They did everything they could for her, but it was too late. She was just too sick. In her last hours she was still an example of confidence and

14

thoughtfulness. She had seen the liberation, and she was very happy about that. Her last words were of love and affection for her family and her friends—especially for you, John. She said she hoped you had gotten through the war without being arrested. She died in the arms of her friends. We buried her there near the camp."

The news stunned Weidner. In just six months the Germans had killed Gabrielle. In the five months she had been held in Paris, with decent treatment, she was healthy and reasonably happy, certainly full of courage; and Weidner felt that with even remotely similar treatment she could go through the next months all right. But he had not reckoned objectively about the Nazi cruelty he knew so well from personal experience. John could hardly believe his ears; so many were returning from the camps, it almost seemed that if he only waited long enough, Gabrielle, too, would return. But now he knew she would never walk through the door of the reception center.

Another returnee, the Countess de Renty, also brought news about Gabrielle. She, too, had been with the girl in her final hours. As Weidner listened to the countess, a strange mixture of emotion welled inside him. This little woman, telling him of his sister's death, had great sorrow of her own, he knew. Her husband had died in the concentration camp just a few months earlier. A fierce wave of hatred for the war and all that had happened in it raced through John as he sat listening to her.

That night in bed Weidner spent hours in tears. "Why should Gabrielle have died?" he asked himself repeatedly.

"She was not a part of what we were doing. She had no part, and yet she has died." He blamed himself for her death; but even as he formed the thought, he knew that it was not so, that she herself had not believed that. Hundreds of lives had been saved because of John's work, and the life-saving and life-taking in the war had been so intermingled in many instances that blame was not easily placed. Certainly Gabrielle never blamed her brother for her capture.

When he awoke the next morning, he set off for Holland to tell his parents of the tragedy. He didn't know how he would break the sad news; he was afraid the shock might be too much. First he told his father that Gabrielle had been very ill since February and there was not much hope for her recovery. Then, a few hours later, he told them the rest of the story, repeating the information given him by Madeleine Billot and the Countess de Renty.

Despite their grief his parents received the news with more calmness than John had expected. Some special wisdom, born of the terrible years under Nazi rule, seemed to have made them already know that Gabrielle's chances of survival, once she had been deported to Germany, were slim. So many were taken; so few came back. Both John and his parents, however, took courage in their firm belief that Gabrielle would be resurrected to life again at the time of Christ's second coming to earth as promised in the Scriptures.

Through their own grief John's parents could see the shock that the news about Gabrielle had on their son. Because of this they held their emotions back so that he would not be hurt even more than he was. They realized that their conduct was a key to help him overcome the deep grief he felt about Gabrielle's death.

When he returned to Paris, there was more bad news. Pastor Paul Meyer, of the Lyons Seventh-day Adventist Church, wouldn't be coming back either. He had died in the concentration camp at Dachau. Benno Nykerk, whose trip years earlier to Lyons from Brussels to see John had really started the large-scale concept of Dutch-Paris, was also a victim of the concentration camps. Caubo was dead, and so was Miss Meunier. And there were many other Dutch-Paris members, about forty in all, for whom the concentration camps had been the end of a desire to help others stay alive.

Gilbert Beaujolin, John's close friend, survived the days of terror when a high price was put on his head by the Gestapo. As hostilities came to an end, he used his influence to see that the contribution made by Dutch-Paris members of French nationality was recognized. With such help as Beaujolin's the French army quickly saw their obligation to the underground members with French nationality, and they were taken into the French military service to receive the benefits that would ensue. John was made an honorary major in the French army for the outstanding service he had given. Belgium and Holland also assumed responsibility for their Dutch-Paris members.

Not long after he had carried the sad news about Gabrielle to his parents, word reached John in Paris that Suzy Kraay had been liberated and was back in Holland. The news brought with it a flood of feelings, many of them disturbing. In his mind he was completely convinced that Suzy had been responsible for the mass arrest of Dutch-Paris members in February, 1944. But as far as Herman Laatsman and some of the others were concerned, there was still no feeling that she was responsible.

"She was always trustworthy before," Laatsman insisted. "Why should she change suddenly? She had been in difficult places before, and she always kept her head."

The only answer was to get Suzy's version of what had happened. Caubo was gone, so he could not help. The same day word came that Suzy had returned to Holland, Weidner and Salomon Chait went to Amsterdam, where the girl was reportedly living. They found her at home.

"John, Salomon—I——" Suzy's voice trailed off in surprise when she opened the door.

"You must come with us," John said as she stared at them. "I am placing you under arrest. It is believed that you have certain responsibility for the arrest of many Dutch-Paris members. Get the things you will need; we will be going to police headquarters."

When they arrived at the police headquarters, John asked Chait to question Suzy. He knew his own personal feelings might prejudice his conduct should he question her. In a short time, under the calm but persistent questioning of Chait, Suzy began to confess that her role had been very much as Weidner suspected, that under torture and threats to the lives of her parents, she had given the names of key leaders of Dutch-Paris. Finally the questioning and her confession ended.

"Now, Suzy, you should go back home," Weidner told her when Chait announced that he was through. "You will be under house arrest until we have decided what will happen to you. You are not to leave your home until you hear from us again."

After he and Chait had discussed Suzy's confession, John went to see his parents again. A decision about what to do with Suzy had to be made, and he felt that his parents could help shape his own decision, since their daughter had died because the girl had talked.

The three discussed Suzy's case for a long time. Then John's father expressed a point of view that wasn't entirely unexpected.

"So much that is bad in this war has happened," he said. "There has been suffering and death on every side. Even our own family has been struck by the tragedy of the war. And now here is Suzy, who has caused so much sorrow because she broke down and gave information to the Nazis. She did wrong, and that is a most serious thing. But the war is over, the bloodshed has stopped, thank God. And I don't want to have any part in extending the horror of the war. I believe we should forgive the girl, that we should tell her we will not attempt to prosecute her for what her acts have done to our family. Nothing we do to her will aid Gabrielle or bring her back to us, but something which we might do to her might make us sorry all the rest of our lives."

"I am ready to accept that, Father," said John, "but the decision about Suzy is not ours alone to make. There are the others in the organization; they have a say, too."

"That is true, but you can tell them we have already made our decision," his father said. "When they hear that, they might decide to do likewise."

Meeting with Dutch-Paris members a few days later, Weidner told them the decision he and his parents had reached about Suzy. After some discussion they agreed that it was a decision they should all adopt. Weidner returned to Suzy's home and informed her that she was free once again. Suzy was told, however, that all those voting to set her free had agreed that she should not expect any financial consideration or award of any kind for the work she had done earlier during the war.

John's father, an ordained minister, went to visit Suzy a short time after this. Later he wrote a letter of encouragement, telling her he hoped her life in the future would be given to helping those in need around her. After several months Suzy sent the following letter to Mrs. Weidner:

"Dear Mrs. Weidner:

"I am short of words to express my feelings. It is for that reason that I have waited so long to send you this letter. I am afraid that it will be more painful for you to read than it is for me to write it. I am the cause of such great sorrow in your life. If I did not feel it was my duty to show you some consolation, I would have spared you this letter.

"I have told your husband as best I could how all this affair developed. I cannot understand how I could have done this. I hope you will believe me, Mrs. Weidner, when I say to you that even now I do not understand how I could do something like that. When the Gestapo read my statement to me the day after I had given it, I could not believe that *I* had betrayed my friends. That your family, to whom I have so much to be thankful, that you have been touched so deeply, gives me more sorrow than the death of my own father in the concentration camp.

"The long year that I passed in the concentration camp myself is much easier to stand than that one moment when I was called to account for what I had done before your son, who had so much confidence in me and who had done so much for others. Very often I have asked myself, 'Why was *I* the one who came back?' After all that has happened, I have the feeling that there is little sense in my going on living. Maybe it is possible to repair our faults and mistakes, but you cannot bring back those who have paid with their lives as victims.

"These seven months that I have been back in Holland, I have done nothing. I lack the courage and confidence to start anything. In spite of the fact that you have not heard from me, yet I have thought very often of you. I haven't given you any news, but don't think I have forgotten you— I've thought about you very much.

"Then your husband came to see me. What that has meant to me you can understand only partially. It has touched me very deeply. Now I know for sure the reason I had to come back. The confidence that he has shown in me has brought me back to life. I know now that my duty will be to show that this confidence is not misplaced, that I am worthy of his confidence. Maybe it will not be of much consolation for you, but I will tell you that, because of your attitude, someone completely down and morally broken is saved.

"Mrs. Weidner, I know that I can never make good for what I have done to you, but I have more soul than you think. Maybe if it is not too difficult for you, I would appreciate very much to get from you a word of receiving this letter. I finish this letter to wish you from all my heart that God and this new year will give you strength to carry your load.

"With high regard,
"Suzy Kraay"

With the judgment of Suzy ended, Weidner returned again to his work in Paris. As he continued to help pick up the tragic fragments of the war, the reports of war-crimes trials began to capture headlines in all the newspapers.

When the trial of Commissioner Bissoir, who had been responsible for Suzy's torture, began, John was called to testify. Weidner told of the consequences of Suzy's arrest, how this had led to the arrest of so many Dutch-Paris members. Finally Bissoir was condemned to hard labor for life, escaping the death sentence only because of protection from high authorities.

One day Weidner noticed that the trial of officers from the Milice prison in Toulouse, where he had been held prisoner, was beginning. The newspaper stories brought back a rush of memories about the torture and days of terror he had suffered there. It also made him recall the young, impressionable Milice officer, Rene Brunner, who had helped Jacques and him to escape.

Brunner, John remembered from conversations with him in the prison, had come from a family of magistrates. His father was from Alsace and was considered a good man of high reputation. But Brunner was easily influenced, working at doing good when in the company of good associates, turning bad when with those of bad reputation. John recalled, too, that the young officer had given aid to others besides himself. He felt obliged to speak in Brunner's behalf, at least to declare that his own life had undoubtedly been saved through Brunner's action.

Weidner placed a call to Brunner's lawyer to see if he could help.

"I am certainly pleased that you have the courage to testify in favor of a case which is not very popular," the lawyer said. "This case, of course, could be a dangerous one for you if your testimony is not clearly understood as a purely humanitarian act. I am very much concerned, because Brunner may get the death sentence. We can surely use your help. What we really need is the use of influence at higher levels. If you have any way to speak a word to some higher magistrates, it would be most helpful."

Following the lawyer's plea for help at higher levels, John contacted some of his friends who had communication with the French Minister of Justice. Through these friends Weidner told his story of Brunner's help. Weidner also tried another method of helping the young officer. He appealed to Gen. Charles de Gaulle, who was the top war hero of

362

France at that time. The general knew John through several contacts, the latest of which occurred in September, 1944. Weidner had gone back to Switzerland then to renew communication with Dr. Visser 't Hooft, General Van Tricht, and others who had been working closely with Dutch-Paris. In Switzerland he had met Xavier de Gaulle, the general's brother, whose escape from the Annecy area Weidner had arranged earlier.

"My brother is in France with the liberation forces, I understand," Xavier had told him. "You will be going back to France in a few days. I wonder if you would deliver a letter to General de Gaulle for me, as that is the only sure way I know to get word to him."

Weidner had said he would be happy to deliver the letter. A short time later he met the general in Lyons and handed him the letter from his brother—the first direct news the general had received from Xavier in several years—in the presence of General de Gaulle's aide-de-camp, Capitaine Guy.

Now John appealed to General de Gaulle in behalf of young Brunner. When the day of judgment finally came for the Toulouse Milice officers, l'Intendant Marty and his associates were condemned to death. Some days later they were executed. But Brunner was given a sentence of twenty years at hard labor. Later John received a deeply moving letter of thanks from Brunner's parents, in which they expressed their gratitude for his intervention in behalf of their son.

Punctuating the routine of John's work came several occasions when bands played and words of gratitude were spoken for Weidner's role in saving lives during the war. Each award ceremony was as unexpected as the previous one to John, for he had desired no glory for his work.

Shortly after the liberation of Paris he was called to Versailles, where he met General Eisenhower, supreme commander of the Allied Forces. The general spoke of the appreciation he felt for the work of underground leaders such as John.

The award ceremonies came with considerable regularity during the four-year period from 1946 to 1950. The first indication Weidner had that he was to receive decorations was word from the Dutch ambassador in Paris that France had inquired if she might bestow decorations on him. He was summoned to the Cour des Invalides in the huge building erected by Napoleon, where the famed warrior now lies entombed. There, with ten other heroes, John stood at attention in the imposing court with hundreds of persons looking on as a general representing the French government pinned the French Legion of Honor on Weidner's military jacket.

A short time later the second highest order, the Croix de Guerre was conferred on Weidner in a private ceremony in Paris. Then later he received the French Medaille de la Resistance.

In 1947 about one hundred of the more than one thousand Jews of all nationalities whom John had helped escape the Nazi death sentence gathered in Amsterdam to honor him. Each contributed a substantial amount of money, which guaranteed that Weidner's name would be entered in the Golden Book of Jerusalem in the newly formed state of Israel. A grove of trees was also planted in the new country in his honor.

Then he was ordered to The Hague in Holland, where a special ceremony was held in the Binnenhof Court in front of the Dutch parliament building. There, with high officials of the Dutch government looking on, he received from the American military attaché the American Medal of Freedom with Gold Palm, a medal for acts of heroism by civilians or members of other nations' armed forces. The medal's citation read: "Captain John H. Weidner, Subject of the Netherlands, for outstanding heroism performed with great courage and magnificent fortitude in the service of the Allied Nations from November, 1944, during which time the vast international escape route known as 'Dutch-Paris,' organized and commanded by him, successfully conveyed 112 Americans and other Allied airmen out of Holland, through Belgium and France, across the Pyrenees into Spain. A great patriot, typifying the spirit of the underground, Captain John H. Weidner, for indomitable courage and unexcelled leadership in his priceless contribution to the defense of liberty has gained the profound gratitude and highest admiration of all freedom-loving peoples. 16 May 1946."

At the British embassy the British ambassador pinned on Weidner's jacket the honor and gratitude of that country through the Military O.B.E. (Order of the British Empire), most coveted of British honors. Later the British Air Chief Marshal also presented him with a certificate of gratitude and appreciation.

From his own country came high honors, too. One day he received a summons to the Dutch embassy in Paris. There the ambassador conferred the Order of Orange Nassau on behalf of the government of the Netherlands, one of its highest awards. On another occasion the queen received John and other members of Dutch-Paris in her palace at Het Loo.

In another ceremony, at the Dutch embassy in Paris, Holland's Queen Juliana, escorted by Prince Bernhard, handed John another award—one which moved him deeply. It was the country's highest wartime decoration, the Kruis Van Verzet, given in posthumous honor to his sister Gabrielle.

Some years after the war had ended, members of the Dutch parliament prepared an official volume citing all known acts which aided the Dutch cause during the war. In this volume John's name was associated with Dr. Visser 't Hooft's as having rendered highest service to their country.

Another official certificate of the American government honoring Weidner read, "The President of the United States of America has directed me to express to Captain John H. Weidner the gratitude and appreciation of the American people for gallant service in assisting the escape of Allied soldiers from the enemy." It was signed "Dwight D. Eisenhower, General of the Army, Commanding General, United States Forces European Theater."

As the machinery of changing from wartime back to peaceful life ground to a stop, John felt one project still remained unfinished among the many plans and programs he

366

had aided in the immediate postwar years. Finally it too was accomplished.

A small memorial cemetery was established about sixty miles from Paris at Senlis. There, in the middle of a small plot where lie about one hundred Dutch soldiers, a crypt was erected. Inscribed on it were the names of Dutch and Allied citizens who had died in France aiding the Allied cause. Chiseled deep into the white marble went the names of John's sister Gabrielle, Paul Meyer, Caubo, Benno Nykerk, and many others. Here was a memorial which meant much more to John personally than any of the gleaming medals that were pinned to his chest.

Worldwide interest and appreciation for what underground leaders like John had done during World War II continued unabated. The government of Israel in 1963 honored him by entering his name among the heroes in the Golden Book in Jerusalem. Trees, purchased through the gifts of Jews in different parts of the world, were planted as a growing, living tribute to him on the Hill of Rememberence along the Avenue of the Righteous at *Yad Vashem* in Jerusalem.

The government of Poland honored John by conferring on him the Polish Medal of Resistance. In Jerusalem, Gideon Hausner, who gained world attention as the prosecutor of the infamous Adolf Eichmann, conferred on John, in behalf of the Israeli government, the Medal of the Righteous Gentile. In 1993 John was chosen as one of seven persons in North America to light a candle in honor of the rescuers of Jews at the opening of the United States Holocaust Memorial Museum in Washington, D.C.

In 1993, Prince Baudoin awarded John the Medal of Officer of the Order of King Leopold II, Belgium's most prestigious decoration. Also in 1993, French President François Mitterrand conferred on him the most prestigious of French decorations, the medal marking him as Officer de L'Ordre de la Legion D'Honneur, an award created by Napoleon.

Atlantic Union College in Massachusetts conferred on John an honorary Doctor of Laws degree. It also created the John Henry Weidner Center for Cultivation of the Altruistic Spirit. The center not only houses John's extensive memorabilia, but it also presents classes, lectures, concerts, exhibitions, social programs, and creative activities to help society understand and act with compassion and altruism.

La Sierra University in Riverside, California, initiated an annual lectureship that will serve as a continuing reminder of the life of service for others that John lived on a daily basis.

XXII

epilogue

IN THE years following the war's end, the days and nights of anxiety felt as he moved along his escape routes helping save refugees no longer gripped John Henry Weidner. He became just one of thousands of persons living quiet lives in Pasadena and then Monterey Park, California. But his days were still full of hard work in his chain of health-food stores and manufacturing business. He was also a very active member in the Pasadena and then the Temple City Seventh-day Adventist churches, and he maintained a lively contact with scores of comrades who worked with him in Dutch-Paris. He married a vivacious lady named Naomi, whom he met at the White Memorial Medical Center in Los Angeles.

Although he made no attempt to draw attention to his unusual role in World War II, the cloak of obscurity was lifted from Weidner's life by numerous requests for him to speak before church groups, in synagogues, in civic club meetings, and on radio and television. In early 1963 the American Jewish Congress brought his wartime activities to the attention of millions in southern California. Searching for names of persons who had helped Jews during World War II, Haskell Lazere, director of the Jewish organization for southern California, uncovered Weidner's record. At a public ceremony, attended by scores of dignitaries, the American Jewish Congress honored him for his record of service with an unusual inscribed plaque that reads: "John H. Weidner—Above all that thou guardest, 'keep thy heart, . . . for out of it are the issues of life.' Proverbs 4:23. For the heroic rescue of hundreds of Jews from occupied Europe during World War II. For highest courage and service to humanity. . . . For exemplifying the finest traditions of charity, justice and righteousness. . . ."

Although his days were full, John always took time out to stay in contact with former members of his old underground organization. He stayed in contact with Raymonde Pillot, his former secretary and helper in Dutch-Paris, who had married and was the mother of twins. Mrs. Annie Langlade, Beaujolin's sister and a very close friend of Weidner's, came through the war safely despite her heroic work in the underground. Maurice Jacquet, with whom John worked so closely until Jacquet was imprisoned, became consul general of the Netherlands in Lyon after the war. In 1961 he died as a result of torture to which he had been subjected in the concentration camps during the war.

John's sister Annette completely recovered from her shock at the loss of Gabrielle and married a dentist. She lived in Switzerland, becoming the mother of two children. Jacques Rens married, became a successful businessman, and the father of four children. Paul Veerman, another of

John's lieutenants, also became a successful businessman and the father of two children.

Solomon Chait made a success of a business career after the war. During the war he had been an unselfish but quietly courageous leader, always thinking of the welfare of others. He maintained that keen interest in others, especially those with whom he had served in the underground. He made regular visits to Dutch-Paris members in Lyons and Brussels, throughout Holland, and elsewhere.

Arie Sevenster retired after having served as minister of the Netherlands in Prague and then as consul general of the Netherlands in Genoa. Gilbert Beaujolin found wealth as a result of a successful business career before he died in early 1994. Herman Laatsman became chancellor of the Dutch Embassy in Brussels, and Mario Janse chancellor of the Dutch Embassy in Bern. Dr. Gabriel Nahas became a prominent medical researcher in the United States.

General A. G. Van Tricht became a representative of the Netherlands army on the combined Allied Chiefs of Staff in Washington, D.C., after the war, before retiring in Holland. Dr. W. A. Visser 't Hooft, although retired from his position as general secretary of the World Council of Churches, continued to be vigorously active in many duties. For his courageous work during the war Dr. Visser 't Hooft was given high honors by Holland.

For his selfless actions in behalf of the Dutch people, Pastor Marc Boegner was presented the Order of Orange Nassau by the government of the Netherlands. He was also elected as one of the 40 members of the French Academy, the highest distinction that can come to a Frenchman. All members of John's underground group received full recognition and decorations from their respective governments for heroic actions during the days of terror.

After the adventures of war in which he so narrowly escaped death many times, John felt that each new day was one more opportunity added to his life, by divine grace, to do something special for God. He felt that this "added time" as he called it, should be spent working for the welfare of others and furthering the proposition that he is his brother's keeper.

"I am happy in my work, in my friends, and in my service to God," Weidner would say. "There are many joys in remembering the past, knowing that I have helped as best I could, and in contemplating the future with faith in a God who never makes a mistake!"

On Sabbath, May 21, 1994, John Henry Weidner, a "Righteous Gentile"—friend of man, child of God—died at his home in Monterey Park, California. Upon learning of his death the world's major news wire services flashed the news to newspapers, magazines, radio and television around the world.

"His daring earned him medals from France, Belgium, Britain and the U.S.—and the ultimate tribute, a 5 million-franc price on his head issued by the Gestapo," observed *Time* magazine in an account of his death.

A memorial service honoring John at the Temple City Seventh-day Adventist Church on Sabbath, May 28, drew hundreds from his ever-widening circle of friends and those who had read the extensive coverage of his death in the media. Participants in the service included the consul general or consular representatives from Holland, France, Belgium, and Israel.

Norman Rosen, who had first brought the record of John's service to the attention of the American Jewish Congress, was at the memorial service, as were those representing the rescuers and the rescued and the children of the resistance during World War II. Rabbi Harold Schulweis, long an advocate of greater honor for non-Jews who had helped save Jews during the war, read the Kaddish, the prayer for the dead.

The service also included representatives of the John Henry Weidner Center for Cultivation of the Altruistic Spirit at Atlantic Union College in Massachusetts, where John's personal reflections, diaries and correspondence are housed, along with his medals and citations for heroic action.

At the memorial service John's biographer quoted from "Fragments," the radio dramatization of *Flee the Captor,* written by Milton Geiger. It was aired three times on "The Eternal Light," the National Broadcasting Company's radio program of the Jewish Theological Seminary of America. In the dramatization Geiger in a poetic, endearing way puts words in John's mouth that aptly express his philosophy of life.:

"I believe in Man because I must, if I am to believe in God—who believed enough in man to create him and remain patient with him. What no cruelty or madness can ever destroy—is Man's belief in himself—which is in the end his trust in his Maker."